Marx, Engels, and Marxisms

Series Editors

Marcello Musto, York University, Toronto, ON, Canada
Terrell Carver, University of Bristol, Bristol, UK

The Marx renaissance is underway on a global scale. Wherever the critique of capitalism re-emerges, there is an intellectual and political demand for new, critical engagements with Marxism. The peer-reviewed series Marx, Engels and Marxisms (edited by Marcello Musto & Terrell Carver, with Babak Amini, Francesca Antonini, Paula Rauhala & Kohei Saito as Assistant Editors) publishes monographs, edited volumes, critical editions, reprints of old texts, as well as translations of books already published in other languages. Our volumes come from a wide range of political perspectives, subject matters, academic disciplines and geographical areas, producing an eclectic and informative collection that appeals to a diverse and international audience. Our main areas of focus include: the oeuvre of Marx and Engels, Marxist authors and traditions of the 19th and 20th centuries, labour and social movements, Marxist analyses of contemporary issues, and reception of Marxism in the world.

Dong-Min Rieu

A Mathematical Approach to Marxian Value Theory

Time, Money, and Labor Productivity

palgrave
macmillan

Dong-Min Rieu
Department of Economics
Chungnam National University
Daejeon, Korea (Republic of)

ISSN 2524-7123 ISSN 2524-7131 (electronic)
Marx, Engels, and Marxisms
ISBN 978-3-031-07807-1 ISBN 978-3-031-07808-8 (eBook)
https://doi.org/10.1007/978-3-031-07808-8

This Palgrave Macmillan imprint is published by the registered company Springer Nature Switzerland AG
The registered company address is: Gewerbestrasse 11, 6330 Cham, Switzerland

In memory of J. K. Rieu (1936–1988)

Titles Published

1. Terrell Carver & Daniel Blank, *A Political History of the Editions of Marx and Engels's "German Ideology" Manuscripts*, 2014.
2. Terrell Carver & Daniel Blank, *Marx and Engels's "German Ideology" Manuscripts: Presentation and Analysis of the "Feuerbach chapter,"* 2014.
3. Alfonso Maurizio Iacono, *The History and Theory of Fetishism*, 2015.
4. Paresh Chattopadhyay, *Marx's Associated Mode of Production: A Critique of Marxism*, 2016.
5. Domenico Losurdo, *Class Struggle: A Political and Philosophical History*, 2016.
6. Frederick Harry Pitts, *Critiquing Capitalism Today: New Ways to Read Marx*, 2017.
7. Ranabir Samaddar, *Karl Marx and the Postcolonial Age*, 2017.
8. George Comninel, *Alienation and Emancipation in the Work of Karl Marx*, 2018.
9. Jean-Numa Ducange & Razmig Keucheyan (Eds.), *The End of the Democratic State: Nicos Poulantzas, a Marxism for the 21st Century*, 2018.
10. Robert X. Ware, *Marx on Emancipation and Socialist Goals: Retrieving Marx for the Future*, 2018.
11. Xavier LaFrance & Charles Post (Eds.), *Case Studies in the Origins of Capitalism*, 2018.

12. John Gregson, *Marxism, Ethics, and Politics: The Work of Alasdair MacIntyre*, 2018.
13. Vladimir Puzone & Luis Felipe Miguel (Eds.), *The Brazilian Left in the 21st Century: Conflict and Conciliation in Peripheral Capitalism*, 2019.
14. James Muldoon & Gaard Kets (Eds.), *The German Revolution and Political Theory*, 2019.
15. Michael Brie, *Rediscovering Lenin: Dialectics of Revolution and Metaphysics of Domination*, 2019.
16. August H. Nimtz, *Marxism versus Liberalism: Comparative Real-Time Political Analysis*, 2019.
17. Gustavo Moura de Cavalcanti Mello and Mauricio de Souza Sabadini (Eds.), *Financial Speculation and Fictitious Profits: A Marxist Analysis*, 2019.
18. Shaibal Gupta, Marcello Musto & Babak Amini (Eds.), *Karl Marx's Life, Ideas, and Influences: A Critical Examination on the Bicentenary*, 2019.
19. Igor Shoikhedbrod, *Revisiting Marx's Critique of Liberalism: Rethinking Justice, Legality, and Rights*, 2019.
20. Juan Pablo Rodríguez, *Resisting Neoliberal Capitalism in Chile: The Possibility of Social Critique*, 2019.
21. Kaan Kangal, *Friedrich Engels and the Dialectics of Nature*, 2020.
22. Victor Wallis, *Socialist Practice: Histories and Theories*, 2020.
23. Alfonso Maurizio Iacono, *The Bourgeois and the Savage: A Marxian Critique of the Image of the Isolated Individual in Defoe, Turgot and Smith*, 2020.
24. Terrell Carver, *Engels before Marx*, 2020.
25. Jean-Numa Ducange, *Jules Guesde: The Birth of Socialism and Marxism in France*, 2020.
26. Antonio Oliva, Ivan Novara & Angel Oliva (Eds.), *Marx and Contemporary Critical Theory: The Philosophy of Real Abstraction*, 2020.
27. Francesco Biagi, *Henri Lefebvre's Critical Theory of Space*, 2020.
28. Stefano Petrucciani, *The Ideas of Karl Marx: A Critical Introduction*, 2020.
29. Terrell Carver, *The Life and Thought of Friedrich Engels, 30th Anniversary Edition*, 2020.
30. Giuseppe Vacca, *Alternative Modernities: Antonio Gramsci's Twentieth Century*, 2020.

31. Kevin B. Anderson, Kieran Durkin & Heather Brown (Eds.), *Raya Dunayevskaya's Intersectional Marxism: Race, Gender, and the Dialectics of Liberation*, 2020.
32. Marco Di Maggio, *The Rise and Fall of Communist Parties in France and Italy*, 2020.
33. Farhang Rajaee, *Presence and the Political*, 2021.
34. Ryuji Sasaki, *A New Introduction to Karl Marx: New Materialism, Critique of Political Economy, and the Concept of Metabolism*, 2021.
35. Kohei Saito (Ed.), *Reexamining Engels's Legacy in the 21st Century*, 2021.
36. Paresh Chattopadhyay, *Socialism in Marx's Capital: Towards a Dealienated World*, 2021.
37. Marcello Musto, *Karl Marx's Writings on Alienation*, 2021.
38. Michael Brie & Jörn Schütrumpf, *Rosa Luxemburg: A Revolutionary Marxist at the Limits of Marxism*, 2021.
39. Stefano Petrucciani, *Theodor W. Adorno's Philosophy, Society, and Aesthetics*, 2021.
40. Miguel Vedda, *Siegfried Kracauer, or, The Allegories of Improvisation: Critical Studies*, 2021.
41. Ronaldo Munck, *Rethinking Development: Marxist Perspectives*, 2021.
42. Jean-Numa Ducange & Elisa Marcobelli (Eds.), *Selected Writings of Jean Jaurès: On Socialism, Pacifism and Marxism*, 2021.
43. Elisa Marcobelli, *Internationalism Toward Diplomatic Crisis: The Second International and French, German and Italian Socialists*, 2021.
44. James Steinhoff, *Automation and Autonomy: Labour, Capital and Machines in the Artificial Intelligence Industry*, 2021.
45. Juan Dal Maso, *Hegemony and Class Struggle: Trotsky, Gramsci and Marxism*, 2021.
46. Gianfranco Ragona & Monica Quirico, *Frontier Socialism: Self-organisation and Anti-capitalism*, 2021.
47. Tsuyoshi Yuki, *Socialism, Markets and the Critique of Money: The Theory of "Labour Notes,"* 2021.
48. Gustavo Moura de Cavalcanti Mello & Henrique Pereira Braga (Eds.), *Wealth and Poverty in Contemporary Brazilian Capitalism*, 2021.
49. Paolo Favilli, *Historiography and Marxism: Innovations in Mid-Century Italy*, 2021.

50. Levy del Aguila Marchena, *Communism, Political Power and Personal Freedom in Marx*, 2021.
51. V. Geetha, *Bhimrao Ramji Ambedkar and the Question of Socialism in India*, 2021.
52. Satoshi Matsui, *Normative Theories of Liberalism and Socialism: Marxist Analysis of Values*, 2022.
53. Kei Ehara (Ed.), *Japanese Discourse on the Marxian Theory of Finance*, 2022.
54. Achim Szepanski, *Financial Capital in the 21st Century*, 2022.
55. Stephen Maher, *Corporate Capitalism and the Integral State: General Electric and a Century of American Power*, 2022.

Titles Forthcoming

Vesa Oittinen, *Marx's Russian Moment*
Kolja Lindner, *Marx, Marxism and the Question of Eurocentrism*
Adriana Petra, *Intellectuals and Communist Culture: Itineraries, Problems and Debates in Post-war Argentina*
George C. Comninel, *The Feudal Foundations of Modern Europe*
Spencer A. Leonard, *Marx, the India Question, and the Crisis of Cosmopolitanism*
Joe Collins, *Applying Marx's Capital to the 21st century*
Jeong Seongjin, *Korean Capitalism in the 21st Century: Marxist Analysis and Alternatives*
Marcello Mustè, *Marxism and Philosophy of Praxis: An Italian Perspective from Labriola to Gramsci*
Shannon Brincat, *Dialectical Dialogues in Contemporary World Politics: A Meeting of Traditions in Global Comparative Philosophy*
Francesca Antonini, *Reassessing Marx's Eighteenth Brumaire: Dictatorship, State, and Revolution*
Thomas Kemple, *Capital after Classical Sociology: The Faustian Lives of Social Theory*
Xavier Vigna, *A Political History of Factories in France: The Workers' Insubordination of 1968*
Attila Melegh, *Anti-Migrant Populism in Eastern Europe and Hungary: A Marxist Analysis*

Marie-Cecile Bouju, *A Political History of the Publishing Houses of the French Communist Party*
Peter McMylor, Graeme Kirkpatrick & Simin Fadaee (Eds.), *Marxism, Religion, and Emancipatory Politics*
Mauro Buccheri, *Radical Humanism for the Left: The Quest for Meaning in Late Capitalism*
Rémy Herrera, *Confronting Mainstream Economics to Overcome Capitalism*
Tamás Krausz, Eszter Bartha (Eds.), *Socialist Experiences in Eastern Europe: A Hungarian Perspective*
Martin Cortés, *Marxism, Time and Politics: On the Autonomy of the Political*
João Antonio de Paula, Huga da Gama Cerqueira, Eduardo da Motta e Albuquer & Leonardo de Deus, *Marxian Economics for the 21st Century: Revaluating Marx's Critique of Political Economy*
Zhi Li, *The Concept of the Individual in the Thought of Karl Marx*
Lelio Demichelis, *Marx, Alienation and Techno-capitalism*
Salvatore Prinzi, *Representation, Expression, and Institution: The Philosophy of Merleau-Ponty and Castoriadis*
Agon Hamza, *Slavoj Žižek and the Reconstruction of Marxism*
Éric Aunoble, *French Views on the Russian Revolution*
Terrell Carver, Smail Rapic (Eds.), *Friedrich Engels for the 21st Century: Perspectives and Problems*
Patrizia Dogliani, *A Political History of the International Union of Socialist Youth*
Alexandros Chrysis, *The Marx of Communism: Setting Limits in the Realm of Communism*
Paul Raekstad, *Karl Marx's Realist Critique of Capitalism: Freedom, Alienation, and Socialism*
Alexis Cukier, *Democratic Work: Radical Democracy and the Future of Labour*
Christoph Henning, *Theories of Alienation: From Rousseau to the Present*
Daniel Egan, *Capitalism, War, and Revolution: A Marxist Analysis*
Genevieve Ritchie, Sara Carpenter & Shahrzad Mojab (Eds.), *Marxism and Migration*
Emanuela Conversano, *Capital from Afar: Anthropology and Critique of Political Economy in the Late Marx*
Marcello Musto, *Rethinking Alternatives with Marx*

Vincenzo Mele, *City and Modernity in George Simmel and Walter Benjamin: Fragments of Metropolis*
David Norman Smith, *Self-Emancipation: Marx's Unfinished Theory of the Working Class*
José Ricardo Villanueva Lira, *Marxism and the Origins of International Relations*
Bertel Nygaard, *Marxism, Labor Movements, and Historiography*
Fabio Perocco (Ed.), *Racism in and for the Welfare State*
Marcos Del Roio, *Gramsci and the Emancipation of the Subaltern Classes*
Marcelo Badaró, *The Working Class from Marx to Our Times*
Tomonaga Tairako, *A New Perspective on Marx's Philosophy and Political Economy*
Matthias Bohlender, Anna-Sophie Schönfelder, & Matthias Spekker, *Truth and Revolution in Marx's Critique of Society*
Mauricio Vieira Martins, *Marx, Spinoza and Darwin on Philosophy: Against Religious Perspectives of Transcendence*
Jean Vigreux, Roger Martelli, & Serge Wolikow, *One Hundred Years of History of the French Communist Party*
Aditya Nigam, *Border-Marxisms and Historical Materialism*
Fred Moseley, *Marx's Theory of Value in Chapter 1 of* Capital*: A Critique of Heinrich's Value-Form Interpretation*
Armando Boito, *The State, Politics, and Social Classes: Theory and History*
Anjan Chakrabarti & Anup Dhar, *World of the Third and Hegemonic Capital: Between Marx and Freud*
Hira Singh, *Annihilation of Caste in India: Ambedkar, Ghandi, and Marx*
Salvatore Engel-Di Mauro, *An Introduction to Ecosocialism*

Preface

The basic ideas presented in this book date to the early 1990s when I was doing my Ph.D. studies at the Seoul National University in South Korea. The political democratization that occurred in the late 1980s led me to the midst of the "Marx Renaissance," which enabled young students to approach Marx's text seriously. Unfortunately, then and now, Marxian economics did not develop rapidly not only due to the breakdown of the "actually existing socialism" as seen on the case of the Soviet Union, but also due to its specific character as a paradigm of critique to mainstream economics rather than an alternative toolkit for pragmatic economic policies. Nevertheless, at least in the field of the labor theory of value, Marxian economics saw pathbreaking development in the early 1980s. New light has been shed on the topic with the emergence of a single-system interpretation that regards labor value and price as an intertwined, mutually penetrating system and not as two independent and logically successive systems. In particular, the "monetary expression of labor time," which already existed in Marx's own text, albeit in an implicit form, became one of the essential concepts in the literature of Marxian value theory. Ironically, my first encounter with the mathematical formulation of Marxian value theory was within this theoretical development form because I had few opportunities to read Marxian literature prior to that due to the political censorship. My former teacher, late Joseph W. Chung, who had just returned from his studies at University of Louvain introduced the concept in his course for which I had enrolled as a graduate student.

The possibility of directly connecting labor time to monetary variables impressed me and soon became the guiding thread for my further study as a dissenting, heterodox economist. In fact, the novel distinction I drew between the "value expression of labor time" and the "monetary expression of value," which is, in a certain sense, what this book is all about, was elaborated through dialogues with him, which frequently developed into heated debates. This book emerged from my intermittent research spanning more than 25 years after completing my degree. My research was, in fact, a continuum of trial and errors, sometimes due to my misunderstanding of related concepts and at other times due to the difficulty I faced in representing my ideas in accurate language. I continue to believe that this topic has potential for further development. Although my achievement may not be considered breakthrough study, I hope that the decomposition of the monetary expression of labor time into these two concepts can be a small steppingstone for the survival of Marxian value theory as a pragmatic tool for the analysis as well as a theoretically fundamental critique of the capitalist economy.

Daejeon, Korea (Republic of) Dong-Min Rieu

Acknowledgments

Since this book is the result of a long journey of thrashing out the relation between labor value and price, some parts of the book are thoroughly reorganized versions of already published papers, with changes to exposition, discussions about new literature, and correction of errors. I would like to thank Hyeon-Hyo Ahn, Duncan Foley, Keehyun Hong, Makoto Itoh, Sangyong Joo, Namhoon Kang, Fred Moseley, Takeshi Nakatani, Hiroshi Ohnishi, Ji-Ung Park, Lefteris Tsoulfidis, Hiroyuki Uni, Roberto Veneziani, and Kiichiro Yagi. Seongjin Jeong encouraged me to initiate the project of writing this book. Sang B. Hahn ran computer simulations for Chapter 9 apart from making helpful suggestions. Hyun Woong Park not only helped me in my approach toward using empirical data in Chapter 8, but also offered many suggestions and held discussions with me both online and offline. Sungkye Kim prepared the illustrations in the book. I am also grateful for the support provided by the Ministry of Education of the Republic of Korea and the National Research Foundation of Korea (NRF-2020S1A5A2A01041412).

Contents

List of Figures

List of Tables

CHAPTER 1

Introduction

On July 11, 1868, Marx wrote to Ludwig Kugelman;

> Every child knows a nation which ceased to work, I will not say for a year, but even for a few weeks, would perish. Every child knows, too, that the masses of products corresponding to the different needs required different and quantitatively determined masses of the total labor of society. That this necessity of the distribution of social labor in definite proportions cannot possibly be done away with by a particular form of social production but can only change the mode of its appearance, is self-evident......Science consists precisely in demonstrating how the law of value asserts itself.[1]

This paragraph is self-evident in that nobody can deny the logic of this in everyday life. If "the law of value" quoted in the last sentence implied merely this common knowledge, it would not have been the object of much dispute in the history of economics, at least in the last century. Is this really the case? The answer is partly "yes," and partly "no."

Let us start with why it is partly "yes." When we say that the economic growth of a certain nation depends on the quality of its labor or labor productivity, and therefore, investment in education or "human

[1] Marx to Kugelman in Hanover. Available at: https://www.marxists.org/archive/marx/works/1868/letters/68_07_11-abs.htm (Accessed: April 1, 2022).

D.-M. Rieu, *A Mathematical Approach to Marxian Value Theory*, Marx, Engels, and Marxisms,
https://doi.org/10.1007/978-3-031-07808-8_1

capital" is an impetus for economic development, then Marx's assertion can be widely accepted. Interestingly, this proposition periodically appears in times of periodical crises in the capitalist economy. There have been discourses on the development of "the information economy," or "weightless economy," etc. However, when the global financial crisis led to the burst of the bubble, these discourses immediately changed and the crisis was attributed to "It's labor, stupid!" Recent futurological prediction of the dismal labor-less society with the emergence of artificial intelligence is, in a certain sense, nothing but the notion that labor is so important that it can never be overlooked.

The economy is usually analyzed based on three keywords: time, money, and labor productivity. On the one hand, labor is measured by time. On the other hand, even in mainstream economics, time is considered a resource scarcer than any other goods and services. Time is innately equally distributed to all human beings. In the capitalist society, however, time cannot be transformed into money easily while money can buy time. In other words, we are confronted with a fundamental asymmetry between time and money. The Marxian labor theory of value is an analytical framework for understanding this very relation among time, money, and labor productivity usually defined as the ratio of the former two.

The main aim of this book is to clarify on the quantitative relation among time, money, and labor productivity as indicated by the book's subtitle. In standard intermediate-level microeconomics textbooks, leisure, defined as the residual time after labor, other than labor can always be transformed into money in proportion to its opportunity cost measured by wage. A representative consumer just maximizes her utility by making a rational choice between leisure and income. If time and money are freely reversible, serious analysis is not necessary. In this sense, therefore, Marxian value theory starts from the fact that this relation is never as transparent as alleged. As per the title of this book, "A mathematical approach to Marxian value theory," one may expect a mathematical approach does not necessarily exclude qualitative analysis as well. However, in this book, I focus on clarifying the quantitative relations among time, labor, and money.

The book is divided into four main parts.

Part I introduces the main theme of the book, the relation between time and money in the context of Marxian value theory. Without examining the conventional literature specifically, I straightaway begin with the investigation of the quantitative relationship between labor value and price.

In Chapter 2, I emphasize the strict distinction among the three categories of labor time, value, and price, in the sense of how they capture the reality of capitalist production from their respective viewpoints. Although the qualitative connection between value and price is not examined further, the logic of socialization and homogenization are shown to be fundamentally different to clarify the meaning of abstract, social, and homogeneous labor. Based on this notion, it is suggested that the monetary expression of labor time (MELT) is decomposed into the "value expression of labor time" (VELT) and the "monetary expression of value" (MEV), which is the main thrust of the entire book. In particular, determining the value of labor-power as a special commodity is necessary to uncover the quantitative connection between value and price. At this stage, it becomes inevitable to examine the "New Interpretation" (NI) developed by Gérard Duménil, Duncan Foley, and others, who formulated the relation between time and money systematically. Unlike the original version of the NI focusing on the aggregate relationship between macro-variables, the issue of quantitatively connecting values and prices on an industry level is the main objective here. In regular economic analysis, one must consider the perspective of inverse transformation from market prices into values. Under general conditions, however, it is impossible to recover the values of individual commodities starting from observable data on market prices, sectoral rates of profit, and technology. I clarify how assuming a uniform rate of exploitation is essential in quantitatively connecting values and prices on an industry level. Although this point has recently been accepted by the NI theorists, one must recognize that the mechanism to determine the VELT on a sectoral level should be explained first.

Chapter 3 turns to the NI itself. I demonstrate how the NI relies on two postulates regarding the MELT and the value of labor-power. The aim of this chapter is to follow the inherent logic of the NI and thus clarify why the constant capital part, unlike the conventional literature of Marxian value theory, is necessarily excluded in the transformation procedure from values into prices of production. This is related to the issue of double counting of the profit contained in constant capital, which was raised at an earlier stage of the NI and soon forgotten. I show that double counting is inevitable insofar as one accepts the NI's specific formulation of the relationship between value and price. This also explains why the rate of profit in value terms is always greater than that in price terms in the NI. Albeit in a modified form from Marx's original one, the quantitative relation between the organic compositions of capital and value-price disparities can also be determined consistently. Continuing the decomposition of the MELT into the VELT and the MEV made in Chapter 2, the construction of a disaggregated model is also described. It will be shown that the NI, at least its original form, implicitly assumes a uniform rate of exploitation, or, more precisely, the VELTs are proportional to wage rates. Last, I explain Cogliano-Foley's recent trials to validate the equal rate of exploitation assumption. I introduce the method of inverse transformation of the labor income share into the rate of surplus value at the industry level. Although this method does not theoretically dominate the Cogliano-Foley method, its advantage lies in its ability to estimate the sectoral differences in the rate of exploitation starting from the observable data. Nevertheless, as it is just another approximate solution to the problem of estimating sectoral rates of surplus value, one should wait for the discussion in Part IV.

In Part II of the book, I explore the theory of labor exploitation. Considered one of the most remarkable achievements of the mathematical Marxian economics in the last century, the Fundamental Marxian Theorem (FMT) needs to be discussed.

Chapter 4 introduces the history of making the FMT in Japanese Marxian economics. A relatively unknown, especially to the Western world, theoretical connection between Nobuo Okishio and Kei Shibata is introduced. First, this would seem to be a topic of interest to historians of economic thought. By clarifying the Shibata-Okishio connection, however, one can understand the central role played by the FMT in the Marxian theory of value and profit. In particular, it will be shown that Samuelson-Steedman's redundancy critique of the labor theory of value was already anticipated by Shibata in the 1930s, and Okishio proposed the FMT to refute the critique. In this chapter, I finally examine the various strands of the Marxian value theory. It will be shown that the FMT only works at a certain level of abstraction with some specific assumptions in each interpretation. This ultimately leads us to recognize what mathematical Marxian economics can and cannot do, a point that has often been misunderstood. The FMT can never "prove" the existence of labor exploitation in the sense that one also needs sociological and political insight to experience the reality of exploitation in the capitalist economy.

This is why the so-called temporal single-system interpretation's alleged proof of the exploitation "under all possible conditions" misses the point.

Chapter 5, as a digression, examines a novel interpretation of the Marxian theory of labor exploitation titled, an "axiomatic approach." This approach, proposed by Roberto Veneziani and Naoki Yoshihara, is based upon a Roemer-like theoretical setup with the analytical tools used in standard graduate-level microeconomics such as a general convex cone technology, etc. Starting from a few desirable axioms required to consistently explain labor exploitation is a promising research direction, but it is not incompatible with my understanding of abstract labor as the substance of value as an axiom, as is explained in Chapter 2. As the basic structure of the NI is also premised on the given postulates, it is but natural for the axiomatic approach to support the NI. Rather than discussing the axiomatic approach squarely, I focus on its relation to the NI. It is shown that beneath the sophisticated mathematical analysis of the axiomatic approach lies the NI's core insight about the Marxian value theory. The axiomatic approach's novel definition of "labor embodied" is conceptually similar to Keynes's "wage-unit" rather than Marxian value, which implies that the approach is premised on more restricted conditions than the NI. No doubt, the axiomatic approach is still in the making and, above all, open to the possibility of being combined with an interpretation other than the NI. However, just as is in the case with the NI, the introduction of heterogeneous labor into the axiomatic approach necessarily requires the assumption of equal rate of surplus value, which is easily predictable from the main argument of this book.

Part III turns to the analysis of the rate of profit which is one of the most prominent characteristics of classical and Marxian economics when compared with the mainstream one. As is well known, the law of the tendency of the rate of profit to fall (TRPF) is a central issue in Marx's project critiquing the political economy.

Chapter 6 discusses the Okishio theorem, which is the most important, and at the same time the most misunderstood, critique of the TRPF. Rather than presenting my argument outright, I start from the Japanese prehistory of the theorem related to the making of the FMT already explained in Chapter 4. Examining a prototype of the theorem provided by Shibata will help to understand its character as a counterfactual explanation. This implies that the Okishio theorem, or more fundamentally, the TRPF should not be considered as a real "disproof" or "proof" of the falling rate of profit under any condition. In this regard, I critically examine a recent critique of the Okishio theorem by the "temporal single-system interpretation" (TSSI) and demonstrate how the TSSI's refutation of the theorem cannot be regarded an internal critique in any sense. More importantly, I clarify the relative movement of three different definitions of the rate of profit by a simple numerical simulation. The main thrust of this chapter, to establish the Okishio theorem as a counterfactual thesis, is pursued by comparing the former with the Foley-Laibman theorem, which reformulated the Okishio theorem by assuming constant wage share instead of constant real wage. This will elucidate the meaning of Okishio's pursuit of the dynamics of competition in his later years, especially related to his seemingly embarrassing recognition of the theorem's limitations.

Chapter 7 critically evaluates the other extreme interpretation of the TRPF put forth by Alfredo Saad-Filho along the lines of Ben Fine's understanding of Marx's *Capital*. I show that although their specific interpretation of the organic composition of capital sheds new light on related issues, the interpretation has serious limitations. The logical difficulties in the organic composition of capital are analyzed. The most serious defect in Saad-Filho's interpretation is that it made the Marxian value theory and related issues, such as the TRPF, unfalsifiable claims in the sense that every downward or upward movement in the rate of profit could neither verify nor disprove the TRPF. While it is also true that Fine and Saad-Filho's interpretation brought about an openness to the TRPF by considering complicated elements affecting the rate of profit, it runs the risk of making the Marxian value theory a degenerating research program in the Lakatosian sense by adhering to highly abstract methodological discussions.

In Chapter 8, as a digression, Thomas Piketty's *Capital in the Twenty-First Century* is reviewed from the perspective of its relationship to Marxian economic theory, especially focusing on the TRPF as an analytical tool. Piketty's analysis is in the same vein as the long-run dynamics pursued by Ricardo, Marx, and other classical economists, or, in other words, it draws a powerful implication from the simple relationships among the several fundamental macro-variables. It will be argued that Marx's theory and Piketty's theory are not necessarily incompatible. By providing simple empirical results of the South Korean economy from 1995 to 2020, I show that the TRPF framework can bridge the gap between Piketty's empirical study and its theoretical explanation. One needs to go beyond the narrow boundary of the neoclassical framework, such as the elasticity of factor substitution, to explain Piketty's famous relationship between profit share and wealth-income ratio. This research direction of "Piketty after Marx," as I call it, will revitalize the TRPF as a useful analytical tool of capital accumulation, rather than as the fundamental proof of the falling rate of profit or an abstract tendency without explanatory power.

Last, Part IV is devoted to suggesting a new research direction in light of the main conceptual innovation of this book, the decomposition of the MELT into the VELT and the MEV.

As will be clear at this stage, my interpretation is a sympathetic critique of the NI focusing on the distinction between labor time and value. In this context, Chapter 9 approaches the issue of labor heterogeneity by a simulation analysis, rather than by collecting empirical data. Introducing the distinction between the VELT and the MEV into Richard E. Greenblatt's stochastic model, I show that regularly observed price-value proportionality continues to be maintained even under the assumption of differential rates of surplus value between sectors, let alone in the standard version of the NI. The direct proportionality between price and labor content obviously weakens only by decomposing the MELT into the VELT and the MEV. This confirms the main point raised in Part I in a roundabout way that the value concept is analytically necessary only if price and value are not directly proportional.

Chapter 10, as a digression, provides an exegetic study of Marx's concept of productive power. The chapter examines the differences between the concepts of Produktivkraft and Produktivität in Volume 1 of *Das Kapital* and draws the following conclusions. First, compared with Produktivität, Karl Marx used the term Produktivkraft in a narrower sense because he chose Produktivität only when explaining the effects of labor intensity being strengthened or machinery being introduced. Second, Marx avoided using Produktivkraft for factors of production other than labor-power.

In Chapter 11, in the concluding part of the book, I propose a tentative method for specifying the distinction between the VELT and the MEV, which are only explained at a purely theoretical level in Chapters 2, and 3 or through a simulation analysis in Chapter 9. In particular, in the analysis of this chapter, I attempt to integrate the two strands of the Marxian value theory, the dual-system approach, and the single-system approach. The conventional input–output analysis is combined with the MELT analysis, thus introducing the main contribution of this book.

PART I

Value and Price

CHAPTER 2

The Quantitative Connection Between Value and Price

2.1 Basic Setup

Prices are given to all commodities traded in the capitalist market. The objective of value theory is to pursue the main factor that regulates these market prices beyond considering them as self-evident facts determined by the interaction of demand and supply. Many factors, including purely coincidental factors, affect prices in the market, forming a series of causal chains. Prices can be explained starting from consumers' subjective satisfaction or from the quantity of socially necessary labor required to produce commodities. Specifying or choosing a certain causal relation itself presupposes a specific viewpoint on the capitalist society, or to put it another way, the research agenda of economics. Therefore, the validation of a specific value theory, the labor theory of value here, should be premised upon whether or how it captures the *differentia specifica* of capitalist society. In this sense, the labor theory of value is a "deductive reasoning starting from given premises (axioms)" (Veneziani & Yoshihara, 2017, p. 1610). Without a doubt, the appropriateness of the axioms or the correctness of the problem setting does not necessarily guarantee the logical consistency. In particular, the measurement of the magnitude of value and the specification of its quantitative connection with market prices should be carefully examined.

D.-M. Rieu, *A Mathematical Approach to Marxian Value Theory*, Marx, Engels, and Marxisms,
https://doi.org/10.1007/978-3-031-07808-8_2

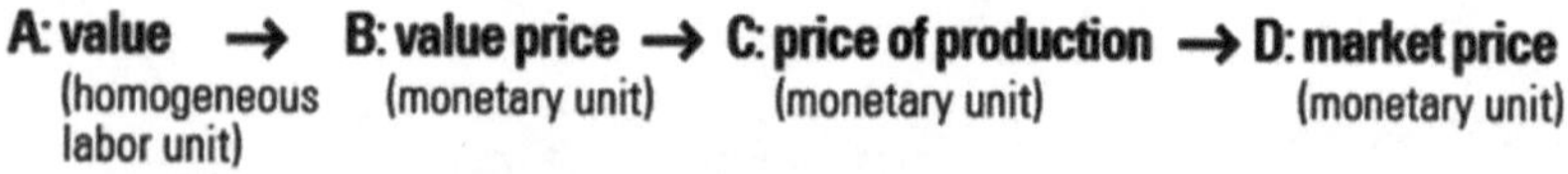

Fig. 2.1 The logical order from value to price

The labor theory of value measures the magnitudes of market prices according to a different principle based on homogenized labor time. As not only the units of measure but also measuring principles are entirely different, prices and values are not directly comparable, and are therefore represented as different magnitudes in two different systems: the price system and the value system. A logical order from value to market price including mediating concepts can be represented as shown in Fig. 2.1.

As the value-price (B)[1] is defined as the price proportional to the magnitude of value, the quantitative magnitude is assumed to be conserved in the process from A to B while the unit of measure changes. However, it is impossible to compare value with value price quantitatively because the latter, unlike the former, belongs to the category of price. However, the quantitative magnitude changes twice in the process from B to C, and further to D. Here B, C, and D are commensurable because all of them are measured by monetary units. In a nutshell, value is represented as market price through three consecutive transformations: mediation by money (A → B), competition between sectors with mutually different organic compositions of capital (B → C), and coincidental changes by demand and supply which leads to differential rates of profit between sectors (C → D).

As only market price (D) is empirically observable, the logical order from A to D is reversed to D → C → B → A in reality. This reversal is consistent with Marx's methodological distinction between "inquiry" and "presentation" (Marx, 1973). The concept of value is found in the process of inquiry from the concrete to the abstract. It is then presented as a starting point to explain the market price. To clarify the quantitative connection between value and price in the present procedure, the "inquiry" is once again needed. Let us consider which method can be applied to compare price categories (B, C, D) with value category (A)

[1] Value price is the term conventionally used in the literature of Japanese Marxian economics. See, for example, Okishio (1965). Bródy (1970) also used the same terminology. The same notion is also called "direct price" (Shaikh, 1984).

on the same dimension.[2] In the literature on Marxian value theory, the process from A to B is regarded as the object of the value-form analysis. However, the quantitative connection between the value system and the price system should be analyzed separately from the value-form analysis.

A good place to start is to imagine a gold standard system in which money itself is a produced commodity. If we denote the price of commodity x and gold, respectively, by p_x and p_g, the relative price of commodity x is equal to its relative value, that is, $\frac{p_x}{p_g} = \frac{v_x}{v_g}$, where v_x and v_g denote, respectively, the value of commodity x and gold (Moseley, 2011, p. 96). However, p_x here is not equal to the price of production of commodity x unless the organic composition of capital in this sector is equal to that in the gold-producing sector. By the same token, reducing the price of production (C) to the corresponding homogenized labor time (A) makes it difficult to remove the change resulting from the differential organic composition of capital between sectors. Even if the price of production of a particular commodity is inversely transformed into a certain magnitude in value space, it is not "value." To paraphrase, it may be called "value of production."

In conclusion, the problem of the relative value not being equal to the relative price emerges as soon as one makes the dimensions of value and price equal. Without some restrictive assumptions, therefore, it is impossible to directly measure value (A) or value price (B) starting from market price (D).

Based on the discussion so far, this chapter aims to clarify the quantitative connection between value and price. Section 2.2 clarifies the meaning of "labor" in the labor theory of value by precisely defining abstract labor, social labor, and homogeneous labor. It is emphasized that the logic of homogenization and socialization should be clearly distinguished. In Sect. 2.3, I show that the connection between value and price can be captured by determining the value of labor-power. A diagrammatical exposition is given in Sect. 2.4. Section 2.5 provides a mathematical formulation using a standard linear production model.

[2] The confusion about the dimension by which the four concepts in Fig. 2.1 are measured has often been reproduced. For details, see Bródy (1970, pp. 95–100) and Okishio (1982).

2.2 Labor: Abstract, Social, and Homogeneous

Regarding the Marxian labor theory of value, it is important to specify similarities and differences between the pair of concepts, abstract/concrete labor, social/private labor, and homogeneous/heterogeneous labor. Let us start with the concept of abstract labor, which is generally regarded as the substance of value despite all the differences between various strands of the Marxian value theory. Two mutually related crucial issues are: whether abstract labor is a concept specific to capitalism, and its relation to social labor and homogeneous labor. Whether abstract labor is a trans-historical concept representing the social division of labor in general which "constitutes the common material basis for all societies" (Itoh, 2021, p. 97) or a historically specific concept only applicable to capitalist societies, it should be approached from a perspective of social and historical situations that make such an abstraction possible.

A working hypothesis in this chapter is that abstract labor as the substance of value is a starting point, or an axiom of Marx's economic analysis of capitalism. Axioms are not produced out of thin air but are determined by the goal of theory, or differently put, an ideological position.[3] Without a doubt, the reason a specific axiom is chosen should be verified in reality. However, the reality depends upon which object of analysis is chosen. If the issue of distributing goods (and services) that are scarce relative to human wants is posited as the object of analysis, it is necessary to have an axiom about principles between human beings and scarce resources such as utility maximization through rational behavior of economic agents. However, as Marx noted in the first paragraph of the first volume of *Capital*, the object of his critique of political economy is the capitalist mode of production with "an immense collection of commodities" (Marx, 1976, p. 125). With this in mind, the concept of abstract labor should be derived from some specific characteristics of

[3] According to methodological instrumentalism, axioms or basic assumptions of a certain theoretical system can be chosen for analytical or pragmatic conveniences such as easier mathematical modeling and empirical data collecting. Instrumentalism, however, is also ideological in the sense that it keeps our eyes away from the historical and social contexts of the theoretical system.

capitalist reality.[4] It is in this sense that "preanalytical vision" with "definite and important ethical implications" should be demonstrated (Hunt, 1983, p. 335).

Now we are faced with the following two points.

First, the commodification of labor-power itself is compatible with any notion of value. The problem is that the labor-power and commodities should be defined without presupposing any specific concept of value. Alternatively, the concept of labor-power logically precedes the concept of abstract labor. This is why the commodification of labor-power is historically explained in the last chapters of "the so called primitive accumulation" in the first volume of *Capital*, after it was previously provided on the purely logical grounds of explaining the origin of capitalist profit. Abstract labor, therefore, includes the moment of the commodification of labor-power itself.

Second, the definition of the value of labor-power can easily run the risk of a circular reasoning. This is because abstract labor itself is premised upon the fact that labor-power is commodified, while labor-power, insofar as it is a commodity, has its value and its substance is nothing other than abstract labor. To avoid this vicious cycle, the value of labor-power should also be introduced as an axiomatic definition.[5] Viewed in this light, the logical structure of *Capital*, volume 1, which tries to prove the existence of exploitation starting from the equal exchange of labor-power should be reexamined (Obata, 1988, p. 161).

In summary, the proposition that abstract labor is a concept specific to the society in which labor-power is commodified has the following two foundations.

First, the main object of economics is not the interchange between human beings and nature but the social relationship between people and people in their historical context. This concept is a theoretical position that results from historical materialism.

[4] Matters would be different if one posits a commodity producing society in general as the object of economics. As is well known, Engels's "simple commodity production" is applied to all the pre-capitalist societies.

[5] In the case of the utility theory of value, the commodity character of labor-power does not cause any problems. Suffice it to say that labor-power is actually traded as a commodity and therefore it can be exchanged against money as a source of utility.

Second, the concept of labor should be determined consistent with the commodification of labor-power. Labor in this case must contain the determination of labor-power as one of its important moments.[6]

As abstract labor is a concept that extracts common, general characteristics of all human labor, by definition, it contains a moment of homogenization. In other words, abstract labor should be commensurable to "construct a homogeneous economic space" (Bidet, 2007, p. 12). This point is directly related to the question of whether abstract labor has a quantity. If abstract labor as the substance of value does not have a quantity, there are two possible solutions. One is to introduce another concept that reflects the substance of value and is measurable at the same time. The other is to argue that price is the expression of abstract labor as the essence, or more significantly, that money itself is abstract labor (Reuten & Williams, 1989). However, it is difficult to accept the latter as value becomes a redundant concept in the sense that it is neither qualitatively nor quantitatively differentiated from price insofar as abstract labor is represented only by money. On the contrary, the former is an inefficient theory because an additional concept is required to make it a self-contained theory. In short, it should be concluded that abstract labor has a quantity out of theoretical necessity.

The quantity of abstract labor is determined by the logic of homogenization included in the concept of abstract labor itself. Real grounds for the process of homogenization are found in the free mobility of labor, the "versatility of labor" (Lee, 1990) strengthened by the expansion of commodity exchange. Homogenization is realized through the repetition of capitalist commodity exchanges. It is impossible, and even meaningless to posit the concept of abstract labor without homogenization. Excluding homogeneous labor a priori leads to the redundancy critique of the value concept (Bowles & Gintis, 1977), or else, de facto determination of value

[6] From a more orthodox viewpoint, the commodification of labor-power is regarded as a precondition for the concept of abstract labor as follows: "...under conditions of petty commodity production (self-proprietorship), even if all the means of production are monetized (exchanged for), commodities will not, except as an exception, exchange at their values. This is because a portion of the labor time embodied in commodities so produced remains concrete labor. The living labor expended in production is that of the proprietor and family and is not monetized, and, therefore, not normalized by exchange" (Weeks, 1981, p. 36). While Weeks emphasizes that the quantity of abstract labor cannot be measured without the commodification of labor-power, this chapter focuses on the theoretical consistency to maintain the axiom that the substance of value is abstract labor.

by price (Krause, 1982). To summarize, abstract and homogeneous labor refer to the same thing in a capitalist society. Abstract labor can be defined as labor homogenized through capitalist commodity exchange. This point is indirectly confirmed by the following paragraph of *Capital*, Volume 1. Here, the substance of value is homogeneous labor; in other words, abstract labor.

> the labour that forms the substance of value is equal human labour, the expenditure of identical human labour-power. The total labour-power of society, which is manifested in the values of the world of commodities, counts here as one homogeneous mass of human labour-power, although composed of innumerable individual units of labour-power. Each of these units is the same as any other, to the extent that it has the character of a socially average unit of labour-power and acts as such. (Marx, 1976, p. 129)

Now let us turn to the distinction between private and social labor.

Private labor is validated as social labor when its product is recognized as socially useful. The concept of social labor itself is trans-historical. For example, in the so-called simple commodity production, the distinction between private and social labor is valid without commodification of labor-power. However, a mode of socialization is historically specific. In capitalist societies, social labor is a concept that reflects the anarchy of capitalist production.

The primary object of socialization is the use-value of a commodity. Private labor fails in socialization if its product is not sold on the market, and therefore regarded as socially useless. The following paragraph from Marx clearly shows this point:

> ...they [commodities-Rieu] must stand the test as use-values before they can be realized as values. For the labour expended on them only counts in so far as it is expended in a form which is useful for others. However, only the act of exchange can prove whether that labour is useful for others, and its product consequently capable of satisfying the needs of others. (Marx, 1976, pp. 179–180)

Without a doubt, as commodities in capitalist societies have both use-value and value, invalidation of use-value simultaneously implies the invalidation of value. However, as capitalist commodity exchange prevails, socially useful goods and services without value can also be validated through market sales. Land and natural resources are representative examples. However, in pre-capitalist societies, the product of labor is validated as useful, without all human labor being considered equal. Therefore, the logic of socialization is independent of the logic of homogenization which is the basis for the concept of abstract labor. In this sense, they are two theoretical pillars of the interpretation of capitalist market exchange. Without a clear distinction between these two logics, it is concluded that value is explained by price, or else value is redundant to explain price.[7]

The logic of homogenization and socialization are related to the reproduction of the relations of production and individual agents, respectively.

The logic of socialization is directly connected to the reproduction of individual agents. In a capitalist society, commodity producers (independent or capitalist) can realize the value produced through social validation by selling their products on the market. The reproduction of individual workers also depends on whether they succeed in socialization by selling their labor-power. By contrast, the logic of homogenization is always accompanied by tendency of differentiation. Capitalists, insofar as they increase profit, try to differentiate labor by using the strategy of divide and rule. Divided labor market or differentiation according to social and cultural elements such as gender and race can be understood in this context. The logic of homogenization is, therefore, "a cyclical movement showing the alternate realization of first the tendency and then the counter-tendency" (Carchedi, 1991, p. 5).[8] Although the tendency of differentiation prevailed for a long time (Roemer, 1978), the logic of homogenization is the main tendency because the organization of the process of capitalist production is practiced through the initiative of capitalists.

Another point to note is that the conflict between the tendency and the counter-tendency is reflected in the determination of the rate of surplus value, which leads to the uneven evolution of the rates of surplus value between industrial sectors or the groups of workers such as skilled vs.

[7] It is Lipietz (1985, p. 163) who clearly distinguishes the logic of socialization and that of homogenization when he argues that the contradiction solved by exchange is that between private and social labor, neither use-value/value nor concrete/abstract labor.

[8] Carchedi (1991, pp. 4–5) calls this "a tendency of the second type" while "a tendency of the first type" indicates "a movement towards a point or an area in which most realized phenomena are clustered." According to this terminology, the logic of socialization is the first type while the logic of homogenization is the second type.

unskilled, male vs. female, etc. While the logic of homogenization implies that the potential use-value of labor-power is given as the value-creating capacity at the point of employment contract, the equalization of the rates of surplus value implies that the value-creating capacity is equalized in the process of labor expenditure after the point of the employment contract. Unlike other commodities, in the case of labor-power, the potential use-value and the actual use-value are neither proportional nor in a fixed quantitative relation. While socialization in general commodities is the transformation of the potential use-value into the actual use-value, this transformation in the case of labor-power occurs in the production process after the point of the employment contract.

To conclude, the distinction between labor time, value, and price is related to the logic of homogenization and socialization as shown in Fig. 2.2. Labor time, value, and price, respectively, correspond to the physical system, value system, and price system of the capitalist production. In particular, labor time here implies the expenditure of human labor-power in a concrete useful form measured by clock hours. The arrow denoted by ③ indicates the logic of socialization in which the product of this concrete labor is exchanged against money, thereby being socially recognized. This process can be set between concrete labor and money directly without the mediation of value or abstract labor. By contrast, the arrow ① indicates the process of transforming heterogeneous concrete labor into homogeneous abstract labor while arrow ② represents the qualitative and quantitative connection between value and price or differently put, abstract labor and money.

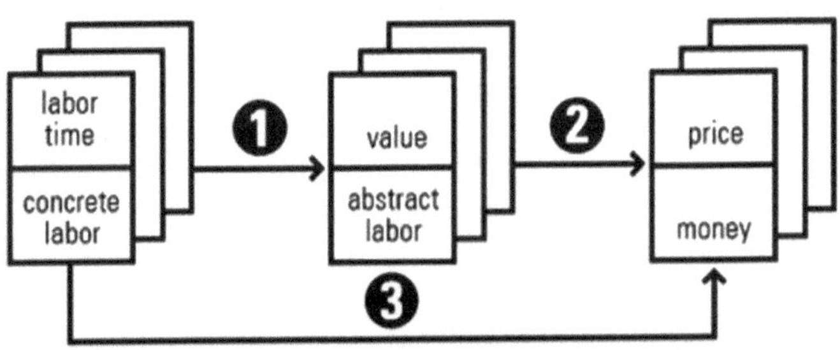

Fig. 2.2 The relation between labor time, value, and price

2.3 The Determination of the Value of Labor-Power

In exploring the quantitative connection between value and price, this section will focus on determining the value of labor-power. As labor-power is not a product of capital, the category corresponding to the price of production cannot be defined. Therefore, the logical order of the transformation is from the value of labor-power to the price of labor-power, and finally to the market wage. Namely, A → B → C → D in the case of general commodities in Fig. 2.1 becomes A → B → D in the case of labor-power. In other words, differential organic compositions of capital or sectoral rates of profit do not have any impact in the case of labor-power because there is no "labor-power producing" sector. Labor-power has either a value price or market price. Therefore, it is possible to "inversely transform" market wages into the value of labor-power through the process of D → B → A.[9]

To explain the existence of capitalist exploitation, Marx introduced the distinction between labor and labor-power. This distinction has two meanings. One is that labor-power also has its use-value insofar as it is a commodity. The other is that, unlike other commodities, value and use-value are homogeneous in the case of labor-power. Labor-power as a commodity is not a qualitatively new concept; rather, novelty can be found in the fact that the non-commodity character of labor-power is emphasized. Therefore, emphasis should be upon "peculiar" rather than "commodity" when labor-power is defined as a "peculiar commodity" (Marx, 1976, p. 274). The specific domain of Marxian value theory is the analysis of the capitalist labor process in which the class conflict around the production and appropriation of value emerges. This domain can be captured by recognizing the non-commodity characteristics of labor-power.

Value and price are two different systems that measure the same physical system according to two different principles. In the case of general commodities, their weight in one system is different from that in the other

[9] Marx himself discussed "the transformation of the value of labor-power into wages" in the chapter 19 of *Capital*, Volume 1 before he tackles the issue of the transformation problem in general in the Volume 3. This may be plausible because the connection between the value of labor-power and wage only requires the abstraction level of the Volume 1. In this sense, the argument here is not necessarily inconsistent with Marx's own idea.

system. Alternatively, the relative value and relative price are different. However, in the case of labor-power, this incongruence does not occur. Therefore, a thread to pursue the quantitative connection between value and price is given by determining the value of labor-power.

Despite its non-commodity character, labor-power is regarded as a commodity, albeit peculiar, because it is traded on the market with its price. It must be noted that the total value of net product in all industries is equal to the total price.[10] Now, suppose a hypothetical sector that "produces" labor-power. This sector can neither be conceptualized as a combination of constant capital and variable capital nor the sectoral rate of profit calculated; therefore, it cannot be the object of capital mobility between sectors. As the product of this hypothetical sector, labor-power should be regarded as composed of only net product. According to the proposition on the net product above, the price of labor-power equals to the value of labor-power. In other words, the value of labor-power is determined as the quantity of abstract labor corresponding to the money wage that workers receive. Even though we do not know how much abstract labor corresponds to one hour of concrete labor, it can easily be calculated how much money corresponds to the quantity of all concrete labor of the whole economy. This calculation can be called the "monetary expression of concrete labor time" (Duménil et al., 2009). The value of labor-power is, by definition, directly represented by this parameter. Furthermore, according to Marx's theory of the relative surplus population, excess supply is prevalent in the labor market. In other words, in the case of labor-power commodity, unlike other commodities, non-market-clearing prices should also guarantee the exchange according to the magnitude of value. To solve this issue, the price of labor-power is assumed to exist only as the value price which is strictly proportional to the magnitude of value.

The objection may be raised that determining wages prior to the value of labor-power is a circular reasoning. However, the value of labor-power is determined not simply by wage, but by referring to the total values produced in the whole economy. The value of labor-power may fluctuate even when the price of labor-power is stable. Value is the concept of capturing the mutual articulation of production and circulation spheres.

[10] This is a postulate of the "New Interpretation" provided by Duménil (1980), Foley (1982), Lipietz (1982) and others. However, in all the major solutions or interpretations to the Marxian transformation problem, this proposition has been commonly accepted.

The aggregate equalities in the transformation procedure validate this mutual articulation in a specified form. The logical priority of the value system is derived from the logical primacy of the production process over the exchange process. The quantitative aspect of this articulation can be captured by the relationship between the value of labor-power and wages because labor-power has a special position in the world of commodities.

When the value of labor-power is determined as above, the rate of surplus value (or exploitation) should be known to determine the magnitude of value produced in each sector. If the sectoral rates of surplus value are equalized ($e_i = e$), the sectoral values produced are calculated as the value of labor-power multiplied by $1 + e$.[11] If not, this method could not be applied. Therefore, we have two options: either to calculate the sectoral value magnitudes with the assumption of the equalized rate of surplus value, or to examine the change in the value of labor-power over time with unequal rates of surplus value between sectors. If one understands the Marxian transformation procedure in its narrowest sense as proof of the compatibility between value and price systems under the assumption of the equalized rate of surplus value, the former method can be accepted. In a more general situation, however, the latter is desirable to pursue the change in value relation over time.

Having made these points, it is time to formulate the quantitative relationship between value and price with regard to the issue of dimension. Abstract labor as a substance of value cannot be measured by clock hours because it is constructed from the common characteristics of various existing concrete labors. If one could find a particular type of concrete labor that has the average coefficient of reducing heterogeneous to homogeneous labor, it would be plausible to use labor as a numéraire. However, it is improbable to identify such a labor type without resorting to price information.

Following Bródy's proposal, the dimension of value $[v]$ can be defined in a roundabout way (Bródy, 1970, p. 98).[12] First, the total labor time

[11] In this case the rate of surplus value is calculated from the ratio of total profit to total wage on the entire economy. As is well known, total profit is equal to total surplus value while total wage in this case is equal to total value of labor-power. Considering the distinction between productive and unproductive labor, this result should be modified because the wages of unproductive workers result from the surplus value produced by productive workers. For details, see Rieu and Park (2020, pp. 290–293).

[12] Bródy used [W] denoting "Wert" which means "value" in German.

($\sum l_i$), total quantity of abstract labor ($\sum v_i$), and total price of net product ($\sum p_i$) should be equal insofar as the dimension of each variable is appropriately adjusted. Each variable captures the same reality from mutually different perspectives, namely, the physical, value, and price systems. This relationship can be represented as follows:

$$\left(\sum l_i\right) \times \alpha = \sum v_i \tag{2.1}$$

$$\left(\sum v_i\right) \times \beta = \sum p_i \tag{2.2}$$

Here α denotes the number of units of abstract labor corresponding to an hour of concrete labor and its dimension is [v /hour]. This can be called the "value expression of labor time." Additionally, the dimension of β is [dollar/v] because it denotes the number of units of money corresponding to a unit of abstract labor. This can be called the "monetary expression of value."

From (2.1) and (2.2), Marx's aggregate equality between value and price is as follows:

$$\sum p_i = \alpha\beta \sum l_i \tag{2.3}$$

The "monetary expression of labor time" or the MELT (m)[13] in the "New Interpretation" (NI) literature of Marxian value theory (Duménil, 1980; Foley, 1982) connects total monetary value-added to total labor time as follows, where the dimension of m is [dollar/hour].

$$m = \sum p_i \Big/ \sum l_i = \alpha\beta \tag{2.4}$$

While the magnitude of m is easily known from observable data, it is impossible to identify the magnitudes of α and β separately.

At a given point in time, some assumptions about the absolute measure of value such as $\alpha = 1$ are required. The value of labor-power calculated

[13] This concept substantially existed in Marx's *Capital*, although he did not use the same terminology. To the best of my knowledge, the first usage of the MELT dates back to Aglietta's "l'expression monétaire de l'heure de travail" (Aglietta, 1976, p. 37). In the English edition (Aglietta, 1979), it was translated into the "monetary expression of the working hour," however, it can also be translated into the "monetary expression of labor time."

under this assumption implies the ratio of the value of labor-power to the total value of all commodities. However, the magnitude of α itself changes over time reflecting the change in value productivity.[14] In this sense, the quantity of abstract labor represented by a clock hour of labor time (α) constantly changes and it is an increasing function of value productivity. Value productivity is determined by labor intensity and the degree of skill.

In light of these considerations, the relationship between the value of labor-power and money wages can be formulated more specifically. Dividing the total money wage ($w_i l_i$) by the monetary expression of value (β), the value of labor-power (VLP) is as follows, where w_i denotes the hourly wage.

$$VLP = \frac{w_i l_i}{\beta} = \frac{w_i l_i}{{}^{m}/_{\alpha}} = \alpha\left(\frac{w_i l_i}{m}\right) \tag{2.5}$$

According to the NI, the value of labor-power is considered to be constant if the money wage and the MELT change proportionately. Strictly speaking, however, it is the relative value of labor-power in terms of the total value of all commodities that remains unchanged. Alternatively, the wage-profit ratio of the whole economy remains unchanged. However, in this case, the sectoral effect is different.

Now the sectoral rate of surplus value (e_i) is summarized as follows, where V_i,S_i, and α_i denote the variable capital, surplus value, and value productivity of the ith sector, respectively.

$$e_i = \frac{S_i}{V_i} = \frac{\alpha_i l_i - w_i l_i/\beta}{w_i l_i/\beta} = \frac{\alpha_i l_i}{w_i l_i/\beta} - 1 = \frac{\alpha_i l_i}{w_i l_i/\frac{m}{\alpha}} - 1 = \frac{\alpha_i m}{w_i \alpha} - 1 \tag{2.6}$$

14 "Value productivity" is not a generally accepted concept. While value is related to abstract labor, productivity is basically related to concrete labor producing use-value of commodities. Here "value productivity" is an analogue indicating the expenditure of abstract labor within the unit of time. An essentially same usage of "value productivity" is found in Reuten (2017, p. 15), in which "value productivity of labor" is defined as "the value produced per unit of time." For example, the intensification of labor in a certain sector increases the value productivity of the sector. Upgrading the skill of workers in a certain sector will also increase the value productivity of the sector. Duménil et al. (2009, p. 561) and Basu (2021, p. 67) also used the term, "value productivity" in a similar sense. See also Chapter 11.

Therefore, the change rate of $1 + e_i$ over time is summarized as[15];

$$(1 \dot{+} e_i) = (\dot{\alpha}_i - \dot{\alpha}) - (\dot{w}_i - \dot{m}) \tag{2.7}$$

The first term on the right-hand side represents the differences in value productivity between the *i*th sector and the entire economy. If the value productivity of the *i*th sector develops more rapidly than the social average ($\dot{\alpha}_i > \dot{\alpha}$), the rate of surplus value in the sector may increase even when the value of labor-power increases ($\dot{w}_i - \dot{m} > 0$). By contrast, the rate of surplus value in the *i*th sector may decrease when the value of labor-power decreases if the value productivity of the *i*th sector develops more slowly than the social average.

It must be noted that the increase in α is consistent with the decreasing tendency of socially necessary labor time required to produce commodities or the "law of decreasing labor content" (Cogliano et al., 2018). The increase in α implies the increase in the quantity of value created within the unit of time due to the increase of the value productivity. Conversely, the total value quantity in a unit of commodity decreases owing to the increase in β. In summary, in a general situation without the equalization of the sectoral rates of surplus value, the value theory centers on the uneven development of sectoral value productivity.

2.4 A Diagrammatical Exposition

The discussion so far can be represented using diagrammatical exposition.

The total labor time OA in the first quadrant of Fig. 2.3 produces a definite quantity of value OB, and it is sold as OC in the market. Reflecting the NI's argument, OB and OC are applied to net product rather than gross product. On the other hand, as OA is equal to OD by definition in the fourth quadrant, the angle between OI and the horizontal axis is 45^0.

The slope of the straight line OE (=OB/OA) represents the number of units of value corresponding to a clock hour. The greater the value expression of labor time (α), the steeper the OE. The slope of the straight line OF (=OB/OC) in the second quadrant depends on the inverse of the monetary expression of value (β). The greater the monetary expression of value, the flatter is OF. Therefore, the quantitative connection among

15 $\dot{x} = \frac{dx/dt}{x}$ where t denotes time.

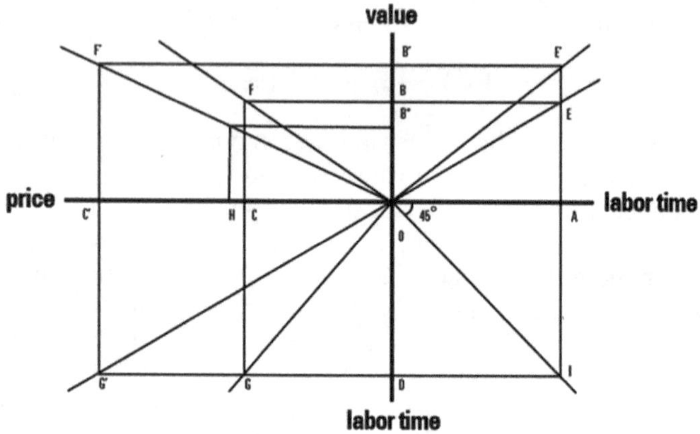

Fig. 2.3 The connection among labor time, value, and price

labor time, value, and price is completely represented in the first and second quadrants. As the MELT directly relates the sum of prices to the sum of labor time, it determines the slope of the straight line OG in the third quadrant. However, focusing only on the third quadrant neglects what happens in the first and the second quadrants. In particular, the issues of reducing heterogeneous labors to homogeneous labor, and the uneven development of value production among sectors are treated as if a black box.

With the development of capitalism, α and β generally increases. This effect is represented by the rotation of OG to OG'; therefore, OA (=OD) corresponds to more monetary units (OC'). Behind this procedure, however, there are two separate processes: OA produces more value (OB') and it is represented by more units of money (OC').

Suppose that the economy OA-OB-OC is changed to OA-OB'-OC', while the composition of products remains unchanged. The even inflation rate CH/OC is assumed to be applied to all commodities. If then, the quantity of use-value represented by OC in the former economy will be equal to OH in the latter economy. Nevertheless, it represents a smaller quantity of value (OB*). This result implies the unit value of each commodity decreases.

Next, the issue of the value of labor-power is analyzed in Fig. 2.4. If the wage is determined as Ow in the economy OA-OB-OC, the value of labor-power is OJ. Suppose that the economy is changed to OA-OB'-OC'

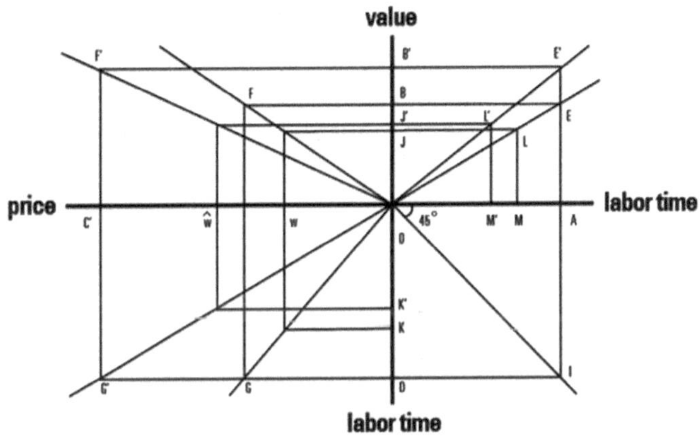

Fig. 2.4 The change in the value of labor-power

and wages also rise to O $\hat{w}$. Then the value of labor-power goes up to OJ'. From the geometrical characteristics, the ratio of the value of labor-power to the total value of net product OJ/OB is equal to OL/OE = OM/OA. However, in the economy OA-OB'-OC', this ratio changes to OJ'/OB' = OL'/OE' = OM'/OA because the total value of product is OB' and the value of labor-power is OJ'. In other words, this ratio decreases from OM/OA to OM'/OA. The value of labor-power in the NI indicates this ratio.

2.5 A Mathematical Formulation

The discussion so far can be formulated using a standard linear production model. For simplicity, each collective labor in each industry is treated as one variety of labor.[16]

The values of individual commodities are defined as

$$\lambda = \lambda A + l = \lambda A + \tilde{l}W^*(I+E) = \lambda A + \left(\frac{\tilde{l}W}{m}\right)\alpha(I+E) \tag{2.8}$$

[16] Without a doubt, there are many heterogeneous labors in each industry. So this assumption is restrictive. However, it does not make any kind of substantive change in the analytical results. For a more general formulation, see Duménil et al. (2009).

Here $\tilde{l}$ denotes the $1 \times n$ vector of the labor purchased by capitalists and l represents the $1 \times n$ vector of abstract labor obtained as a result of reducing heterogeneous labors to homogeneous labor. E, W, and W^* are the $n \times n$ diagonal matrices whose main diagonal is, respectively, the rate of exploitation (e_i), the wage rate (w_i) and the value of labor-power in each industry. It must be noted that neither a uniform rate of exploitation nor a uniform wage rate is assumed here.

The prices are defined as

$$p = (pA + \tilde{l}W)(I + R) \tag{2.9}$$

Here R is the $n \times n$ diagonal matrix whose main diagonal is the rate of profit (r_i) in each industry. Therefore, p defines market prices without the assumption of a uniform rate of profit.

Multiplying both sides of (2.8) by m leads to

$$\tilde{l}W = \left(\frac{1}{\alpha}\right)m\lambda(I - A)(I + E)^{-1} \tag{2.10}$$

By contrast, (2.9) can be summarized as

$$\tilde{l}W = p[I - A(I + R)](I + R)^{-1} \tag{2.11}$$

Equating (2.10) with (2.11) produces the following relationship:

$$\lambda = \left(\frac{\alpha}{m}\right)p[I - A(I + R)](I + R)^{-1}(I + E)(I - A)^{-1} \tag{2.12}$$

Under the assumption of a uniform rate of exploitation ($e_i = e_j = e$), $I + E = (1 + e)I$, (2.12) is changed to:

$$\lambda = \left(\frac{\alpha(1 + e)}{m}\right)p[I - A(I + R)](I + R)^{-1}(I - A)^{-1} \tag{2.13}$$

Therefore, it is possible to recover the values of individual commodities starting from observable data on market prices (p), sectoral rates of profit (R), and technology (A). It must be noted that α can be assumed to be 1 or any other constant. Namely, the assumption of a uniform rate of exploitation plays a role of quantitatively connecting values and prices on an industry level. In a general case, however, we must go back to (2.12) with n equations and $2n$ unknowns (λ_1, ..., λ_n, e_1, ..., e_n). The equation system is underdetermined unless one explains the mechanism of determining the value expression of labor time on a sectoral level.

References

Aglietta, M. (1976). *Régulation et crises du capitalism: L'expérience des États-Unis*. Calmann-Lévy.

Aglietta, M. (1979). *A theory of capitalist regulation: The US experience* (D. Fernbach, Trans.). Verso.

Basu, D. (2021). *The logic of capital: An introduction to Marxist economic theory*. Cambridge University Press.

Bidet, J. (2007). *Exploring Marx's capital: Philosophical, economic and political dimensions*. Brill.

Bowles, S., & Gintis, H. (1977). The Marxian theory of value and heterogeneous labour: A critique of reformulation. *Cambridge Journal of Economics, 1*(2), 173–192.

Bródy, A. (1970). *Proportions, prices and planning: A mathematical restatement of the labor theory of value*. North-Holland.

Carchedi, G. (1991). *Frontiers of political economy*. Verso.

Cogliano, J. F., Flaschel, P., Franke, R., Fröhlich, N., & Veneziani, R. (2018). *Value, competition and exploitation: Marx's legacy revisited*. Edward Elgar.

Duménil, G. (1980). *De la valeur aux prix de production*. Economica.

Duménil, G., Foley, D., & Lévy, D. (2009). A note on the formal treatment of exploitation in a model with heterogeneous labor. *Metroeconomica, 60*(3), 560–567.

Foley, D. K. (1982). The value of money, the value of labor power, and the Marxian transformation problem. *Review of Radical Political Economics, 14*(2), 37–47.

Hunt, E. K. (1983). Joan Robinson and the labour theory of value. *Cambridge Journal of Economics, 7*(3–4), 331–342.

Itoh, M. (2021). *Value and crisis: Essay on Marxian economics in Japan* (2nd ed.). Monthly Review Press.

Krause, U. (1982). *Money and abstract labour*. Verso.

Lee, C.-O. (1990). *On the three problems of abstraction, reduction and transformation in Marx's labour theory of value*. PhD Thesis, University of London.

Lipietz, A. (1982). The so-called transformation problem revisited. *Journal of Economic Theory, 26*(1), 59–88.

Lipietz, A. (1985). *The enchanted world: Inflation, credit and the world crisis* (I. Patterson, Trans.). Verso.

Marx, K. (1973). *Grundrisse* (M. Nicolaus, Trans.). Penguin Books.

Marx, K. (1976). *Capital* (Vol. 1). Penguin.

Moseley, F. (2011). The determination of the "monetary expression of labor time" ("MELT") in the case of non-commodity. *Review of Radical Political Economics, 43*(1), 95–105.

Obata, M. (1988). *Kachiron no Tennkai* [In Japanese, The evolution of value theory]. University of Tokyo Press.
Okishio, N. (1965). *Shihonsei Keizai no Kisoriron* [In Japanese, Basic theory of the capitalist economy]. Sobunsya.
Okishio, N. (1982). Dimensional analysis in economics. *Kobe University Economic Review, 28*, 31–44.
Reuten, G. (2017). The productive powers of labour and the redundant transformation to prices of production: A Marx-immanent critique and reconstruction. *Historical Materialism, 25*(3), 3–35.
Reuten, G., & Williams, M. (1989). *Value-form and the state*. Routledge.
Rieu, D.-M., & Park, H. W. (2020). Unproductive activities and the rate of surplus value at the industry level in Korea, 1995–2015. *Journal of Contemporary Asia, 50*(2), 284–307.
Roemer, J. E. (1978). Differentially exploited workers: A Marxian theory of discrimination. *Review of Radical Political Economics, 10*(2), 43–53.
Shaikh, A. (1984). The transformation from Marx to Sraffa. In E. Mandel & A. Freeman (Eds.), *Ricardo, Marx, Sraffa: The Langston memorial volume* (pp. 43–84). Verso.
Veneziani, R., & Yoshihara, N. (2017). One million miles to go: Taking the axiomatic road to defining exploitation. *Cambridge Journal of Economics, 41*(6), 1607–1626.
Weeks, J. (1981). *Capital and exploitation*. Edward Arnold.

CHAPTER 3

The New Interpretation: Toward a Critical Development

3.1 Introduction

The "New Interpretation" (NI), which was advanced starting in the 1980s (Duménil, 1980; Foley, 1982; Lipietz, 1982; Mohun, 1994) has changed the theoretical terrain of Marxian value theory, especially by changing the approach to dealing with the relationship between labor value and price. Unlike the conventional method using input–output data, the NI, which draws upon "capitalist accounting practice" (Foley, 1986, p. 60), has opened a way to "translate directly back and forth between money and labor time accounting" (ibid., p. 131) through the concept of the "monetary expression of labor time" (MELT). The NI, therefore, by making it possible to "to use widely available real-world money value data" (Foley, 2018, p. 561), has also contributed greatly to Marxian empirical research. Furthermore, as was recently shown by an "axiomatic approach" (Veneziani & Yoshihara, 2017), the NI maintains theoretical robustness regarding the issue of exploitation not only in a standard linear production model but also in general convex cone economies.

However, the "original sin" of the NI lies in its modifications of Marx's proposition, which may not be sustained by textual evidence,[1] as in the

[1] This is the main reason why the NI is criticized for "turning the whole relation between surplus value and profit on its head" (Shaikh & Tonak, 1994, p. 179). Fine et al.

D.-M. Rieu, *A Mathematical Approach to Marxian Value Theory*, Marx, Engels, and Marxisms,
https://doi.org/10.1007/978-3-031-07808-8_3

two issues of the so-called double-counting problem and a new definition of the value of labor-power, of which the most striking feature is, unlike the received view, its dependence on information about price and income.

First, according to the NI, it is net product, and not gross product, that is conserved in the transformation procedure from value to price. Some NI theorists argue that this is because adopting gross product causes the problem of double counting of constant capital (Campbell, 1997; Glick & Ehrbar, 1987; Lipietz, 1982). Although double counting has allegedly been refuted (Ramos-Martinez & Rodriguez-Herrera, 1996) and has not received further explicit discussion, it is still worth examining.

Second, the NI defined the value of labor-power as the money wage divided by the MELT, which implies that the conventional definition of the amount of labor embodied in the workers' consumption bundle should not be used (Duménil, 1980; Foley, 1982; Mohun, 1994). However, some NI theorists argue that these two definitions are compatible (Campbell, 2002; Glick & Ehrbar, 1987; Lipietz, 1982). Although it seems that the latter position has not been submitted to further analysis, this compatibility issue is also relevant to reorganizing the NI.

This chapter evaluates the above two issues from the viewpoint that NI is a critical development of Marxian value theory. It will be shown here that the NI's internal logic necessarily leads to problems in accepting the conventional aggregate on gross product and connecting the value of labor-power to the consumption bundle of workers.

Another important issue regarding NI is its application at the industry or sectoral level. The essential core of the NI lies in its ability to recover value magnitudes starting from observable price data, which can be called the "inverse transformation" in the sense that its direction is contrary to Marx's procedure of transforming values into prices.[2] The NI originally pursued only the aggregate relationship between labor time and price. Recently, however, it has been noted that the NI can also be applied to a disaggregated model (Duménil et al., 2009; Rieu, 2008). As noted earlier in Sect. 2.5 of Chapter 2, it has also become clear that the operationalization of the NI at the sectoral level requires the assumption of a uniform

(2004) also argue that the NI is a "wrong turning" assuming a direct and unmediated relationship between value and money.

[2] See Fig. 2.1 of Chapter 2. While the logical transition from B to C represents the procedure of Marxian transformation, the inverse transformation implies D → C → B → A.

rate of exploitation (Cogliano, 2018; Foley, 2016, 2018; Rieu, 2009a).[3] This chapter explores these issues while devoting attention to the critical development of the NI.

The remainder of this chapter is structured as follows. Section 3.2 summarizes the formal structure of the NI and demonstrates its reliance on two axioms regarding the MELT and the value of labor-power. Section 3.3 examines the problem of double counting and the relationship between the value of labor-power and the bundle of wage goods. It will be shown that the profit contained in constant capital is inevitably counted doubly according to the NI's specific formulation of the relationship between value and price. The compatibility of the two definitions of the value of labor-power will also be reexamined in light of the considerations discussed in Sect. 2.3 of Chapter 2. In Sect. 3.4, the application of NI at the microeconomic level is discussed. Before treating the differential sectoral rates of surplus value, the systematic relationship between the organic composition of capital and value-price disparities will be discussed. Then, the decomposition of the MELT discussed in Chapter 2 will be introduced to construct a disaggregated model. The MELT is decomposed into the "value expression of labor time" and the "monetary expression of value," and the measurement of sectoral rates of surplus value will be clarified based on this decomposition. In light of these discussions, an inverse transformation method is provided. Finally, Sect. 3.5 concludes the paper.

3.2 The Formal Structure of the New Interpretation

Before delving into details of the above-mentioned issues, the basic structure of the NI should be formulated. As this section focuses on the NI's two axioms which are regarded as given from the outset, it is not asked why the aggregates should be modified or why the value of labor-power should be differently defined. The analysis here is devoted to examining what happens if one faithfully follows the logic of NI.

A simple formulation of the NI was provided by Fine et al. (2004) as follows. Here P, R, w, L, S, and m denote the total profit, total

[3] Albeit in a different context, Reuten (2017, p. 20) argues for the unequal rates of surplus value because "there is apparently no mechanism for the equalisation of productive powers (or technique) between sectors."

net revenue, money wage rate, total amount of living labor, total surplus value, and the MELT, respectively.[4]

$$P = R - wL \tag{3.1}$$

$$S = L - \frac{w}{m}L \tag{3.2}$$

$$R = Lm \tag{3.3}$$

It must be noted that Eq. (3.1) is an identity. In contrast, Eqs. (3.2) and (3.3) hold if and only if the following two axioms of NI are accepted[5]:

Axiom 1. MELT (m) is defined with regard to net product.

Changing Eq. (3.3) with respect to m:

$$m = \frac{R}{L} = \frac{py}{lx} \tag{3.4}$$

Here, the $1 \times n$ vectors of $p = (p_1, p_2, ..., p_n)$ and $l = (l_1, l_2, ..., l_n)$ denote prices and labor inputs, respectively, while the $n \times 1$ vectors $x = (x_1, x_2, ..., x_n)^T$ and $y = (y_1, y_2, ..., y_n)^T$ denote gross product and net product, respectively.[6]

Equation (3.4) represents the ratio of transforming the total labor performed over a certain period into the prices of the net product in the same period. Mohun and Veneziani (2017, p. 1399) changed this equation into the form, $py = mlx$, which they call the "conservation principle" in the sense that total value created by labor is conserved in the process of exchange. It should also be noted that the dimension of m is monetary units per hour.

[4] Instead of the MELT, Fine et al. (2004, p. 5) used the "labor equivalent of money," which originated from the "value of money" (Foley, 1982) in the early literature of the NI. As it is defined as the inverse of the MELT, the equations are slightly changed here.

[5] This formulation was elaborated by Nakatani and Rieu (2003) as "two postulates." An essentially identical formulation was recently given by Mohun and Veneziani (2017).

[6] As is well known, the equation relating gross product and net product is $y = (I - A)x$, where A is an $n \times n$ matrix of input coefficients.

Axiom 2. The value of labor-power (VLP) is defined as the ratio of money wage (w) to the MELT:

$$VLP = \frac{w}{m} \tag{3.5}$$

Under the definition given by Eq. (3.5),[7] Eq. (3.2) holds because the total surplus value is equal to the difference between total living labor and total value of labor-power: $S = L - VLP \cdot L = L - \frac{w}{m}L$.

The NI is completely described by Eqs. (3.1)–(3.3) based on the two axioms above (Mohun & Veneiziani, 2017, p. 1400, Theorem 3). For discussing the disaggregated economy already explained in Sect. 2.5 in Chapter 2, however, it is useful to represent the value and price equations using a standard linear production model as follows, where π represents the $1 \times n$ profit vector:

$$\lambda = \lambda A + l = \lambda A + \frac{w}{m}l + \left(1 - \frac{w}{m}\right)l \tag{3.6}$$

$$p = pA + wl + \pi \tag{3.7}$$

At first glance, it is unusual to introduce the money wage rate directly into the value in Eq. (3.6). To remove this awkwardness, $\frac{w}{m}$ must be a dimensionless quantity. As w represents the hourly wage, a parameter is needed to transform the hourly wage into a scalar with the dimension of monetary units per hour. This parameter is the MELT. Furthermore, Eq. (3.7) clearly shows that the NI is not necessarily related to any equilibrium state such as the equalized rate of profit. The following statement by one of the founders of the NI confirms this point:

> As far as the new interpretation of the transformation problem is concerned, the required conditions are *the existence of a positive set of prices regardless of the rates of profit, guaranteeing not necessarily uniform positive wages, and a positive aggregate price of the net output*. (Italics in original; Duménil, 1984, p. 348)

[7] Mohun and Veneziani (2017, p. 1400) named this equation in the form $w = mVLP$ as the "weak single-system," compared with a "strong single-system" such as that of Wolff et al. (1982). The distinction between "weak" and "strong" is related to the treatment of constant capital in the transformation procedure, which will be discussed in Sect. 3.4. See also footnote 14

Now, we can determine how the two aggregate equalities in Marx's transformation procedure are modified in the NI. If one wishes to discuss the aggregate equalities of transformation, dimensional consistency must be obtained. The NI multiplies *m* by value or divides the price by *m*. The former case, denoting ε as the difference between the total profit and the total surplus value represented in terms of price, is as follows:

$$\varepsilon = \pi x - m\left(1 - \frac{w}{m}\right)lx = p(I - A)x - mlx = py - mlx = 0 \quad (3.8)$$

The last equality in (3.8) is derived from Eq. (3.4). Equation (3.8) implies that the total profit and total surplus value are equal. Without loss of generality, adopting the assumption $m = 1$[8] produces the following relation, which implies that the total price of the net product is equal to the total value of the net product.

$$py = lx = l(I - A)^{-1}y = \lambda y \quad (3.9)$$

Therefore, positing the two axioms leads to the modified aggregate equality of the NI, that is, Eq. (3.9).

3.3 Double Counting and the Value of Labor-Power

First, this section clarifies why double counting necessarily arises if one follows the internal logic of the NI. The objective here is not to show that the NI is the only correct view, but rather that the NI is logically consistent with respect to the double-counting issue.

In the NI literature, the so-called double-counting problem was originally pointed out by Lipietz (1982), who noted that the conventional view, in which the aggregate equality is determined with respect to the gross product, is misleading because the profit on the constant capital is counted twice. Therefore, he argued that aggregate equality must be amended to one with respect to the net product. Its implications were

[8] As m is the parameter connecting labor time unit with monetary unit, it can be assumed to be constant at a given point of time. If $m = k(> 0, \neq 1)$, then the original monetary unit can be transformed into a new unit by dividing by k. For example, the dimension of m, [dollar/hour] is changed to [$(1/k)$ dollar/hour]. Under this new monetary unit $(1/k)$ dollar, m comes to be 1.

Table 3.1 A simple reproduction example

Department	C_i	V_i	P_i	PoP_i
I	87.7	63.2	41.7	192.6
II	57.2	28.7	40.5	126.4
III	47.7	34.5	20.9	103.1
Sum	192.6	126.4	103.1	

approved by Glick and Ehrbar (1987), Saad-Filho (1996), and Campbell (1997).[9] Interestingly, double counting is no longer discussed in the NI literature. However, it is closely related to Axiom 1 of the NI, and therefore, to the rectification of the aggregate equality, that is, Eq. (3.9). Maintaining silence regarding the double-counting issue obviates the difference between the NI and other single-system interpretations (Lee, 1993; Moseley, 1993, 2016; Wolff et al., 1982), which sustains aggregate equality with regard to the gross product. Section 3.4 of this chapter shows that the internal logic of the NI implicitly includes a different treatment of constant capital from the latter.

To decipher the meaning of double counting, a good place to start is to examine the alleged refutation of double counting by Ramos-Martinez and Rodriguez-Herrera (1996). Assuming a simple reproduction in a three-department model, Ramos-Martinez and Rodriguez-Herrera (1996, p. 68) presented a numerical example, as seen in Table 3.1, and tried to show that double counting does not arise in any sense. In this example, departments I, II, and III are assumed to represent departments that produce means of production, wage goods, and luxury goods, respectively. C_i, V_i, P_i, and PoP_i denote the constant capital, variable capital, profit, and price of production of the ith department, respectively. As the constant capital and the variable capital are assumed to be transformed into prices from values, each variable is measured by the price unit. The equilibrium condition of simple reproduction is satisfied as the sum of each column is equal to that of each row. For example, the sum of profits in the three departments constitutes the demand for luxury goods, which is set equal to the supply of luxury goods, namely the price of production in department III.

[9] Saad-Filho, however, later denied the existence of the double-counting problem in a coauthored paper (Fine et al., 2004, p. 14).

Table 3.2 Decomposition of the prices of production into the cost price and profit at the previous stage of production

	Constant capital			*Variable capital*			*Profit*			*Price of production*		
	Sum	*Cost price*	*Profit*	*Sum*	*Cost price*	*Profit*	*Sum*	*Cost price*	*Sum*	*Sum*	*Cost price*	*Profit*
I	87.7	68.7	19.0	63.2	43.0	20.2	**41.7**	33.2	8.5	192.6	144.9	47.7
II	57.2	44.8	12.4	28.7	19.5	9.2	**40.5**	32.3	8.2	126.4	96.6	29.8
III	47.7	37.3	10.3	34.5	23.4	11.0	*20.9*	16.7	4.3	103.1	77.5	25.6
Sum	192.6	150.9	**41.7**	126.4	85.9	**40.5**	103.1	82.1	**20.9**	422.1	318.9	103.1

In Table 3.1 the proportion of the cost price $(C_i + V_i)$ to the total price of production in department I is $(87.7 + 63.2)/192.6 = 0.7835$ while the proportion of the profit is $41.7/192.6 = 0.2165$.[10] Applying the same ratio with the assumption of constant technology, $C_I(87.7)$ is decomposed into the cost price (68.7) and profit (19.0) at the previous stage of production. In other words, C_I contains the profit in the department that produces the elements of C_I. In a similar way, Table 3.2 is derived.

Ramos-Martinez and Rodriguez-Herrera (1996) argued that the bold numbers in Table 3.2 clearly show that there is no double counting in any sense. For example, the profit of department I (41.7) is equal to the profits contained in the constant capital of all three departments (19.0 + 12.4 + 10.3). This is also the case in departments II and III.

The above argument can be represented in general notations as follows, where γ_i denotes the proportion of profit to the price of production in the ith department.

$$(C_I + C_{II} + C_{III})\gamma_I + (V_I + V_{II} + V_{III})\gamma_{II} + (P_I + P_{II} + P_{III})\gamma_{III} = P_I + P_{II} + P_{III} \tag{3.10}$$

Dividing both sides of (3.10) by the sum of the prices of production and summarizing gives the following:

$$\frac{\sum C_i}{\sum PoP_i}\gamma_I + \frac{\sum V_i}{\sum PoP_i}\gamma_{II} + \frac{\sum P_i}{\sum PoP_i}\gamma_{III} = \gamma \tag{3.11}$$

[10] All numbers in this chapter are rounded off.

where γ is the ratio of total profit to the sum of the prices of production.

Equation (3.11) is nothing other than the statement that the weighted average of the ratio of profit to the price of production in each department is equal to the ratio of the sum of profits in the entire economy to the sum of prices of production. Here the weight is the relative magnitude of each department in the economy measured by the monetary sum of produced commodities. By definition, $\frac{\sum C_i}{\sum PoP_i} + \frac{\sum V_i}{\sum PoP_i} + \frac{\sum P_i}{\sum PoP_i} = 1$. According to the equilibrium condition of simple reproduction, $\sum C_i$, $\sum V_i$, and $\sum S_i$ are equal to the prices of the means of production, wage goods, and luxury goods, respectively. Therefore, Eq. (3.11) represents a self-evident relationship, which does not deny the possibility of double counting in any sense.

Now let us see why double counting necessarily arises if one follows the internal logic of the NI.

Equations (3.6) and (3.7) can be modified as follows, where s is the surplus value vector:

$$\begin{aligned}\lambda &= \frac{w}{m}l(I-A)^{-1} + \left(1-\frac{w}{m}\right)l(I-A)^{-1}\\ &= \frac{w}{m}l(I-A)^{-1} + s(I-A)^{-1}\end{aligned} \tag{3.12}$$

$$p = wl(I-A)^{-1} + \pi(I-A)^{-1} \tag{3.13}$$

If we adopt an aggregate of the gross product in NI in Eqs. (3.12) and (3.13), respectively, postmultiplying by x, the result may be written as follows:

$$\begin{aligned}\lambda x &= \frac{w}{m}l(I-A)^{-1}x + s(I-A)^{-1}x\\ &= px = wl(I-A)^{-1}x + \pi(I-A)^{-1}x\end{aligned} \tag{3.14}$$

Hence, with the usual assumption that $m = 1$, the total value and total price of the gross product are equal if and only if the following condition is satisfied:

$$s(I-A)^{-1}x = \pi(I-A)^{-1}x \tag{3.15}$$

Under the standard assumptions of the Perron–Frobenius theorem, Eq. (3.15) can be represented as follows:

$$(s + sA + sA^2 + \cdots)x = (\pi + \pi A + \pi A^2 + \cdots)x \qquad (3.16)$$

While the term on the left-hand side represents the total surplus value plus the sum of surplus values contained in constant elements of the capital at all stages of production, the term on the right-hand side represents profits aggregated in the same manner. This implies that if one adopts the conventional aggregate with respect to the gross product, then the profits contained in the constant capital are multiply counted. In this sense, the "double counting" actually means "multiple counting."[11]

It must be noted here, however, that this result is due to the NI's specific definition of the value of labor-power. Unless one accepts the two axioms of the NI, Eq. (3.12) does not hold because $(1 - \frac{w}{m})l$ cannot be regarded as the surplus value. As is well known, in Marx's own interpretation, total living labor minus the labor equivalent of total wage is not equal to the surplus value without restrictive assumptions.

Theorem 3.1 characterizes the double-counting problem in the context of conventional aggregate equality. The two conventional aggregates hold if one defines labor quantity, surplus value, and profit in a similar way to the notion of "vertical integration" (Pasinetti, 1973),[12] which implies a sort of double counting.

Theorem 3.1. If one calculates the profit and labor infinitely regressed, the total value and total price are equal with regard to the gross product.

[11] A flax-linen example was used to demonstrate the double counting by Glick and Ehrbar (1987), Saad-Filho (1996), and Campbell (1997). In this example, 1 unit of flax is produced by 4 hours of labor while producing 1 unit of linen requires 1 unit of flax plus 2 hours of labor. As this example has a specific input–output structure represented by $A = \begin{pmatrix} 0 & 1 \\ 0 & 0 \end{pmatrix}$, Eq. (3.15) becomes $s_1 + s_1 + s_2 = \pi_1 + \pi_1 + \pi_2$ where s_i and π_i denote the ith element of s and π. Without a doubt, this holds only by chance when $s_1 = \pi_1$. As $A^n = \begin{pmatrix} 0 & 0 \\ 0 & 0 \end{pmatrix}$ for $n \geq 2$, the profit and the surplus value in the flax sector are exactly counted twice.

[12] Fujimoto and Valle Baeza (2011) also tried to formulate the relation between values and prices by adopting the concept of vertical integration. Their research is notable as it treats market prices, not prices of production as equilibrium prices.

Proof Let x^* indicate $x(I - A)^{-1}$. Then, Eq. (3.14) can be represented as follows:

$$\lambda x = wl^*x + s^*x = px = wl^*x + \pi^*x \tag{3.17}$$

If $s^*x = \pi^*x$ is assumed, then $\lambda x = px$ holds. (Q.E.D.)

Let us now look at the value of labor-power in detail. Marx defined the value of labor-power as the quantity of labor required to produce commodities whose consumption is necessary to reproduce labor-power. This can be represented as λb, where $b = (b_1, b_2, \ldots, b_n)^T$ denotes the $n \times 1$ vector of the commodities necessary for the reproduction of labor-power. In contrast, as seen from the two axioms in Sect. 3.2, the NI's value of labor-power is equal to the wage divided by the MELT.

As Axiom 2 obviously breaks from the classical-Marxian notion of the subsistence wage, it does not seem that these two definitions of the value of labor-power are compatible. Mohun (1994, p. 401) succinctly stated the NI's position in this respect as follows:

> Labor-power is not a produced commodity; it is a commodified aspect of human beings, and human beings are not produced in any valorisation process. It might be suggestive for some purposes to consider that labour process which (re)produces people, but the relation involved are not class ones,..., and (re)production is neither production for sale nor production for profit. Consequently, there are no input-output data to consider which have any meaning in terms of the market....

The final sentence of the quote requires further examination. It is evident that there are no explicit input–output data in the reproduction of labor-power. However, we can hypothetically imagine the "labor-power (re)producing" (or household) sector in two ways.

First, as explained in Sect. 2.3 of Chapter 2, labor-power as a commodity may be assumed to be composed of only net product. In this case, Axiom 1 of the NI requires that the value of the labor-power be equal to its price, namely, the market wage, because it should be applied to all commodities including labor-power.[13] This refers to Axiom 2 of the NI. Therefore, in this case, Axiom 2 necessarily results from Axiom 1.

Second, as Nikaido (1960, p. 22) suggested, it is possible to endogenize the household sector in the input–output table. Suppose that the nth sector represents the household, then the consumption bundle can be regarded as the "input" vector, $(a_{1n}, a_{2n}, \ldots, a_{nn})$. In this case, the "net product" of the household sector becomes zero. Accepting this suggestion, the input–output structure of the household sector is formulated as follows:

$$(a_{1n} + a_{2n} + \cdots + a_{nn})x_n = x_n \tag{3.18}$$

As $l_n = y_n = 0$, $p_n y_n = l_n x_n$. In other words, if $\sum_{i=1}^{n-1} p_i y_i = \sum_{i=1}^{n-1} l_i x_i$ holds, then $\sum_{i=1}^{n} p_i y_i = \sum_{i=1}^{n} l_i x_i$ automatically holds. This implies that the Axiom 1 of the NI presents no problem. Now, introducing prices changes Eq. (3.18) to the following:

$$\frac{p_1}{m}a_{1n} + \frac{p_2}{m}a_{2n} + \cdots + \frac{p_n}{m}a_{nn} = \frac{w}{m} \tag{3.19}$$

Note that (3.19) is an identity with the proviso that workers do not save. The right-hand side, $\frac{w}{m}$ is the NI's value of labor-power. To be able to connect it with the real wage basket vector, one should provide the economic implications of $\frac{p}{m}$. This is the very way in which another version of the NI tried to put together the two definitions of the value of labor-power. The most sophisticated discussion was provided by Campbell (2002), who introduced the novel concept of "the vector of redistributed value," which is defined as $\frac{p}{m}$. While Duménil et al. (2009) called the NI the "price of net product-unallocated purchasing power" (PNP-UPP), Campbell (2002) introduced the hypothetical allocation of purchasing power according to the MELT. However, this allocation necessarily leads to an effect contrary to the original intention of complementing the NI. If a concept of "redistributed value" is used to explain the connection

[13] The only case of exception is when the difference between the value and the price of the net product in all the sectors except labor-power is exactly canceled out by the difference between the value of labor-power and wage. However, this is possible only by chance.

between the NI's value of labor-power and the real wage basket, then it should also be applicable to constant capital (Moseley, 2000). Although Foley's position (2000, p. 24) appears not to be against the application of the MELT to constant capital, such an application may ultimately lead to the unraveling of the NI, or to the introduction of another redundant concept, which is neither value nor price.[14] Certain economic interpretations such as "redistributed value" can be given to $\frac{p}{m}$ only *ex-post* and in a hypothetical sense. Furthermore, as will be shown in the next section, the NI's implicit explanation of value-price deviation is not compatible with the symmetric treatment of constant capital and variable capital.

3.4 The Application of the New Interpretation at the Microeconomic Level

Equation (3.4) may be rewritten using an axiomatic equality between total living labor and the total value of the net product:

$$m = \frac{py}{lx} = \frac{py}{\lambda y} = \frac{\lambda \Delta y}{\lambda y} = \sum \omega_i \delta_i \tag{3.20}$$

where $\delta_i = \frac{p_i}{\lambda_i}$, $\omega_i = \frac{\lambda_i y_i}{\lambda y}$, and $\Delta = diag(\delta_1, \delta_2, \cdots\cdots, \delta_n)$.

In other words, MELT is the weighted average of the price-value ratio of commodities (δ_i), where the weight (ω_i) is the sectoral ratio of the value of the net product. Therefore, it seems impossible to apply this concept directly to an individual sector level (Saad-Filho, 1996, p. 127). Rieu (2006), however, showed that a specific value-price relation at the sectoral level is implied in the NI. This point will be further pursued in this section. The aim here is to explore the ways in which the NI will be used to estimate Marxian value categories at the microeconomic level.

[14] In particular, as will be shown in the next section, the rate of profit is always smaller than the value rate of profit in the NI. This is critically different from other "single-system" theorists arguing for the symmetric treatment of constant and variable capital such as Moseley (2016). Freeman (2004) also argued for a similar concept as a good approximation for "value," a development predated by Brinkman's (1999) attempt to conceptualize "essential price", which in our notation is, $\frac{p_i}{m}$. Freeman's proposal implies the idea of transforming the NI into a different interpretation, which is similar to the "temporal single-system interpretation(Kliman, 2007; Kliman & McGlone, 1999).

Table 3.3 Three-department model: example

Department	*C*	*V*	*S*	*Total*
I	68.86	20	20	108.86
II	60.25	30	30	120.25
III	51.65	40	40	131.65

3.4.1 Value-Price Deviation

Let us start with a numerical example, shown in Table 3.3, which describes a reproduction scheme in terms of value. Departments I, II, and III denote the department producing the means of production, wage goods, and luxury goods, respectively. These can be analyzed without necessarily assuming simple reproduction.[15]

Based on the NI, the system of simultaneous equations used to solve the prices of production can be set up (Itoh, 2005; Rieu, 2006) as Eqs. (3.21)–(3.24), where δ_1, δ_2, and δ_3 denote the price-value ratio of each department. According to Axiom 2, the value of labor-power is not multiplied by any price-value ratio but merely by the MELT, which is assumed here to be 1. Equation (3.24) represents "the total profit = the total surplus value," which also implies an aggregate of net product assuming $m = 1$. The solutions are $\delta_1 = 1.2547$, $\delta_2 = 1.1274$, $\delta_3 = 1.0233$, and $r = 0.2841$.

$$(68.86\delta_1 + 20)(1 + r) = 108.86\delta_1 \tag{3.21}$$

$$(60.25\delta_1 + 30)(1 + r) = 120.25\delta_2 \tag{3.22}$$

$$(51.65\delta_1 + 40)(1 + r) = 131.65\delta_3 \tag{3.23}$$

$$(180.76\delta_1 + 90)r = 90 \tag{3.24}$$

The results are presented in Table 3.4. Here superscript P implies that the variable is measured in terms of price. It must be noted that the prices

[15] Unlike Bortkiewicz's famous example, the organic composition of capital in department II is assumed here to be equal to the social average.

Table 3.4 New interpretation's solution

Department	C^P	V^p	S^P	*Total*
I	86.4	20	30.2	136.6
II	75.6	30	30	135.6
III	64.8	40	29.8	134.6

of production in all departments are greater than the monetary equivalents of values, and therefore, the average rate of profit calculated in value terms is always greater than that in price terms. This is due to the double counting noted above.[16]

In capitalist reality, we are faced with empirical data, such as shown in Table 3.4. Then. this can be transformed into labor values, such as those seen in Table 3.3, by solving the simultaneous equations system such as (3.21)–(3.24). Table 3.3 is derived under the assumption of the equalized rate of surplus value. As shown in Chapter 2, the distribution of variable capital among departments cannot be uniquely determined. However, this assumption does not cause any problems for the consistency of the NI. In this sense, the NI does not simply assume away constant parts of capital because it is possible to calculate their values consistently when their prices are given.

This analysis can lead to the problem of correspondence between value-price deviation and the composition of capital. Marx presented his famous rule on the deviation of price from value in the third volume of *Capital* as follows:

> The value of the commodities produced by capital II [with higher composition of capital-Rieu] would, therefore, be smaller than their price of production, the price of production of the commodities of III [with lower composition of capital-Rieu] smaller than their value, and only in the case of capital I in branches of production in which the composition happens to coincide with the social average, would value and price of production be equal. (Marx, 1959, p. 164)

[16] This was noted by Cogliano et al. (2018, p. 252), however, without referring to the issue of double counting.

Table 3.5 Numerical example for new interpretation

Department	PCC_i	$PCC_i - PCC_{AVE}$	p_i	$m^*\lambda_i$	$p_i - m^*\lambda_i$	μ_i	$\mu_i - \mu_{AVE}$
I	4.32	1.80	136.6	122.8	13.8	0.6325	0.0750
II	2.52	0	135.6	135.6	0	0.5575	0
III	1.62	−0.90	134.6	148.5	−13.8	0.4814	−0.0761

The above rule can be represented as follows, where OCC_i and OCC_{AVE} denote the organic composition of capital in the ith sector and in social average, respectively:

$$p_i - \frac{\lambda_i}{m} = f(OCC_i - OCC_{AVE}) \qquad f' > 0, \quad f(0) = 0 \tag{3.25}$$

Marx's rule does not hold in the NI because aggregate equality is defined with regard to net product, not gross product. Although the organic composition of capital in department III is lower than the social average in Table 3.3, its price of production (134.6) is greater than the value multiplied by the MELT (assumed to be 1), 131.65. This problem has been ignored in the NI tradition.

However, if we use the ratio of total price to total value with regard to gross product (m^*),[17] then a new rule for value-price deviation in the NI emerges, as shown in Table 3.5.

In this example, $m^* = 406.8/360.76 = 1.1276$. Note that the sectoral composition of capital (PCC_i) and its social average (PCC_{AVE}) are measured here in terms of price, not value. The new rule is as follows:

$$p_i - m^*\lambda_i = g(PCC_i - PCC_{AVE}) \qquad g' > 0, \quad g(0) = 0 \tag{3.26}$$

$$p_i - m^*\lambda_i = h(\mu_i - \mu_{AVE}) \qquad h' > 0, \quad h(0) = 0 \tag{3.27}$$

In (3.27), μ_i denotes the proportion of constant capital in the price of production of the ith department measured in monetary units: $\mu_i =$

[17] Calculation of this *ex-post* ratio is not incompatible with the NI's axiom on net product. It must be noted in passing that a precursor of the NI, De Vroey (1981, p. 190), defined the "monetary expression of social labor-time" as the ratio of the sum of prices to the sum of values with regard to gross product.

$\frac{C_i^P}{C_i^P+V_i^P+S_i^P}$. In addition, μ_{AVE} is the average of the μ_i's. For example, because PCC_{III} is smaller than PCC_{AVE}, its value multiplied by m^* (148.5) is greater than its price of production (134.6). If any economic meaning can be given to $m^*\lambda_i$, then Marx's theory of the relationship between value-price deviation and the composition of capital is supported, albeit in a modified form.

Unlike Marx's original rule, (3.26) and (3.27)[18] relate the value-price deviation to the internal composition of capital measured in prices. This is an inevitable result of the NI's definition of the value of labor-power which is dependent on price-income data. The merit of this rule is that it is operational because one does not have to deal with difficult problems such as different vintages in elements of constant capital. In a certain sense, it can be said that the NI avoids the difficult question of measuring capital raised in the Cambridge controversy.

As explained in Sect. 2.1 of Chapter 2, $m^*\lambda_i$ does not have its own place in the distinction between value and price. However, its counterpart in the price domain, $\frac{p_i}{m^*}$, can be calculated from observable data. In light of these considerations, the following argument provided by an NI theorist requires further examination.[19]

> The labor theory of value therefore says nothing about constant capital, for the price of each individual item is not proportional to its labor-value, and the price of all such items aggregated together is not proportional to their aggregate labor-value. It is value-added that is central to this interpretation, not total value. (Mohun, 2018, p. 11)

3.4.2 *Labor Heterogeneity*

Heterogeneous labor has been one of the most difficult issues in the literature on Marxian value theory. Although Marx constantly emphasized the importance of reducing heterogeneous to homogeneous labor, he assumed away the issue in order to "save…the trouble of making the reduction" (Marx, 1976, p. 135). This assumption was also adopted in the early literature of the NI when Lipietz (1985, p. 41) assumed

[18] This relation is a modified version of the rule provided by Seton (1957).

[19] Interestingly, Mohun (2004, p. 86) reached essentially same result as (3.26). See the Proposition 2 of the paper. However, he noted, "within the DF [Duménil-Foley: Rieu] approach this sort of proposition is at best of only doubtful interest" (ibid., p. 97).

that "value added by skilled labor has been reduced…to a simple labor equivalent."

With respect to the mathematical representation of the labor theory of value, there is serious doubt on the exact meaning of the labor input vector, l. As Fleetwood (2001, p. 61) noted, it seems to be "individual and concrete labor" that "could be observed interacting with the technology (A) and receiving a wage (w)." If there exists a proportional relation between the nominal amount of labor time measured by the clock hour and the amount of abstract labor, this doubt can be dispelled. However, this proportionality is related not only to the reduction of heterogeneous to homogeneous labor, but also to the issue of value productivity noted earlier in Chapter 2. Although Lipietz (1982) advanced the concept of the "tensor of exploitation" to treat this issue, it has been a long time since it was pursued in the NI literature.

A more radical objection regarding the existence of heterogeneous labor was previously raised by Morishima, who accurately predicted future changes in the literature of Marxian value theory including the NI (Morishima, 1973, pp. 180–181):

> …as soon as the heterogeneity of labour is allowed for, the value of theory is seen to conflict with Marx's law of the equalization of the rate of exploitation through society, unless the different sorts of labour are reduced to the homogeneous abstract human labour in proportion to their wage rates. This is a serious dilemma from the point of view of Marxian economists, because on the one hand different rates of exploitation among different classes of workers obviously are not compatible with Marx's view of the polarization of society into two classes, capitalists and workers, and on the other, if different sorts of labour are converted into the abstract human labour in proportion to their wages, then the resulted value system depends on relative wages and hence Marx's intention of obtaining an intrinsic value system completely independent of markets is not fulfilled. There is no easy way out of this predicament.

Let us follow the development of the NI from the perspective of Morishima's statement. As the denominator of the MELT is the total working time measured by the clock hour, not abstract labor hour, it requires further examination if the NI is applied at the microeconomic level. Using the same logic noted in footnote 8, the total working time can be set equal to the total abstract labor time at a given point in time. However, without restrictive conditions, the sectoral distribution of abstract labor time deviates from that of labor time measured by the clock hour. Furthermore, this problem is intertwined with the issue of differential rates of exploitation among different groups of workers or sectors. Foley (2005) may have been the first to seriously address this issue. However, he supported the conventional NI procedure by assuming that "different qualities of labour are present in the same proportions in all sectors of production" (p. 41). Although he "leaves open the question of whether different qualities of labour are subject to the same rate of exploitation" (Foley, 2005, p. 41), Foley still regards the measurement of abstract labor time as a "pragmatic issue" or "econometric problem."[20] Interestingly, Foley (2005, p. 41) himself accepted the necessity of labor quality adjustment in case "we are interested in the degree to which international foreign exchange markets equate social labor across different countries."[21] As the essentially same problem will arise in the case of estimating differential sectoral rates of surplus value, however, some adjustments for the qualitative differences in labor are inescapable and should be integrated into the theory, which goes beyond a merely pragmatic issue.

The issue of estimating the sectoral rates of surplus value was first raised by Rieu (2008), and then was accepted by Duménil et al. (2009). It was finally clarified that this issue is related to the issue of the equalization of the rate of exploitation and the conversion of concrete labor to abstract human labor by wages, as already noted by Morishima (1973).

3.4.3 *Decomposition of the Monetary Expression of Labor Time*

Before exploring the issue of sectoral rates of surplus value, let us determine whether the definition of the value of labor-power (3.5) can be applied at the microeconomic level. A simple application of (3.5) at the sectoral level yields:

$$VLP_i = \frac{w_i}{m} \tag{3.28}$$

[20] As Cartelier (2006, p. 298) notes, however, just assuming averaging out cannot be a "pragmatic" solution to the "unsolved problem" in that it does not in fact pursue the relationship between value and price more deeply.

[21] Recently this issue was thoroughly examined by Ricci (2021) with respect to unequal exchange in international trade.

where w_i denotes the wage rate in the ith sector.

Remembering that the NI's definition of the value of labor-power is premised upon the conception that labor-power is not produced capitalistically, it is logically natural to accept (3.28). Among the NI theorists, Duménil et al. (2009) also accepted Eq. (3.28) while Mohun (2004, p. 75) explicitly stated that this does not necessarily hold.[22] If Eq. (3.28) is accepted, then the sectoral rates of surplus value can be represented as follows:

$$e_i = \frac{m}{w_i} - 1 \tag{3.29}$$

From (3.29), it is clear that $w_i = w_j$ implies $e_i = e_j$. It is obvious, however, that sectoral rates of surplus value also depend on value productivity, not only on the wage rate. As there exists free mobility of labor on the side of workers regarding working conditions such as wage rate and labor intensity, it might be plausible to assume the equalization of the rate of exploitation among sectors, in particular, to find the equilibrium prices in the classical-Marxian long-run equilibrium (Cogliano et al., 2018). However, if one tries to recover sectoral rates of surplus value starting from actual market prices, not equilibrium prices, this assumption cannot be adopted.

Based on the discussion in Chapter 2, two different issues should be pursued separately to apply NI at the microeconomic level. First, sectoral-level exploitative conditions are not equal at a given point in time. Second, equal amounts of clock hours may produce different amounts of socially necessary abstract labor due to differences in the value productivity. Rieu (2008, p. 565) proposed decomposing the MELT into the product of the "value expression of labor time (VELT)" and the "monetary expression of value (MEV)," which correspond to α and β in Chapter 2, respectively. The VELT indicates how many hours of socially necessary abstract labor correspond to an hour of concrete individual labor, while the MEV represents how many units of money correspond to an hour of abstract labor. Duménil et al. (2009) described this composition as follows[23]:

[22] For the details of Mohun's argument and its critique, see Rieu (2008, pp. 560–561).

[23] While Duménil et al. (2009) do not explicitly adopt the terminology, "the values created by one hour of labor" (p. 563) actually implies the VELT. On one hand, it was Gouverneur (1990) who used the term "monetary expression of value" earlier. However, his concept is different from the MEV here because he directly regards an hour of every

> The two notions, the MELT and the MEV, which can also be called the 'Monetary Expression of value-creating (abstract) Labor Time', are distinct. (Duménil et al., 2009, p. 564)

Under this decomposition, Eq. (3.3) or Axiom 1 of the NI becomes as follows:

$$m = \frac{R}{L} = \frac{\lambda y}{lx} \cdot \frac{py}{\lambda y} = VELT \cdot MEV \tag{3.30}$$

The usual assumption of the NI, namely, $m = 1$, is innocuous at the macro-level of the economy. As shown in footnote 8, the absolute magnitude of the MELT is irrelevant in connecting the total labor time and total value-added in prices. At the sectoral level, however, the distinction between the VELT and MEV matters.

Using the numerical examples found in Tables 3.3 and 3.4, the gist of this distinction can be explained. As the MELT is assumed to be 1 in this example, we can safely assume that the VELT and MEV are also equal to 1. Now, the MEV of the ith department (MEV_i) is calculated as the ratio of $V_i^P + S_i^P$ to $V_i + S_i$ in Table 3.6. It is easily confirmed that the MEV is equal to 1 at the aggregate level because $\sum(V_i + S_i) = \sum(V_i^P + S_i^P)$. At the sectoral level, MEV_i depends on the difference between the sectoral organic composition of capital and the social average. As the NI rule (3.26) shows, the price-value difference is an increasing function of the organic composition of capital measured in price terms. This hints at

Table 3.6 Decomposition of the monetary expression of labor time

Department	$\sum L_i$ *(A)*	$\sum(V_i + S_i)$ *(B)*	$\sum(V_i^P + S_i^P)$ *(C)*	MEV_i *(C/B)*	$VELT_i$ *(B/A)*	$MELT_i$ *(C/A)*
I	20	40	50.2	1.2550	2.0	2.51
II	60	60	60.0	1.0000	1.0	1.00
III	100	80	69.8	0.8725	0.8	0.80
Total	180	180	180	1.0000	1.0	1.00

concrete labor as an hour of "value." On the other hand, Ricci's (2021, p. 110) distinction between the "labour expression of value" and the "monetary expression of value" is in the same spirit of the decomposition in this chapter. However, he introduces the physical quantity of the commodity as a medium for connecting labor time with price.

the possibility of that MEV_i is also an increasing function of the organic composition of capital. In addition to the organic composition of capital, market elements, such as monopoly power could also affect the magnitude ofMEV_i. If the capital in the ith sector has some kind of monopoly power that prohibited other capital from entering its business, it could maintain a monopoly price greater than an equal rate of profit price for some time. This implies that the same quantity of abstract labor is exchanged against more units of money in the ith sector, which means that MEV_i is above average. In Table 3.6, only department I has a higher-than-average MEV. To show the importance of the decomposition above, assume that the value productivity is in the order of departments I, II, and III. Therefore, 20 hours in department I creates 40 abstract labor hours, while 100 hours in department III only creates 80 abstract labor hours. In this case, all theVELT_i's are different, although the aggregate VELT is equal to 1.[24] In the case of department II, 60 hours of labor is homogenized to 60 hours of abstract labor, and then transformed into 60 dollars. Therefore, this distinction does not make any difference. If all $VELT_i$'s are equal, then the distinction is meaningless because an hour of individual concrete labor always creates an hour of socially necessary abstract labor.

Now the disaggregated representation for (3.30) is formulated as:

$$m_i = VELT_i \cdot MEV_i \tag{3.31}$$

As already explained in Fig. 2.2 of Chapter 2, Eq. (3.31) describes the logic of homogenization and socialization which are logically successive. In the process of production, the ith concrete, individual labor is homogenized to a certain amount of socially necessary abstract labor by the$VELT_i$. Then in the exchange process, the latter is transformed into a certain quantity of money by the MEV_i. The magnitude of the $VELT_i$ depends on the coefficient of reducing concrete to abstract labor and the "tensor of exploitation" (Lipietz, 1982). If the ith labor is more

[24] This discussion is an application of Itoh's "so-called three tables (instead of the conventional two tables)" (Itoh, 2021, p. 16). However, his distinction between "the substance of value produced" and "the substance of value acquired" (ibid., p. 113) is different from the distinction between labor time and value here. "The substance of value acquired" corresponds to "value of production" noted in Sect. 2.1 of Chapter 2.

skilled-than-average labor, then $VELT_i$ will be greater than 1.[25] Harsher exploitative conditions in the ith sector are also connected with a larger $VELT_i$. The $VELT_i$'s will be equal only when all the concrete labors are homogenized to the same amount of abstract labor, and all the exploitative conditions are equalized across sectors.

Based on the suggested decomposition of the $MELT$, the sectoral rate of the surplus value is as follows:

$$e_i = \frac{VELT_i \cdot L_i - VLP_i L_i}{VLP_i L_i} = \frac{VELT_i - \frac{w_i}{m}}{\frac{w_i}{m}} = VELT_i\left(\frac{m}{w_i}\right) - 1 \tag{3.32}$$

The comparison of (3.32) with (3.29) makes it clear that the sectoral rates of surplus value are systemically distorted according to the conventional NI method, as the following relation shows:

$$VELT_i \geq (<) 1 \rightarrow e_i \geq (<) \frac{m}{w_i} - 1 \tag{3.33}$$

If the concrete labor in the ith sector produces more (less) abstract labor than the social average within an equal number of clock hours, its rate of exploitation is greater (smaller) than that estimated by the simple application of the NI procedure, which assumes that every clock hour is equal to the same amount of socially necessary abstract labor time. Equation (3.29) provides a proximate estimate only if the value productivity in the ith sector is equal to the social average.

It is also shown that the necessary and sufficient condition for the sectoral rates of surplus value being equalized is as follows:

$$e_i = e_j \leftrightarrow \frac{VELT_i}{w_i} = \frac{VELT_j}{w_j} \tag{3.34}$$

[25] The skill scales are assumed to be adjusted so that the coefficient of average labor is equal to 1. The scales can also be adjusted so that the least skilled labor has a coefficient of 1. This, however, would not alter any relevant result. It must also be emphasized that "skill" here is not defined in the narrow sense of the term. As the $VELT_i$ is consistently linked to sectoral differences between concrete, individual labor time and socially necessary, abstract labor time, it is also determined by working conditions such as labor intensity in the sector concerned.

Therefore, equal rates of surplus value require that the relative wage rate must be equal to the relative value expression of labor time, which is not necessarily equivalent to wage rate equalization. This implies that sectoral rates of surplus value are equalized when the $VELT_i$'s are proportional to wage rates, $VELT_i = kw_i$(k is constant), in other words, when "workers receiving the same wage for the same value-creating labor are equally exploited" (Duménil et al., 2009, p. 565).

It is now possible to clarify the hidden assumptions for the NI to be admissible at the sectoral level. First, the earlier NI at the least neglects the distinction between socially necessary abstract labor and individual labor, and therefore it finally amounts to assuming equal value expressions of labor time. Second, the remaining case for the NI is when the value expressions of labor time are proportional to wage rates. This results in assuming equal rates of surplus value at the outset, which was finally admitted by Duménil et al. (2009, p. 561) as follows.

> In order to recover a measure of this value productivity from real-world price and wage data by sector, some additional assumption about relative rates of exploitation (which Marx often assumes to be equal) is required.

On the one hand, this conclusion is frustrating in the sense that it confirms Morishima's (1973) prediction quoted earlier. On the other hand, it inevitably results from the NI's methodology integrating value and price into a single system by newly defining the value of labor-power.[26]

[26] It would be interesting to note here that Keynes's concept of "labour-unit" is also premised upon a similar assumption as the second case above:

> ... in so far as different grades and kinds of labour and salaried assistance enjoy a more or less fixed relative remuneration, the quantity of employment can be sufficiently defined for our purpose by taking an hour's employment of ordinary labour as our unit and *weighting an hour's employment of special labour in proportion to its remuneration*; i.e. an hour of special labour remunerated at double ordinary rates will count as two units. (Italics added: Keynes, 1973, p. 41)

This might hint at a Keynesian origin of the NI regarding the problem of the aggregator, which was emphasized by Morishima (1973) as a common point between Marx and Keynes.

3.4.4 The Inverse Transformation Method

Foley (2016, 2018) and Cogliano (2021) tried to legitimize the equalized rate of exploitation assumption using equilibrating behavior on the side of workers between wage and labor effort formulated by a radical version of the efficiency wage model (Bowles & Gintis, 1990). In the same vein, Cogliano (2018) performed an empirical study of the U.S. economy, finding a divergence between surplus value production and its realization at the industry level. However, as the following quote shows, the Foley-Cogliano analysis is based upon the assumption that workers approximately feel the degree of the exploitation, or differently put, "worker does have access to his own subjective experience" (Foley, 2016, p. 381):

> Even though it is impossible to measure labor effort "objectively," workers do know how much labor effort is required in various employments and "vote with their feet" so as to equalize the ratio of total labor effort to money wages. (Foley, 2018, p. 565)

Although this assumption is plausible, it only provides "an abstract benchmark" (Foley, 2016, p. 382). It is never guaranteed that the real economy is in the long-run equilibrium state of an equal rate of surplus value across industries.

It will be shown here that the rate of surplus value at the industry level can be estimated, using the methodology of the inverse transformation, starting from the data on the labor income share at the industry level under the assumption of equal $VELT_i$'s.[27]

The $MELT_i$ is defined as follows:

$$m_i = \frac{VA_i}{L_i} \tag{3.35}$$

where VA_i and L_i represent the money value-added and total labor time of the ith industry, respectively.[28]

[27] From (3.34), $VELT_i = VELT_j$ does not necessarily equal to $e_i = e_j$ unless $w_i = w_j$.

[28] Without a doubt, only productive industries are counted here. Albeit using different terminology, the $MELT_i$ was already anticipated by Okishio (1956). His concept of "the rate of income" is defined as income per unit of direct labor. It was introduced to analyze

Under the assumption of the equalized $VELT_i$'s, the value of labor-power and the rate of surplus value of the ith industry are as follows:

$$VLP_i = \frac{w_i}{m} \tag{3.28}$$

$$e_i = \frac{m}{w_i} - 1 \tag{3.29}$$

Now the inverse transformation of the labor income share into the rate of surplus value at the industry level can be performed according to the following procedure.

First, the labor income share of the ith industry, denoted by LS_i, is computed as:

$$LS_i = \frac{w_i L_i}{VA_i} = \frac{w_i}{VA_i/L_i} = \frac{w_i}{m_i} \tag{3.36}$$

On the other hand, the value equivalent of the labor income share of the ith industry (LS_i^{VALUE}) is defined as:

$$LS_i^{VALUE} = \frac{V_i}{V_i + S_i} = \frac{1}{1 + e_i} \tag{3.37}$$

Here, V_i, S_i, and e_i are the variable capital, surplus value, and rate of surplus value of the ith industry, respectively.

Combining (3.29), (3.36), and (3.37) yields:

$$LS_i^{VALUE} = \frac{1}{1 + e_i} = \frac{1}{1 + \frac{m}{w_i} - 1} = \frac{w_i}{m} = \frac{m_i}{m} LS_i \tag{3.38}$$

Using (3.37) and (3.38), the rate of surplus value of the ith industry is calculated as:

$$e_i = \frac{1}{LS_i^{VALUE}} - 1 = \frac{1}{\frac{m_i}{m} LS_i} - 1 = \frac{m}{m_i \times LS_i} - 1 \tag{3.39}$$

the unequal exchange between industries. See footnote 7 of Chapter 6. See also Rieu (2009b) for details on the usage of "the rate of income" in the literature of Japanese Marxian economics.

Given m and the m_i s, one can calculate the rate of surplus value by inversely transforming the labor income share at the industry level using Eq. (3.39).

On the other hand, the profit-wage ratio of the ith industry, denoted by e_i^{PRICE}, which is the price equivalent of the rate of surplus value, is expressed as

$$e_i^{PRICE} = \frac{VA_i - w_i L_i}{w_i L_i} = \frac{VA_i}{w_i L_i} - 1 = \frac{1}{LS_i} - 1 \quad (3.40)$$

Equations (3.39) and (3.40) demonstrate that the relationship between the MELT and the $MELT_i$ s determines the relationship between the rate of surplus value and the profit-wage ratio at the industry level. If $MELT > MELT_i$, then $e_i > e_i^{PRICE}$. This implies that the exploitation is more intense than when it is measured in terms of price. This also means that some of the surplus value produced in the ith industry is transferred to other industries. On the other hand, $MELT < MELT_i$ implies that surplus value produced in other industries is transferred to the ith industry.

From Eq. (3.34), it can be seen that the wage rate equalization plus our assumption means the equalized rate of surplus value, namely, the Foley-Cogliano assumption. This does not necessarily mean that our alternative is a weaker assumption than Foley-Cogliano because the latter permits differential $VELT_i$ s in so far as they are proportional to wage differentials. However, a critical difference is that our alternative focuses on the transfer of the value already produced in each sector, while Foley-Cogliano assumes the equalized rate of surplus value as an end result from the start. In summary, the determination process of the labor income share at the industry level is composed of the following two procedures:

1. The determination of the $VELT_i$ in the process of production.
2. The determination of the MEV_i through capital mobility for the rate of profit equalization and labor mobility for wage-effort equalization.[29]

[29] While MEV_i is an increasing function of the organic composition of capital, degree of protection, sectoral financial capability, etc., $VELT_i$ is affected positively by the labor intensity of the ith sector (Rieu et al., 2014, p. 195). As the labor intensity is closely related to labor effort of workers, the determination of $VELT_i$ is not independent of procedure (2). This is another simplification of our methodology.

Under the condition that the $VELT_i$ is proportional to w_i, Foley-Cogliano assumes that procedure (2) is determined by procedure (1). Furthermore, the uniform rate of surplus value as an end result of the two procedures is de facto presupposed from the start. Contrariwise, our methodology tries to estimate the sectoral rate of surplus value by focusing on procedure (2) by setting procedure (1) unknown. This is also related to the pursuit of unequal exchange between sectors using the difference between MELT and $MELT_i$.

As neither method is free from the defects pointed out by this chapter's critique of the NI, it cannot be concluded that any one of them dominates the other. Without directly estimating the $VELT_i$ s, however, we should choose one or the other.[30] In particular, given that an economy may or may not be in the long-run equilibrium position, it seems that the assumption proposed in this chapter that notes the sectoral difference is better justified.

3.5 Conclusion

The NI argues that Marxian value categories can be measured using price variables through the concept of the MELT. Under the two axioms of the NI, it can be shown that the profit in constant capital is multiply counted. This implies that the NI is internally consistent with regard to the adoption of the net product as the object of conservation in the Marxian transformation procedure. To maintain the logical consistency of the NI, the value of labor-power must be defined separately from the real wage basket, especially regarding the asymmetrical treatment of constant and variable capital. It has also been shown that, unlike the received conception, the NI signifies a definite value-price relation at the microeconomic level. As a corollary, a new relationship between value-price deviation and the organic composition of capital measured in monetary terms can be established.

Although in the earlier NI literature the MELT was considered a tool to capture value-price connections only on an aggregate level, recent literature has cultivated the possibility of applying the NI at the microeconomic level. Reflecting these discussions, the issue of estimating the sectoral rates of surplus value has been examined. In so doing, it was

[30] The issue of estimating $VELT_i$s (or "value productivity" in Chapter 2) will be discussed in Part IV.

suggested that the MELT be decomposed into two concepts: namely, the "value expression of labor time" and the "monetary expression of value." As a result of this general theoretical consideration, it has been confirmed that the NI's conventional procedure can only be hold if all the concrete labors are homogenized to the same amount of abstract labor and all the exploitative conditions are equalized across sectors. Finally, the methodology of the inverse transformation is provided to estimate the sectoral rates of surplus value starting from the data on the sectoral labor income share.

References

Bowles, S., & Gintis, H. (1990). Contested exchange: New microfoundations for the political economy of capitalism. *Politics and Society, 18*(2), 165–222.

Brinkman, R. (1999). *On the relation between labor time and money in a two sector system of commodity production and exchange*. Unpublished manuscript.

Campbell, A. (1997). The transformation problem: A simple presentation of the "new solution." *Review of Radical Political Economics, 29*(3), 59–69.

Campbell, A. (2002). The nature of surplus value in the "new solution." *Review of Radical Political Economics, 34*(1), 69–73.

Cartelier, J. (2006). Book review. F. Moseley (Ed.), Marx's theory of money: modern appraisals. *The European Journal of the History of Economic Thought, 13*(2), 293–300.

Cogliano, J. F. (2018). Surplus value production and realization in Marxian theory—Applications to the U.S., 1990–2015. *Review of Political Economy, 30*(4), 505–533.

Cogliano, J. F. (2021). *Marx's equalized rate of exploitation* (Working paper 2021-01). Department of Economics, University of Massachusetts, Boston,

Cogliano, J. F., Flaschel, P., Franke, R., Fröhlich, N., & Veneziani, R. (2018). *Value, competition and exploitation: Marx's legacy revisited*. Edward Elgar.

De Vroey, M. (1981). Value, production, and exchange. In I. Steedman (Ed.), *The value controversy*. Verso.

Duménil, G. (1980). *De la valeur aux prix de production*. Economica.

Duménil, G. (1984). The so-called 'transformation problem' revisited: A brief comment. *Journal of Economic Theory, 33*(2), 340–348.

Duménil, G., Foley, D. K., & Lévy, D. (2009). A note on the formal treatment of exploitation with heterogeneous labor. *Metroeconomica, 60*(3), 560–567.

Fine, B., Lapavitsas, C., & Saad-Filho, A. (2004). Transforming the transformation problem: Why the "new interpretation" is a wrong turning. *Review of Radical Political Economics, 36*(1), 3–19.

Fleetwood, S. (2001). What kind of theory is Marx's labour theory of value? A critical realist inquiry. *Capital and Class, 73*, 41–77.
Foley, D. (1982). The value of money, the value of labor-power, and the Marxian transformation problem. *Review of Radical Political Economics, 14*(2), 37–47.
Foley, D. (1986). *Understanding capital: Marx's economic theory*. Harvard University Press.
Foley, D. (2000). Recent developments in the labor theory of value. *Review of Radical Political Economics, 32*(1), 1–39.
Foley, D. (2005). Marx's theory of money in historical perspective. In F. Moseley (Ed.), *Marx's theory of money*. Palgrave Macmillan.
Foley, D. (2016). What is the labour theory of value and what is it for?". In G. Freni, H. D. Kurz, A. M. Lavezzi, & R. Signorino (Eds.), *Economic theory and its history: Essays in honor of Neri Salvadori* (pp. 370–384). Routledge.
Foley, D. (2018). The "New Interpretation" after 35 years. *Review of Radical Political Economics, 50*(3), 559–568.
Freeman, A. (2004). The case for simplicity: A paradigm for the political economy. In A. Freeman, A. Kliman, & J. Wells (Eds.), *The new value controversy and the foundation of economics*. Edward Elgar.
Fujimoto, T., & Valle Baeza, A. (2011). Prices distorted from labor values. In N. Salvadori & C. Gehrke (Eds.), *Keynes, Sraffa and the criticism of neoclassical theory: Essays in honour of Heinz Kurz*. Routledge.
Glick, R., & Ehrbar, H. (1987). The transformation problem: An obituary. *Australian Economic Papers, 26*(49), 294–317.
Gouverneur, J. (1990). Productive labour, price/value ratio and rate of surplus value: Theoretical viewpoints and empirical evidence. *Cambridge Journal of Economics, 14*(1), 1–27.
Itoh, M. (2005). The new interpretation and the value of money. In F. Moseley (Ed.), *Marx's theory of money: Modern appraisals*. Palgrave Macmillan.
Itoh, M. (2021). *Value and crisis: Essays on Marxian economics in Japan* (2nd ed.). Monthly Review Press.
Keynes, J. M. (1973). *The general theory of employment*. Macmillan.
Kliman, A. (2007). *Reclaiming Marx's capital: A refutation of the myth of inconsistency*. Lexington Books.
Kliman, A., & McGlone, T. (1999). A temporal single-system interpretation of Marx's value theory. *Review of Political Economy, 11*(1), 33–59.
Lee, C. O. (1993). Marx's labour theory of value revisited. *Cambridge Journal of Economics, 17*(4), 463–478.
Lipietz, A. (1982). The so-called transformation problem revisited. *Journal of Economic Theory, 26*(1), 59–88.
Lipietz, A. (1985). *The enchanted world: Inflation*. Verso.
Marx, K. (1959). *Capital* (Vol. III). Progress Publishers.
Marx, K. (1976). *Capital* (Vol. I). Penguin.

Mohun, S. (1994). A re(in)statement of the labour theory of value. *Cambridge Journal of Economics, 18*(4), 391–412.
Mohun, S. (2004). The labour theory of value as foundation for empirical investigations. *Metroeconomica, 55*(1), 65–95.
Mohun, S. (2018). A celebration of the labour theory of Value (In Japanese), *Keizai Seminar*, April: 24–30. English version. Available at https://simonmohun.com. Accessed April 1, March 2022.
Mohun, S., & Veneziani, R. (2017). Value, price, and exploitation: The logic of the transformation problem. *Journal of Economic Surveys, 31*(5), 1387–1420.
Morishima, M. (1973). *Marx's economics*. Cambridge University Press.
Moseley, F. (1993). Marx's logical method and the "Transformation Problem". In F. Moseley (Ed.), *Marx's method in capital: A reexamination*. Humanities Press.
Moseley, F. (2000). The "new solution" to the transformation problem: A sympathetic critique. *Review of Radical Political Economics, 32*(2), 282–316.
Moseley, F. (2016). *Money and totality: A macro-monetary interpretation of Marx's logic in capital and the end of the 'Transformation Problem'*. Brill.
Nakatani, T., & Rieu, D.-M. (2003). On the "new interpretation" of Marxian labor theory of value. *Kobe University Economic Review, 49*, 51–62.
Nikaido, H. (1960). *Mathematical methods for modern economics* (In Japanese). Iwanami Shoten.
Okishio, N. (1956). Kokuminsyotoku to Roudou (In Japanese: National income and labor). *Kokumin Keizai Zassi* (Journal of National Economics), *94*(4), 48–64.
Pasinetti, L. L. (1973). The notion of vertical integration in economic analysis. *Metroeconomica*, *25*(1), 1–29.
Ramos-Martinez, A., & Rodriguez-Herrea, A. (1996). The transformation of values into prices of production: a different reading of Marx's text. In A. Freeman & G. Carchedi (Eds.), *Marx and non-equilibrium economics*. Edward Elgar.
Reuten, G. (2017). The productive powers of labour and the redundant transformation to prices of production. *Historical Materialism, 25*(3), 3–35.
Ricci, A. (2021). *Value and unequal exchange in international trade: The geography of global capitalist exploitation*. Routledge.
Rieu, D.-M. (2006). A reexamination of the quantitative issues in the new interpretation. *Review of Radical Political Economics, 38*(2), 258–271.
Rieu, D.-M. (2008). Estimating sectoral rates of surplus value: Methodological issues. *Metroeconomica, 59*(4), 557–573.
Rieu, D.-M. (2009a). The "New Interpretation": Questions answered and unanswered. *Metroeconomica, 60*(3), 568–570.
Rieu, D.-M. (2009b). The Shibata-Okishio connection: Labor theory of value and rate of profit. *Journal of the History of Economic Thought, 31*(3), 325–339.

Rieu, D.-M., Lee, K., & Ahn, H.-H. (2014). The determination of the monetary expression of concrete labor time under the inconvertible credit money system. *Review of Radical Political Economics, 46*(2), 190–198.

Saad-Filho, A. (1996). The value of money, the value of labour power and the net product: An appraisal of the "new approach" to the transformation problem. In A. Freeman & G. Carchedi (Eds.), *Marx and non-equilibrium economics*. Edward Elgar.

Seton, F. (1957). The 'transformation problem.' *Review of Economic Studies, 24*(3), 149–160.

Shaikh, A., & Tonak, E. A. (1994). *Measuring the wealth of nations: The political economy of national accounts*. Cambridge University Press.

Wolff, R., Roberts, B., & Callari, A. (1982). Marx's (not Ricardo's) 'Transformation Problem': A radical reconceptualization. *History of Political Economy, 14*(4), 564–582.

Venezini, R., & Yoshihara, N. (2017). One million miles to go: Taking the axiomatic road to defining exploitation. *Cambridge Journal of Economics, 41*(6), 1607–1626.

PART II

Exploitation of Labor

CHAPTER 4

Labor Exploitation as the Origin of Profits

4.1 Introduction

The Fundamental Marxian Theorem (FMT), with the Okishio theorem which will be discussed in Chapter 6, is one of the representative achievements in mathematical Marxian economics in the last century.

As is well known, the main goal of Marx's labor theory of value was to reveal that the origin of capitalist profit lies in the exploitation of labor. The FMT is nothing other than a mathematical representation of this central insight. In the first volume of *Capital*, Marx assumed equal exchange according to which every commodity is traded at the price proportional to its value.[1] In reality, however, commodities are exchanged at the prices that are not necessarily proportional to their values not only due to coincidental elements such as short-run discrepancies between demand and supply but also due to the transformation of values into prices of production as long-run equilibrium prices. The FMT tries to bridge the gap between the surface of market exchange characterized by unequal exchange and the domain in which capitalist exploitation happens.

[1] As already noted in Chapter 2, the usual expression "value is equal to price" cannot hold in a strict sense because of the dimensional difference between value and price.

D.-M. Rieu, *A Mathematical Approach to Marxian Value Theory*, Marx, Engels, and Marxisms,
https://doi.org/10.1007/978-3-031-07808-8_4

On the other hand, it may be asked if "what economic theory determines must be what one directly observes" (Petri, 2012, p. 20). This is a more profound question than it looks at first because it fundamentally asks what mathematics can and cannot do for economics. More specifically, this issue is related to the FMT's role as the theoretical bridge mentioned above in the sense that one should first determine the level of abstraction at which the so-called proof of exploitation is provided.

This chapter approaches the FMT focusing upon these two mutually related issues in a roundabout way. First, the history of the development of FMT in Japan is examined in relation to the theory of Nobuo Okishio (1927–2003), who originally proved the theorem. In particular, the theoretical relation between Okishio and Kei Shibata (1902–1986), Okishio's precursor, is explained to clarify the theoretical status of the FMT in the entire structure of the Marxian theory of value and exploitation. Second, the specific assumptions of recent interpretations of Marxian value theory with regard to the FMT are clarified to elucidate the level of abstraction at which the theorem works.

The chapter is structured as follows. In Sect. 4.2, the basic content of the FMT is summarized for heuristic purposes. Section 4.3 examines the Shibata-Okishio-Morishima connection focusing on the issues of the Markov process solution to the transformation problem and the necessity of the labor value concept. Section 4.4 discusses the recent claim of the Temporal Single-System Interpretation that the FMT should hold without any restrictive conditions by comparing it with the New Interpretation. It will be shown that each interpretation "proves" the FMT in its own way. Section 4.5 concludes.

4.2 The Fundamental Marxian Theorem

Although the FMT was named by Morishima (1973, p. 53), it was first proven by Okishio (1955).[2] It can be formulated as follows (Cogliano et al., 2018, pp. 201–202);

FMT: The rate of profit and the rate of surplus value are always positive, zero, or negative simultaneously.

[2] As this paper was written in Japanese, it was not well known outside Japan. Morishima (1973, p. 53) also cited its English version, Okishio (1963), which soon became well known to the English-speaking world.

Proof. Although the theorem can be proved in a more general condition assuming just positive profits, it is proved here for prices of production with equalized rate of profit for simplicity. Using the Perron–Frobenius theorem, the following relation can be obtained where A, b, l, and x denote the conventional input-coefficient matrix ($n \times n$), real wage basket vector (n × 1), direct labor input vector ($1 \times n$), and gross output vector ($1 \times n$), respectively. Note that x is a right eigenvector of $A + bl$.[3]

$$x = (1 + r)(A + bl)x \tag{4.1}$$

Labor values are represented as follows, where λ is the $1 \times n$ value vector.

$$\lambda = \lambda A + l = \lambda A + \lambda bl + (1 - \lambda b)l \tag{4.2}$$

Combining (4.1) and (4.2), the equilibrium rate of profit can be given as a function of the rate of exploitation, $e = (1 - \lambda b)/\lambda b$.

$$r = \frac{(1 - \lambda b)lx}{\lambda(A + bl)x} = e\frac{\lambda blx}{\lambda(A + bl)x} \tag{4.3}$$

Therefore, insofar as $\lambda blx > 0$, $r > 0$ implies $e > 0$ and vice versa (Q.E.D.).

Two points must be noted here.

First, although Morishima (1973, p. 53) completed the theorem by proving sufficiency, i.e., "$e > 0 \Rightarrow r > 0$,"[4] the FMT's main thrust lies in its necessity, i.e., "$r > 0 \Rightarrow e > 0$." This is because the FMT tries to go from the visible world of market prices to the invisible world of capitalist exploitation, which was Okishio's original intention of elaborating the theorem. Furthermore, it is also consistent with the spirit of the inverse transformation explained in Chapter 2.[5] In a certain sense, the proof of sufficiency is redundant for the theoretical task of the theorem.

[3] The Perron–Frobenius theorem also guarantees the existence of the equal rate of profit equilibrium prices in the classical-Marxian sense because $p > 0$ is a left eigenvector of $A + bl$ from $p = (1 + r)p(A + bl)$.

[4] "This result, whose necessity is due to Okishio, while its sufficiency, although not discussed by him, is also easily proved, may be claimed as the Fundamental Marxian Theorem..." (Morishima, 1973, p. 53).

[5] Okishio repetitively emphasized this point in his works. For example, see his interview with a Korean journal (Okishio, 1995).

Second, the FMT is premised upon some restrictive conditions. As the theorem expresses the idea that "there is capitalist exploitation of labor in production when the workers' productive contribution is higher than their wage" (Screpanti, 2003, p. 163), it simultaneously assumes that the real wage is given below a certain level. In Eq. (4.2), the existence of exploitation implies that the surplus value vector $(1 - \lambda b)l$ should be positive. This is called the "surplus condition" (Okishio et al., 1978) and can only be guaranteed by political and social mechanisms in each society. In other words, the FMT is not sufficient to prove the labor exploitation as the origin of profits. This was already noted by Okishio.

> If, however, one interprets this theorem [FMT-Rieu] from *a wider perspective*, the issue is supposed to be of under the assumption of positive profit. Regarding the issue, it is obvious that the existence of surplus labor is necessary, but not sufficient. (Okishio, 1977, p. 134, translated from Japanese, emphasis in original)

Beyond the formal setup of the FMT, therefore, it is necessary to analyze the dynamic process of capital accumulation and the labor market. As will be seen in Sect. 6.4.3 of Chapter 6, Okishio pursued this issue in his later years.

Much ink has been spilled over whether the FMT truly proves the existence of labor exploitation in the sense that "…with the same eigenequation [for values-Rieu] any other product could be cast in the same role" (Bródy, 1970, p. 85). Bowles and Gintis (1981) cynically illustrated the peanut as an example of a "basic commodity" that can be shown to be "exploited" by the same mathematical logic as the FMT. In a different context, the FMT was also criticized for holding only in a linear production model, not in a general convex cone economy (Yoshihara, 2017). All these issues are directed to the determination of the appropriate level of abstraction at which the FMT works, which will be discussed in Sect. 4.4.

4.3 Historical Background

4.3.1 Shibata-Okishio-Morishima Connection

As the FMT is an economic application of the Perron–Frobenius theorem in linear algebra, there were many predecessors of Okishio. Particularly notable is French mathematician Maurice Potron (1872–1942), who was the first to give a de facto proof of the equality between positive surplus value and positive profit (Mori, 2008).[6] This section, however, focuses on the connection between Japanese scholars. As mathematical Marxian economics has exceptionally developed in Japan since the 1930s, it makes us anticipate all the bifurcations in the literature of Marxian value theory in the 1970s.

Michio Morishima (1923–2004), who introduced the achievements of Japanese mathematical Marxian economics to English-speaking readers with his own contribution, explicitly stated that much of his analysis was derived from Okishio (Morishima, 1973, p. viii). As explained in the previous section, the central insight of the Marxian theory of profit as labor exploitation is related to the necessity aspect of the FMT. In this sense, it is natural to examine Okishio's contribution here. Furthermore, this Japanese contribution dates back to a prewar economist, Kei Shibata, who already raised almost all the controversial issues in Marxian value theory. Shibata's contribution was noted in the literature on the history of Marxian economics (Groll & Orzech, 1989; Howard & King, 1992); however, it was usually regarded as an earlier critique of Marxian value theory. This is somehow similar to the reception of Okishio's contribution, particularly regarding the Okishio theorem, in the Western literature. Shibata, as a professor at Kyoto University (Kyoto Imperial University at the time) during the prewar period, published many articles on Marxian value theory and Walrasian economics, mainly in the *Kyoto University Economic Review*.[7] The main reason why Shibata became a "forgotten economist" (Tsuru, 2006 [1985], p. 237) is due to his unusual political career. To make matters worse, strong antipathy toward the mathematical methods of Marxian economists (Akama, 2000, p. 130) caused his contribution to be underestimated. One can glimpse this from Itoh (2021), who comprehensively introduced Japanese Marxian economics to the Western world, and did not comment on Shibata.

These three economists overlapped each other in their academic lives and theoretical trajectories. Furthermore, their relation was subtle, and it is worth examining not only from the perspective of historians of

[6] In particular, Potron introduced a general model with heterogeneous labor. For an English translation of Potron's manuscripts, see Bidard and Erreygers (2010).

[7] For biographical notes on these three economists, see Rieu (2009, pp. 326–329). See Sugihara et al. (1996) for the entire list of Shibata's works. Makino (2015) also provides a comprehensive biography of Shibata.

economic thought but also from the viewpoint of elaborating Marxian theory of value and profit.

Above all, attitudes toward Marxian value theory were subtly different between these three economists despite similar mathematical formulations they had in common.

Although he formulated the FMT, Morishima emphasized that he was an anti-Marxist in his memoir (Morishima, 2007 [1997], p. 19). On the other hand, Okishio consistently argued that capitalism should be replaced by a "new society" in which all members of society can take part in making decisions about production (Okishio, 2004). More importantly, Morishima and Okishio had different theoretical positions not only on political and ideological issues but also in the acceptance of Marxian value theory. After providing a sophisticated analysis of Marxian theories of value, exploitation, and capital whose basic formal structure is similar to Okishio's in his famous book, Morishima somehow surprisingly suggested the abandonment of the labor theory of value:

> One of the conclusions of this book is that Marx's economics can acquire citizenship in contemporary economic theory by detaching it from its root, the labour theory of value, and grafting it onto the von Neumnn stock so as to produce Marx-von Neumann flower! (Morishima, 1973, p. 194)

It is natural for Okishio to respond to this conclusion as follows:

> I can never agree with the conclusion that the labor theory of value should be abandoned. Does he abdicate or support what he calls the "Fundamental Marxian Theorem"? If he wants to support it, the value concept is indispensable. (Okishio, 1977, translated from Japanese, pp. 274–275)

This paragraph is quoted from Okishio's book review on Morishima (1973) which was originally written in 1974. In the book review, Okishio raised several issues mainly related to analytical assumptions such as the characteristics of the input-coefficient matrix. Morishima responded to this review (Morishima, 2004); however, interestingly, he did not directly discuss the implications of FMT. His indirect answer to the above quote can be found in the reply to Samuelson saying that "Marx without the labor theory of value" is possible "as long as…the Fundamental Marxian Theorem is the core of his economic theory" (Morishima, 1974, p. 73). Itoh (2021, p. 41) correctly noted this difference between Okishio and

Morishima: "His [Morishima's-Rieu] theoretical direction seems contrary to that of Okishio, and even more opposed to most other Japanese Marxian economists." In summary, the Morishima-Okishio connection is more complicated than it looks in the sense that Morishima reached a fundamentally antithetical conclusion starting from adopting Okishio's mathematical framework.

Shibata's attitude toward Marxian value theory is more ambiguous than Okishio's, however, he basically supported it. In his 1933 paper[8] discussing Marxian economics and Walrasian theory of general equilibrium, Shibata concluded the following:

> What is it, then, that makes Marxian economics so powerful and the general equilibrium theory of the mathematical school so inert? It is simply this, that whereas in the Marxian economics the organization of capitalistic production and the laws of its development are analyzed in a direct way, in the general equilibrium theory the main attention is directed to the analysis of the mental structure of the individuals who take part in the organization of capitalistic production. (Shibata, 1933a, p. 108)

This is somewhat embarrassing if one considers Shibata's meticulous analysis to show that any theory of value is redundant which will be discussed in Sect. 4.3.3. Furthermore, Shibata's political position was very peculiar in that he was suspected of being an ultra-nationalist, rather than a Marxist.[9] This explains partly why Shibata was only indirectly and negatively described by Morishima, an undergraduate student of Kyoto University at the time, in his memoir.

> As the postwar period saw the rise of rampant Marxist professors in the faculty of economics, Kyoto University was not such a cozy place for me. In contrast, at the time of my entrance, it was an unbearable place due to right-wing teachers. As the agents of the military and Nazis, they

[8] This was a translated version of a Japanese paper published in the same year. The original Japanese version was republished in the volume celebrating a century's anniversary of *Keizai-Ronso* which is the annals of the Faculty of Economics at Kyoto University (Shibata, 2015).

[9] Cooperating with fascists, Shibata proposed a "new economic mode" in which capitalists should be deprived of the power to appoint (and dismiss) "firm leaders" and profits must remain under state control (Yagi, 1999). The atmosphere at the time can be glimpsed from Chapter 3 of Morris-Suzuki (1989). As a result of his career in this period, Shibata was expelled from Kyoto University after the Second World War.

> taught weird bubble-like theories such as the logic of Japanese economy, the theory of new order,[10] imperialist economics and etc. (Morishima, 2007 [1997], translated from Japanese, p. 84)

> When I was a freshman, assistant professor S taught the history of economics. As he immersed himself in Professor Kei Shibata's bizarre theory of the so-called logic of Japanese economy, I regarded him as one of those who jumped on the bandwagon [of nationalism-Rieu]. (ibid., translated from Japanese, p. 93)

These recollections are not compatible with Tsuru's (2006 [1985], p. 237) statement that Morishima regarded Shibata as one of "the three representative prewar Japanese economists." Nevertheless, the Shibata-Morishima connection is not such a simple one. Above all, Morishima's book on Walras' economics emphasizing that "Walras' theory of exchange and production is...but an overture to his general equilibrium theory of capital formation and circulation" (Morishima, 1977, pp. vii–viii) was in a similar vein as Shibata's project to "attain great potency in analyzing both the organization of capitalistic production and the laws of its development" "by settling [some] points" of "the general equilibrium theory" (Shibata, 1933a, p. 109). When Morishima (1973, p. 9) emphasized "the superiority of Marxian economics over modern economics in dynamic analysis" with quotes from Lange (1935), it should have been impossible for Morishima not to recognize Shibata's 1933 article which was explicitly referred to in the first sentence.[11]

During the postwar period, Shibata continued research to argue for "the theory of human emancipation." In a book (Shibata, 1959) published in English by a Japanese publisher, Shibata tried to synthesize all major economic theories, including those of Marx and Keynes, as well as general equilibrium theory.[12] Although his project in this book was

[10] "New order" here is a translation of "Shin Taisei" which was used in the name of a study group organized by Shibata in 1940.

[11] "In a recent issue of the *Kyoto University Economic Review* Professor Shibata brought up the question of the relative merits of Marxian economics and the modern theory of economic equilibrium" (Lange, 1935, p. 189).

[12] According to his memoir (Shibata, 2009, pp. 199–201), Shibata sent copies of this book to Maurice Dobb, M. Kalecki, and Oscar Lange in the spring of 1954. Most likely, he had already completed the book before it was commercially published. The author gives thanks to Kiichiro Yagi for noting this point.

not as ambitious as a nonstandard one, Shibata's evaluation of Marxian value theory, at least from a purely analytical perspective, did not change compared with his prewar position.

On the other hand, Okishio's connection with Shibata is more conspicuous and transparent than the Morishima-Shibata connection. In his seminal English paper proving the Okishio theorem (Okishio, 1961), Okishio attributed his theorem to Shibata's two articles (Shibata, 1934, 1939). This is why Negishi (1989) coined the term the "Shibata-Okishio theorem," which will also be used in Chapter 6 of this book. Okishio always regarded Shibata as both his predecessor and main antagonist. Specifically, his two-volume work, *Marukusu Keizaigaku* (In Japanese, Marxian Economics), published in 1977, clearly shows his theoretical relationship to Shibata's works.

Conclusively, the Shibata-Okishio-Morishima connection provides a miniature of the modern controversy around the issues in Marxian value theory. The divergence between Morishima and Okishio, more generally, two antithetical attitudes toward the labor theory of value, were already extant in Shibata's works in the 1930s. This section focuses on the FMT. Another important issue, Marx's law of the tendency of the rate of profit to fall will be discussed in Sect. 6.2 of Chapter 6.

4.3.2 From the Fundamental Marxian Theorem to the Transformation Problem

As is well known in the Marxian literature, prices of production deviate from values unless very restrictive assumptions are made. Marx himself provided a numerical example of the transformation of values into prices of production in the third volume of *Capital*. Although he showed the first step of the transformation, Marx noted that it is not required to go into further detail (Marx, 1981, p. 265). This is where Ladislaus von Bortkiewicz raised the so-called transformation problem. The iterative solution tries to solve the problem by resuming this interrupted procedure infinitely using a Markov process. It was first given by Okishio and Shaikh independently.[13]

[13] Okishio (1972) was the first general proof of the iterative solution, and it was soon translated into English (Okishio, 1974). While Shaikh (1977) was the first in western literature, it was already mimeographed in 1973 (Morishima & Catephores, 1978, p. 166).

Okishio-Shaikh's iterative solution can be represented as the following relation where p^t is the price at the tth stage in the iterative process and the initial price, $p^0 = \lambda$.

$$\lim_{t\to\infty} p^{t+1} = \lim_{t\to\infty}\left[1 + \frac{p^t x - p^t(A+bl)x}{p^t(A+bl)x}\right]p^t(A+bl) \tag{4.4}$$

Relation (4.4) implies that developing the iterative procedure makes the price system converge to the system of prices of production, $p = (1+r)p(A+bl)$. Furthermore, $p^0 = \lambda$, $p^{t+1}x = p^t x = \cdots = p^0 x = \lambda x$ holds, where x is the gross output vector. This implies that total price of production becomes equal to the total value while the total profit is not equal to the total surplus value.

As the rule of iteration can be chosen arbitrarily, the iterative solution has many variations. Instead of relation (4.4), choosing rule $r^t = \frac{S}{p^t(A+bl)x}$ where S represents surplus value leads to the equality between total profit and total surplus value. In this case, the equality between the total price of production and the total value does not hold (Nakatani, 1995).

It must be noted that even Glick and Ehrbar (1987) gave an iterative solution that is based on the "New Interpretation" (NI) of Marxian value theory. This can be represented as follows (Nakatani & Rieu, 2003, p. 56) which leads to the NI's modified aggregate equalities already explained in Chapter 3.

$$\lim_{t\to\infty} p^{t+1} = \lim_{t\to\infty}\left[1 + \frac{\lambda y - (\frac{w}{m})lx}{p^t Ax + (\frac{w}{m})lx}\right](p^t A + \frac{w}{m}l) \tag{4.5}$$

Regarding the iterative solution, the following two points should be noted.

First, the result of convergence does not necessarily presuppose the starting point $p^0 = \lambda$. In this sense, the iterative procedure does not exactly describe the transformation process from values into prices of production but rather a process of equilibrating in logical time.

Second, the iterative procedure can be replaced by the corresponding simultaneous equation system. For example, the NI solution of procedure (4.5) can be obtained by solving the NI's simultaneous equation system incorporating "the total profit = the total surplus value" as Eqs. (3.21)–(3.24) in Chapter 3. In this sense, the rule of iteration is simply a matter of choosing the constraint.

Now let us examine a precursor of the Okishio-Shaikh solution, Shibata (1933b) which provided a Markov process solution to the problem of transforming Marxian values into prices of production.[14] This was a result of the controversy between Shibata and Yasuma Takada (1883–1972) who was his colleague at Kyoto University. Takada (1931) tried the iterative process, only to fail to obtain the convergence result. Takada reached the conclusion that price-value deviation diverged to infinity because he assumed the constancy of the average rate of profit in the iteration process (Okishio, 1977, p. 207). Starting from a von Bortkiewicz-like simple reproduction scheme, Shibata (1933b, p. 61) argued that "it is necessary to iterate the process of averaging the rates of profit a second and a third time" and gave a numerical example to show the possibility of the solution. Most likely because the Perron–Frobenius theorem was not commonly known to economists at the time, Takada-Shibata controversy was composed of tedious calculations of numerical examples.

Without a doubt, Okishio's contribution was to provide a general proof of the Markov process described in (4.4). For him, given that the equality between total profit and total surplus value should be abandoned, the FMT was essential to show the causal relation between profit and labor exploitation, which was the main objective of his entire theory. Therefore, Okishio's theory eventually comes down to the establishment of the FMT which preceded the proof of the Markov process not only in logical but also in chronological order.[15] Nishi (2012, p. 172) argued "Shibata, albeit in numerical examples, was the first who showed that the existence of exploitation is the condition for the existence of profit by a successivist method [iterative method-Rieu]." However, at least in Okishio's problem setup, the iterative solution itself cannot prove the FMT. Thus, it must be that the logical reasoning in his mind ran from the FMT to the transformation problem.

[14] As Shibata knew the literature of Georg von Charasoff and Natalie Moszkowska who had already pursued the same direction (Howard & King, 1992, pp. 230–231), Shibata could not take full credit for the iterative solution.

[15] Unlike Howard and King's notes (1992, p. 286), the FMT must be traced back to the year 1955, not Seton (1957) or Okishio's English paper (Okishio, 1963). Okishio already provided the outline of the FMT in his Japanese paper (Okishio, 1955).

4.3.3 *The Necessity of the Labor Theory of Value*

Shibata's attitude toward the Marxian labor theory of value was ambivalent in that he consistently argued for its necessity while he logically disproved its necessity as price theory. More specifically, Shibata emphasized the role of the labor theory of value as the viewpoint of society, in some senses such as normative economics based on value judgment while he provided a prototype of Samuelson-Steedman, such as the "redundancy" critique (Samuelson, 1971; Steedman, 1977) of the labor value concept.[16]

Let us examine Shibata (1939), in which he provided a general discussion about the redundancy of the labor theory of value. Shibata's logic is very simple in that the general rate of profit and prices are determined from the following system of prices of production.

$$p = (1 + r)(pA + pbl) \tag{4.6}$$

As is well known, (4.6) is composed of n equations with $n+1$ unknown variables, i.e., n prices and the general rate of profit, r. Therefore, relative prices with a numéraire $p_i = 1$ and r can be determined by directly solving equations. Letting the price-value ratio, $d_i \equiv p_i/\lambda_i$, the Eq. (4.6) is transformed into:

$$\lambda D = (1 + r)(\lambda DA + \lambda Dbl) \tag{4.7}$$

where $D = diag(d_1, d_2, \ldots, d_n)$.

As (4.7) is the simultaneous equation system with regard to the value-price,[17] $\lambda_i d_i$ and the general rate of profit, it is easily reduced to (4.6) and relative prices with the general rate of profit can also be uniquely determined. In this procedure, the value equation $\lambda = \lambda A + l$ and the rate of exploitation are not required, in other words, just a "complicating detour" (Samuelson, 1971). According to Shibata (1939, p. 47), "reference to value does not affect the results concerning prices and general profit rate."

[16] In the latter sense, Howard and King (1992, p. 138) noted Shibata's work as a milestone in the value theory debate.

[17] Value-price is defined as "value divided by money's value" or "the value expressed in its relation to the value of money" (Shibata, 1939, p. 46). This term was also used by Okishio to emphasize that the dimensions of value and price are different (Okishio, 1974 [1993], p. 43).

This general discussion in 1939 seems to completely refute Shibata's (1933b) iterative solution introduced above. It would be rational to ask what the use is of iterating to show the convergence to prices from something redundant. Shibata, however, consistently emphasized the importance of the labor theory of value as "a specific viewpoint of the world" (Shibata, 1933b, p. 68). This is more evident in his book, *Riron Keizaigaku* (In Japanese, Theoretical Economics) published in 1935:

> Marx's theory...may be criticized for using the value concept ...because one can explain exchange value without referring to the value concept. This, however, does not imply that the value concept is generally redundant, but that the value concept is redundant from the viewpoint of specifying exchange value determination. (Shibata, 1935, translated from Japanese, p. 35)

Alternatively, the labor theory of value is not valid as the explanation of the relative prices; however, it is still necessary. Furthermore, in his postwar book, Shibata repeated the same argument, however, with a strong flavor of normative economics such as the expression of "emancipation":

> It [value theory – Rieu] is really necessary in economics, because economics is not a mere purpose-less positive science but is one of those sciences which are dedicated to the cause of some purpose or other just as the medical science is, which is dedicated to the cause of maintaining and improving human physiological health...Economics is dedicated to the cause of emancipation of the laboring masses...The impropriety of the Ricardian theory of value – as developed further by Marx – consists in the fact that it overlooks the role played by the entrepreneurs. (Shibata, 1959, p. 28)[18]

It is not surprising that Okishio strongly objected to Shibata's "redundancy thesis":

> ... It is difficult to agree with Shibata's argument that it is sufficient to start with price equations with an abrupt assumption of equal-rate-of-profit,

[18] The last sentence is related to Shibata's peculiar opinion that the economy should maximize the rate of income defined as the ratio of value-added to capital invested. See Sect. 6.2 of Chapter 6.

> without a labor theory of value, because the concept of embodied labor is indispensable to elucidate why equal-rate-of-profit is a positive constant. (Okishio, 1977, p. 207, translated from Japanese)

Once again, the FMT here plays the role of connecting the value system and the price system. As already explained, the necessity aspect of the theorem proves that $r > 0$ in Eq. (4.6) implies the positive rate of exploitation which cannot be caught by the Eq. (4.7) itself. Okishio's method starting from market prices is different from Marx's presentation in *Capital*, which assumes equal exchange in the first volume to show the existence of labor exploitation, and then explains the unequal exchange according to the transformation of values into prices in the third volume.

The Shibata-Okishio-Morishima connection is also worth examining here.

Morishima (1973, pp. 6–7) speaks of "an interesting example of the non-univalence of the correspondence between economics and mathematics" in that his discussion of the transformation problem is very different from Samuelson's in its conclusions, "in spite of the surprising similarity in the mathematics used." In other words, he is "very much more sympathetic than he [Samuelson-Rieu] is." This very "non-univalence," however, is equally applied to the relation between him and Okishio, especially regarding the FMT. Okishio is supportive of the labor theory of value through the theoretical role of the FMT, while the FMT's status is questionable in Morishima's rejection of the labor theory of value. Without a doubt, Shibata's attitude toward the value concept is different from that of either Okishio or Morishima.

In summary, the Shibata-Okishio connection can be summarized as follows. While Shibata supports the labor theory of value from the perspective of normative standards, Okishio tries to maintain it as a positive economic theory that explains capitalist exploitation starting from price variables. Shibata's work contained two lines of reasoning running from general equilibrium theory to the labor theory of value, combining the redundancy thesis with the normative aspect of economic theory. Beyond generalizing Shibata's analysis, Okishio tried to revive the analytical aspect of the labor theory of value. The FMT has a central place in Okishio's theory not only in connecting the price sphere to the value sphere but also in the presentation of the Okishio theorem which will be discussed in Chapter 6. Insofar as the FMT is proven, the equality between total profit and total surplus value can be abandoned.

Furthermore, a new technology should be chosen in terms of prices (not values), which necessarily requires rectification of Marx's law of the tendency of the rate of profit to fall. All this considered, in Okishio's view, the FMT is a logical refutation of the so-called redundancy critique. Whether Okishio's trial succeeded or not, it can be said that the value controversy in the 1970s reversed the order of his reasoning.

4.4 Interpretations of the Fundamental Marxian Theorem

4.4.1 Introduction

Following the paradigm shift in Marxian value theory that began in the early 1980s, represented by the "New Interpretation" (NI), the FMT came to play a smaller role in the NI than conventional interpretations, such as those of Okishio and Morishima. Undoubtedly, there have been many discussions that generalize the FMT beyond linear production theory (Yoshihara, 2017) and combine it with the Class-Exploitation Correspondence Principle (Roemer, 1982). However, the "Temporal Single-System Interpretation" (TSSI) is notable because it reintroduced the FMT in the literature on Marxian value theory. As the TSSI belongs to the same single-system interpretation, from a wider perspective, as the NI,[19] its FMT approach is distinct from the conventional dual-system approach. Nevertheless, unlike the NI, the TSSI gave a crucial meaning to the FMT by "reclaiming Marx's *Capital*" (Kliman, 2007). Hence, the controversy between the two streams within the single-system interpretation has been very harsh (Kliman & Freeman, 2006, 2008; Mohun & Veneziani, 2007). This section tries to intervene in the controversy, in a roundabout way, by showing that each interpretation adopts its own specific assumptions to integrate the FMT into its entire theoretical body. In Sect. 4.4.2, the TSSI's interpretation of the FMT will be examined. A comparative analysis of this and the NI's interpretation in Sect. 4.4.3, will show that the FMT only works at a certain level of abstraction with different conceptual definitions. In Sect. 4.4.4, it will be demonstrated that the proof of the FMT is not a critical experiment for identifying the correct interpretation of Marxian value theory.

[19] Duménil and Foley (2008) identify the NI with "the single-system labor theory of value."

4.4.2 The Temporal Single-System Interpretation

A useful starting point is the summary of the basic formal structure of the TSSI.

In the TSSI, value and price are defined in the form of first-order differences as follows:

$$\lambda_{t+1} = p_t A + l \tag{4.8}$$

$$p_{t+1} = p_t A + l + g_t \tag{4.9}$$

Here the subscript denotes time defined discretely, and g represents the price-value difference. Since the TSSI theorists emphasize continuous technical change, A and l should also be time-indexed. However, for analytical simplicity, they usually start with (4.8) and (4.9) (Kliman & McGlone, 1999, p. 37). Notably, g also represents the profit-surplus value difference. Denoting the wage rate as w, profit (π) and surplus value (s) per unit of commodity are as follows:

$$\pi - s = (p_{t+1} - p_t A - wl) - (l - wl) = (l + g_t - wl) - (l - wl) = g_t \tag{4.10}$$

The first equality holds here because the value of labor-power in the TSSI is equal to wl when the monetary expression of labor time (MELT) is assumed to be 1.[20]

According to Eq. (4.8), the values of the constant capital should be calculated by their historical costs, not their current costs. However, the context of historical versus current cost, which had been implicitly accepted, was negated in the following discussion.

> ...it is complete misnomer to treat the distinction between the above [sequential valuation-Rieu] and equilibrium valuations as a distinction between 'historical' and 'current' cost. The value transferred to the product is not given by the magnitude of capital when purchased; it is given by the magnitude of this capital when it is used. This is its 'current' cost. The equilibrium determination substitutes a completely different notion,

[20] The TSSI's MELT is essentially similar to the NI's concept, but the related variables are defined intertemporally. See Akinci and Karahanogullari (2015) for an elaborated formulation of the TSSI's MELT.

redefining the word 'current' to mean 'future'; it says that the value transferred by the cotton is given by what the cotton *will* cost when it has been produced using a technology that does not exist at the time it is used. (Freeman, 1999, p. 10. Italics in original)

To follow the internal logic of the TSSI, we now examine whether the TSSI is consistent with the above argument by introducing continuous time (Rieu, 2003, pp. 91–92). We assume that the price of constant input changes at the instantaneous rate of $\sigma(< 0)$ from t_0 to t_1. The physical quantity of constant input is assumed to remain unchanged as q_0. Then, prices of constant inputs should be calculated as follows:

$$\int_{t_0}^{t_1} p_0 q_0 e^{\sigma t} dt = \frac{p_0 q_o}{\sigma}\left(e^{\sigma t_1} - e^{\sigma t_0}\right) \tag{4.11}$$

In the TSSI in the discrete time framework, however, the prices of constant inputs are $p_0 q_0 e^{\sigma t_0}$. This calculation is compatible with (4.11) only when $\sigma = 0$, which implies that there is no technical progress. As Kliman and McGlone (1999, p. 34) admit, in its early stage, the TSSI was not a homogenous body of work. Therefore, the time concept that the TSSI is premised on might differ between theorists. Contrary to the other TSSI theorists regarding the intertemporal setting, Freeman (1996, 1999) consistently worked on a continuous time framework. Therefore, the context emphasizing the distinction between historical and replacement costs (Laibman, 2001) cannot be attributed to Freeman's work. As the TSSI evolved, however, Freeman's framework was implicitly adopted. For example, Kliman's (2007) "pre-production reproduction cost" tries to integrate continuous time into the discrete time framework. As another TSSI theorist noted, however, this causes a new difficulty when valuing commodities in the presence of a stock of commodities (Potts, 2016).

Before moving to the main discussion, it should be noted that the TSSI's nonconventional definition of value violates a necessary condition for the existence of labor exploitation, i.e., the "net production possibility condition" (Okishio, 2022, p. 82), which is an economic representation of the Hawkins-Simon condition. This can easily be shown by a one-commodity corn model. When a and l are the quantity of corn and labor required to produce a unit of corn, the unit value of corn (λ_c) is calculated as $\lambda_c = a\lambda_c + l = \frac{l}{1-a}$. If $a \geq 1$, the unit value would be negative or even infinity. Therefore, for an economically meaningful solution, a

should be less than 1. In the TSSI value definition (4.8), however, the value magnitude becomes positive, even when $a \geq 1$.[21]

Accordingly, here, the TSSI is examined in the context of the FMT.[22]

The TSSI differentiates itself from the NI by determining values intertemporally and argues that the NI and any other simultaneist framework cannot prove the FMT, which should work at "the real world" (Kliman, 2007, pp. 175–176) level.[23] The reason why the TSSI is the only possible interpretation for validating the FMT, especially when compared with the NI, is as follows:

> The NI and SSSI [Simultaneous Single-System Interpretation-Rieu] imply that surplus labour and profit must have the same sign when the PNP [price of net product-Rieu] is positive. Assume for the moment that it is indeed always positive. Does this make surplus labour sufficient for profit? No. It is insufficient, because positive profit requires something more than surplus labour—namely a positive PNP. (Kliman & Freeman, 2006, p. 118)

Notably, here, the TSSI focuses on the sufficiency aspect of the FMT, which was not the main interest of Okshio. Furthermore, since Okishio's net production possibility condition is required to obtain an economically meaningful interpretation of the labor value, this quote seems to be a tautology that argues the temporal definition of value is the only correct interpretation. Moreover, the TSSI's alleged proof of the FMT without any restrictive constraint requires further changes to the definitions of profit and inflation.

Above all, the TSSI considers the FMT to propose that "surplus labor is both necessary and sufficient for *real profit* to exist" (Kliman, 2001, p. 106, italics added), which implies that profit in the FMT should be defined as real profit, not nominal profit. In other words, even in the case of a negative price of net product (PNP), real profit is positive while nominal profit is negative (Kliman, 2007, pp. 188–189).

[21] Another difficulty in this case is that value is not equal to price even in one-commodity model, which is inconsistent with the conventional wisdom of the labor theory of value.

[22] For a comprehensive critique of the TSSI, see Veneziani (2005). The Okishio theorem, another main issue raised by the TSSI will be examined in Sect. 6.3 of Chapter 6.

[23] According to Kliman (2007, p. 190), the net production possibility condition noted above is the main cause for the failure of the original FMT, which is unable to clarify "the relationship between surplus labor and profit *at actual output levels*" (Italics added).

Using this chapter's notations, the TSSI's "real profit" (Π_R) can be represented as follows where i denotes the rate of inflation:

$$\Pi_R = \frac{1}{1+i} p_{t+1} x_{t+1} - p_t x_{t+1} - w_t l_t x_{t+1} \tag{4.12}$$

This is different from "nominal profit" (Kliman, 2007, p. 186) due to the first term on the right-hand side, which includes $\frac{1}{1+i}$.

The definition of inflation is critical because it determines whether the FMT of the TSSI holds:

> If the exploitation theory of profit holds under a particular definition of inflation, and one accepts that definition, then one must conclude that surplus labor is the sole source of (real) profit. If one rejects the definition, one must draw the opposite conclusion. (Kliman, 2001, p. 106)

As is well known, the growth accounting equation shows that the change rate of the MELT is the sum of the inflation rate and the change rate of labor productivity because the MELT is defined as the product of price and labor productivity. Nevertheless, the TSSI adopts an unusual definition for the rate of inflation, which includes a rise in labor productivity as well as an increase in price, as follows:

> According to the concept of inflation with which we are most familiar, inflation occurs if there is an increase in the money price of a given set of physical terms. However, Marx employed a different concept of inflation, according to which inflation occurs if there is an increase in the money price of a set of items that has a given cost in terms of labor-time. (Kliman, 2011, pp. 82–83)

In this context, the rate of inflation is defined as

$$i = \frac{m_{t+1} - m_t}{m_t} \tag{4.13}$$

where m_t and m_{t+1} represent input MELT and output MELT, respectively (Kliman, 2007, p. 185).[24]

[24] As explained in the previous chapters, the MELT is decomposed into the value expression of labor time (VELT) and the monetary expression of value (MEV). The increase in the MELT, therefore, results from either the increase in the VELT or the

This unusual definition is derived from Eq. (4.8) which defines values in a temporal setting. Therefore, as Akinci and Karahanogullari (2015, p. 771) formulated, the MELT of TSSI is also temporally defined as:

$$m_{t+1} = \frac{p_{t+1}x_{t+1}}{\frac{p_t A_{t+1} x_{t+1}}{m_t} + l_t x_{t+1}} \tag{4.14}$$

Now Kliman's (2007, pp. 185–187) proof of the FMT proceeds as follows.

The value-added in terms of labor time is:

$$l_t x_{t+1} = \frac{p_{t+1}x_{t+1}}{m_{t+1}} - \frac{p_t A_t x_{t+1}}{m_t} \tag{4.15}$$

On the other hand, surplus labor (S_L) is defined as total labor time minus necessary labor time which is monetary wages divided by the MELT.

$$S_L = l_t x_{t+1} - \frac{w_t l_t}{m_t} \tag{4.16}$$

Combining (4.15) with the TSSI's definition of the inflation rate, (4.13) leads to:

$$m_t l_t x_{t+1} = \frac{m_t}{m_{t+1}} p_{t+1}x_{t+1} - p_t A x_{t+1} = \frac{p_{t+1}x_{t+1}}{1+i} - p_t A x_{t+1}$$

$$\therefore \; p_t A x_{t+1} = p_t A x_{t+1} + m_t l_t x_{t+1} \tag{4.17}$$

Therefore, real profit is calculated as follows:

$$\Pi_R = p_t A x_{t+1} + m_t l_t x_{t+1} - p_t A x_{t+1} - w_t l_t = m_t l_t x_{t+1} - w_t l_t = m_t S_L \tag{4.18}$$

In Eq. (4.18), there is no possibility of negative MELT, as the initial value of the MELT is positive and finite (Kliman, 2001, p. 108).

This proof, however, entirely depends on a teleological construction to "make Marx's exploitation theory of profit make sense" (Kliman, 2007,

increase in the MEV. Even if one adopts Kliman's definition of the inflation, the former should be assumed away.

p. 189). As a result, the TSSI's proof of the FMT has a tautological character. Namely, transforming Eq. (4.13) into

$$m_t = m_0(1+i)^t \tag{4.19}$$

shows that the rate of inflation must be greater than -1 to avoid making m_{t+1} negative or zero. That is, the positiveness of m_t requires not only the positiveness and the finiteness of m_0, but also that the rate of inflation must be greater than -1, which implies $m_{t+1} > 0$ from Eq. (4.13).

As will be shown in Sect. 4.4.3, the tautological character of the FMT is inevitable not only in the TSSI but also in the NI, and, more generally, in any single-system interpretation. The TSSI's alleged proof, however, requires another unusual assumption to clarify whenever a negative PNP appears.

Using (4.12), the relation between real profit and nominal profit (Π_N) is obtained as:

$$\Pi_R = \Pi_N - \frac{i}{1+i} p_{t+1}x_{t+1} = m_t S_L \tag{4.20}$$

In Eq. (4.20), positive real profit with negative nominal profit implies the negative $\frac{i}{1+i}$, which means its numerator, the inflation rate (i) should be negative. Combining (4.19) with this requirement leads to $-1 < i < 0$. This is an implausible assumption of declining MELT.[25]

In sum, in contrast to the TSSI's allegation, the FMT is not proved "*under completely general conditions*" (Kliman, 2001, p. 106. Italics in original). Now, we turn to the NI's conception of the FMT.

4.4.3 *The New Interpretation*

As the NI tried to connect price and labor time directly through the MELT, the theoretical status of the FMT is clearly different from that in the conventional literature. In the NI, the FMT was marginalized because the so-called transformation problem became "a trivial exercise in definitions" (Duménil, 1984, p. 349). However, as already noted above, Okishio's original intention for the theorem is not necessarily incompatible with the NI; it attempts to express the essence of capitalist exploitation, starting from the surface of market exchange:

25 The author is indebted to Fred Moseley for noting this point.

> The important issue for Marx was......that one can therefore use a measure of the monetary expression of labor appropriately defined at the level of the aggregate system of commodity production to translate flows of money in real-world capitalist accounts into flow of labor-time and vice versa. (Foley, 2000, pp. 20–21)

In fact, in an earlier stage, the NI tried to integrate the FMT into its theoretical system. Lipietz (1982) and Duménil and Roy (1982) formulated the relation between the rate of exploitation (e) and the equilibrium rate of profit (r), $r = f(e)$, as "convex, monotonically increasing in e and bounded by R [the maximal rate of profit when wage rate is zero – Rieu]" (Lipietz, 1982, p. 69). This was very similar to Morishima's relation between the wage-profit curve and the exploitation-rate curve (1973, p. 64). Once again, if one faithfully reflects Okishio's original intention, the inverse function form, $e = f^{-1}(r)$ would be more appropriate.

However, in its later stage, the NI was distanced from the FMT, since the theorem failed "to motivate the analysis of the embodied labor coefficients system by showing what explanatory power it has over observable phenomenon" (Foley, 2000, p. 18). According to the NI's critiques, the NI regards positive profit itself as the symptom of exploitation (Saad-Filho, 2002, p. 45). As emphasized repeatedly in this book, this is because the NI's main concern is to provide a unified conception of labor time and money, and to thereby, make it possible to return to the realm of labor time starting from the realm of monetary variables.

Although no NI theorist explicitly gave a "proof" for the FMT, it may be given by using the two axioms of the NI noted in Chapter 3.

$$m = \frac{py}{lx} \tag{4.21}$$

$$VLP = \frac{w}{m} = \frac{wlx}{py} \tag{4.22}$$

Here $y = x - Ax = (I - A)x$ represents the vector of net product.

Using Eqs. (4.21) and (4.22), the total surplus value (S) is related to the total profit (Π)

$$S = lx - VLP \cdot lx = lx - \frac{w}{m}lx = \frac{py - wlx}{m} = \frac{\Pi}{m} \tag{4.23}$$

From (4.23), it is clear that positive surplus value, $S > 0$, is identical to positive profit, $\Pi > 0$. This relation is similar to the TSSI's FMT, (4.18) in its form except that here Π means nominal profit, Π_N in the TSSI. The TSSI's refutation of the NI was that py, and therefore, m may be negative. However, this was already recognized in an earlier stage of the NI:

> As far as the new interpretation of the transformation problem is concerned, the required conditions *are the existence of a positive set of prices regardless of the rates of profit, guaranteeing not necessarily uniform positive wages, and a positive aggregate price of the net output*. (Duménil, 1984, p. 348. Italic in original)

As the MELT is the ex-post relation between monetary value-added and working hours for a given period of time, $py < 0$ if y has any negative element, and some specific composition of the product. Stamatis (1998–1999, p. 43) pointed out this possibility before the TSSI.

In a reply to the criticism of the TSSI, Mohun (2003, p. 98) argued that "economies in disequilibrium still have some structure; if they are technologically and economically viable they can reproduce themselves, prices are not random, and behavior is not arbitrary. A disequilibrium state is not one in which absolutely anything can happen." Strictly speaking, however, this is not a rebuttal of the TSSI's refutation but an admission of its possibility, at least on purely logical grounds.

Clearly, positive PNP is a weaker constraint than the net production possibility condition in the conventional interpretation because py can be positive without necessarily presupposing $y \geq 0$. On the other hand, it does not satisfy the requirement of the conventional labor value concept because PNP is sensitive to changes in relative prices (Cogliano et al., 2018, p. 216). However, as the equations of the NI are "all specified in terms of aggregates" (Mohun, 2004, p. 77), the NI does not require the existence of positive values in more realistic conditions such as joint production. Therefore, one cannot determine the logical superiority of either the NI or the conventional interpretation.

The fact that Eqs. (4.21) and (4.22) are given as axioms implies that the FMT is not the object of a mathematical proof in the NI. This is consistent with the following explanation of why the NI is an interpretation rather than a solution:

> ...the New Interpretation proposes to define the relevant categories of the labor theory of value so that what is regarded as the key Marxian insight, the quantitative equivalence between capitalist gross profit and unpaid labor, holds. The "dual" approach to the labor theory of value..., in contrast, considers whether it is possible to deduce Marx's equivalence from the assumptions (such as the identification of the value of labor power with the labor embodied in the workers' consumption). (Foley, 2000, p. 22)

This implies that categories of the labor theory of value are defined to satisfy Marx's essential requirements, which is in the same spirit as Kliman's (2007) attempt to "make Marx's exploitation theory of profit make sense," which was quoted above in Sect. 4.4.2. Therefore, the NI's FMT, if it exists, only works at a certain level of abstraction, mirroring the TSSI's FMT exactly.

Finally, it is known that any other simultaneous single-system interpretation (Lee, 1993; Wolff et al., 1982) including a "macro-monetary interpretation" (Moseley, 2016) requires positive PNP to connect monetary profit to surplus value. This is because the formal difference between the NI and the other simultaneous single-system interpretations is only in how they measure the constant capital part, which does not affect the relationship between surplus labor and profit.

4.4.4 Summing Up

Table 4.1 summarizes the discussions thus far.

As noted in the introduction of this chapter, the TSSI seems to suggest that "what economic theory determines must be what one directly observes" (Petri, 2012, p. 20). Therefore, it attempts to connect positive profit and positive surplus labor without any unrealistic conditions, which

Table 4.1 The FMT and interpretations of Marxian value theory

	Main goal	*Assumptions*	*Beyond the scope*
The TSSI	Proof of the FMT under general conditions	Specific definition of inflation and profit Declining MELT	
The NI	Connecting money to labor time	Positive PNP	Sufficiency aspect of the FMT

is regarded as proving the FMT under general conditions. On the other hand, as the NI focuses on translating monetary variables into labor time correspondents, the sufficiency aspect of the FMT is particularly beyond its scope.

As the TSSI and the NI "prove" the FMT in their own way at their chosen level of abstraction, one cannot decide which interpretation is logically superior to the other. This is reflected in the assumptions that both interpretations explicitly and implicitly adopted. While the NI should accept positive PNP as a given premise or as a part of its two axioms, the TSSI constructs specific conceptions of inflation and profit, and furthermore assumes a declining MELT.

4.5 Conclusion

In this chapter, we examined the history of the FMT's construction in Japan to emphasize that the central role of the FMT is to connect money variables to labor exploitation, thereby demonstrating the necessity of the labor theory of value. The necessity aspect of the FMT that was originally intended by Okshio is consistent with the NI's problem setting; however, labor value and price are considered two mutually independent dual existences.

Although a recent revival of the FMT by the TSSI raised many important issues, the FMT's original intention and limitations should be recognized. It was shown that the FMT only works at a certain level of abstraction with assumptions that are specific to each interpretation of Marxian value theory. Ultimately, this leads us to recognize what mathematical Marxian economics can and cannot do, which has often been misunderstood. The FMT can never "prove" the existence of labor exploitation; we also need to obtain sociological and political insights to describe the reality of exploitation in a capitalist economy.

References

Akama, M. (2000). Marxian economics. In A. Ikeo (Ed.), *Japanese economics and economists since 1945*. Routledge.

Akinci, U., & Karahanogullari, Y. (2015). Convergence of monetary equivalent of labour times (MELTs) in two Marxian interpretations. *Cambridge Journal of Economics, 39*(3), 769–781.

Bidard, C., & Erreygers, G. (Eds.). (2010). *The analysis of linear economic systems*. Routledge.
Bródy, A. (1970). *Proportions, prices and planning: A mathematical restatement of the labor theory of value*. North-Holland.
Bowles, S., & Gintis, H. (1981). Structure and practice in the labor theory of value. *Review of Radical Political Economics, 12*(4), 1–26.
Cogliano, J., Flaschel, P., Franke, R., Frölich, N., & Veneziani, R. (2018). *Value, competition and exploitation: Marx's legacy revisited*. Edward Elgar.
Duménil, G. (1984). The so-called "transformation problem" revisited: A brief comment. *Journal of Economic Theory, 33*(2), 340–348.
Duménil, G., & Foley, D. K. (2008). The Marxian transformation problem. In S. N. Durlauf & L. B. Blume (Eds.), *The new Palgrave: A dictionary of economics*. Palgrave Macmillan.
Duménil, G., & Roy, C. (1982). Une approche fonctionelle du théorème Marxien fundamental d'Okishio Morishima. *Cahiers d'économie politique, 7*, 129–139.
Foley, D. K. (2000). Recent developments in the labor theory of value. *Review of Radical Political Economics, 32*(1), 1–39.
Freeman, A. (1996). Price, value and profit—A continuous, general, treatment. In A. Freeman & G. Carchedi (Eds.), *Marx and non-equilibrium economics*. Edward Elgar.
Freeman, A. (1999). *The limits of Ricardian value: Law, contingency and motion in economics*. Paper presented at the 6th mini-conference of International Working Group on Value Theory.
Glick, M., & Ehrbar, H. (1987). The transformation problem: An obituary. *Australian Economic Papers, 26*(49), 294–317.
Groll, S., & Orzech, Z. B. (1989). From Marx to the Okishio theorem: A genealogy. *History of Political Economy, 21*(2), 253–272.
Howard, M. C., & King, J. (1992). *A history of Marxian economics* (Vol. 2). Princeton University Press.
Itoh, M. (2021). *Value and crisis: Essays on Marxian economics in Japan* (2nd ed.). Monthly Review Press.
Kliman, A. (2001). Simultaneous valuation vs. the exploitation theory of profit. *Capital and Class, 73*, 97–112.
Kliman, A. (2007). *Reclaiming Marx's capital: A refutation of the myth of inconsistency*. Lexington Books.
Kliman, A. (2011). *The failure of capitalist production: Underlying causes of the Great Recession*. Pluto Press.
Kliman, A., & Freeman, A. (2006). Replicating Marx: A reply to Mohun. *Capital and Class, 88*, 117–126.
Kliman, A., & Freeman, A. (2008). Simultaneous valuation versus the exploitation theory of profit: A summing up. *Capital and Class, 94*, 107–118.

Kliman, A., & McGlone, T. (1999). A temporal single-system interpretation of Marx's value theory. *Review of Political Economy, 11*(1), 33–59.
Laibman, D. (2001). Rising 'material' versus falling 'value' rates of profit: Trial by simulation. *Capital and Class, 73*, 79–96.
Lange, O. (1935 [1968]). Marxian economics and modern economic theory. *Review of Economic Studies, 2*(3), 189–201. In D. Horowitz (Ed.), *Marx and modern economics*. Monthly Review Press.
Lee, C.-O. (1993). Marx's labour theory of value revisited. *Cambridge Journal of Economics, 17*(4), 463–478.
Lipietz, A. (1982). The so-called transformation problem revisited. *Journal of Economic Theory, 26*(1), 59–88.
Makino, K. (2015). *Shibata Kei – Shihonshyugi no Chokoku wo Mezasite* [In Japanese: In pursuit of overcoming capitalism]. Nihon Keizai Hyouronsha.
Marx, K. (1981). *Capital* (Vol. 3). Penguin Books.
Mohun, S. (2003). On the TSSI and the exploitation theory of profit. *Capital and Class, 81*, 85–102.
Mohun, S. (2004). The labour theory of value as foundations for empirical investigations. *Metroeconomica, 55*(1), 65–95.
Mohun, S., & Veneziani, R. (2007). The incoherence of the TSSI: A reply to Kliman and Freeman. *Capital and Class, 92*, 139–145.
Mori, K. (2008). Maurice Potron's linear economic model: A de facto proof of 'fundamental Marxian theorem.' *Metroeconomica, 59*(3), 511–529.
Morishima, M. (1973). *Marx's economics*. Cambridge University Press.
Morishima, M. (1974). The fundamental Marxian theorem: A reply to Samuelson. *Journal of Economic Literature, 12*(1), 71–74.
Morishima, M. (1977). *Walras' economics*. Cambridge University Press.
Morishima, M. (2004). *Marx's economics* (Japanese Edition). (Y. Takasuka, Trans.). Michio Morishima's Collected Works, Vol. 7. Iwanami Shoten.
Morishima, M. (2007 [1997]). *Memoirs* (in Japanese), Vol. 1. Asahi Shimbun-sha.
Morishima, M., & Catephores, G. (1978). *Value, exploitation and growth: Marx in the light of modern economic theory*. McGraw-Hill.
Morris-Suzuki, T. (1989). *A history of Japanese economic thought*. Routledge and Nissan Institute for Japanese Studies.
Moseley, F. (2016). *Money and totality: A macro-monetary interpretation of Marx's logic in capital and the end of the 'transformation problem'*. Brill.
Nakatani, T. (1995). Distribution of surplus value and production price (in Japanese). *The Bulletin of Japan Society of Political Economy, 33*(2).
Nakatani, T., & Rieu, D.-M. (2003). On the 'new interpretation' of Marxian labor theory of value. *Kobe University Economic Review, 49*, 51–62.
Negishi, T. (1989). *History of economic theory*. North-Holland.

Nishi, A. (2012). Ippankinkouriron to marukusu – Shibata Kei no Keizaigaku [In Japanese: General equilibrium theory and Marx: Shibata Kei's economics]. *Hannan Ronsyu (Hannan University Review), 47*(2), 155–176.

Okishio, N. (1955). Kachi to KaKaku [In Japanese, value and price]. *Keizaigaku Kenkyu Nenppo* [Annals of economics research], 1. Kobe University.

Okishio, N. (1961 [1993]). Technical changes and the rate of profit. *Kobe University Economic Review, 7*. In M. Krüger & P. Flaschel (Eds.), *Nobuo Okishio—Essays on political economy: Collected papers*. Peter Lang.

Okishio, N. (1963 [1993]). A mathematical note on Marxian theorems. *Weltwirtschaftliches Archiv, 91*(2). In M. Krüger & P. Flaschel (Eds.), *Nobuo Okishio—Essays on political economy: Collected papers*. Peter Lang.

Okishio, N. (1972). Marukusu no Seisankakakuron ni Tsuite [In Japanese, On Marx's theory of prices of production]. *Kobedaigaku Keizaigaku Kenkyu [Kobe University Economic Studies], 19*, 38–63.

Okishio, N. (1974 [1993]). Value and production price. *Kobe University Economic Review, 20*. In M. Krüger & P. Flaschel (Eds.), *Nobuo Okishio—Essays on political economy*. Peter Lang.

Okishio, N. (1977). Marukusu Keizaikaku: Kachi to Kakaku no Riron [in Japanese]. *Marxian economics: The theory of value and price*. Chikuma Shobo.

Okishio, N. (1995). An interview with professor Okishio (in Korean). *Iron (Theory), 13*, 227–240.

Okishio, N. (2004). *Keizaigaku to Gendai no Syomondai* [In Japanese, economics and contemporary problems]. Otuki Shoten.

Okishio, N. (2022). *The theory of accumulation: A Marxian approach to the dynamics of capitalist economy*. Springer-Verlag.

Okishio, N., Nakatani, T., & Kitano, M. (1978 [1993]). Three topics on Marxian fundamental theorem. *Kobe University Economic Review* (24). In M. Krüger & P. Flaschel (Eds.), *Nobuo Okishio—Essays on political economy*. Peter Lang.

Petri, F. (2012). *On recent reformulations of the labour theory of value*. Department of Economics University of Siena 643, Department of Economics, University of Siena.

Potts, N. (2016). Two temporal single system interpretation of Marx calculations of the MELT. *Marxism 21, 13*(2), 94–122.

Rieu, D.-M. (2003). The temporal single-system interpretation of Marx's value theory: A critical appraisal. *Korean Economic Review, 19*(1), 81–96.

Rieu, D.-M. (2009). The Shibata-Okishio connection: Labor theory of value and rate of profit. *Journal of the History of Economic Thought, 31*(3), 325–339.

Roemer, J. E. (1982). *A general theory of exploitation and class*. Harvard University Press.

Saad-Filho, A. (2002). *The value of Marx*. Routledge.

Samuelson, P. (1971). Understanding the Marxian notion of exploitation: A summary of the so-called 'transformation problem' between Marxian values and competitive prices. *Journal of Economic Literature, 9*(2), 399–431.

Screpanti, E. (2003). Value and exploitation: A counterfactual approach. *Review of Political Economy, 15*(2), 155–171.

Seton, F. (1957). The transformation problem. *Review of Economic Studies, 25*, 149–160.

Shaikh, A. (1977). Marx's theory of value and the transformation problem. In J. Schwartz (Ed.), *The subtle anatomy of capitalism*. Goodyear Publishing.

Shibata, K. (1933a). *Marx's analysis of capitalism and the general equilibrium theory of the Lausanne School* (pp. 107–136). Kyoto University Economic Review.

Shibata, K. (1933b). The meaning of the theory of value in theoretical economics. *Kyoto University Economic Review, VIII*, 49–68.

Shibata, K. (1934). On the law of decline in the rate of profit. *Kyoto University Economic Review, IX*, 61–75.

Shibata, K. (1935). *Riron Keizaigaku* [In Japanese: Theoretical economics]. Koumondou.

Shibata, K. (1939). On the general profit rate. *Kyoto University Economic Review, XIV*, 40–66.

Shibata, K. (1959). *Dynamic and dialectic theories of world capitalism*. Minerva Shobo.

Shibata, K. (2009). *Keizai no Housoku wo Motomete* [In Japanese: In Pursuit of the Law of Economy] (Supplementary). Nihon Keizai Hyouronsha.

Shibata, K. (2015). Shihonron to Ippan-Kinkou-Riron [In Japanese: Capital and the theory of general equilibrium]. *Keizai-Ronso, 189*(1), 31–44.

Stamatis, G. (1998–1999). On the "new solution." *International Journal of Political Economy, 28*(4), 23–46.

Steedman, I. (1977). *Marx after Sraffa*. New Left Books.

Sugihara, S., Kumon, S., & Okamura, M. (1996). Shibata Kei no Nenpo-Tyosaku Mokiroku [In Japanese: Shibata Kei—Career and works]. *Aoyama Kokusai Seikei Ronsyu [Aoyama Journal of International Politics, Economics and Business], 37*, 231–264.

Takada, Y. (1931). *Roudoukachisetsu no Ginmi* [In Japanese: An examination of the labor theory of value]. Nippon Hyoron Sha.

Tsuru, S. (2006 [1985]). *Gendai Keizaigaku no Gunzou* [In Japanese: Figures in modern economics]. Iwanami Shoten.

Veneziani, R. (2005). Dynamics, disequilibrium, and Marxian economics: A formal analysis of temporal single-system Marxism. *Review of Radical Political, Economics, 37*(3), 517–529.

Wolff, R., Roberts, B., & Callari, A. (1982). Marx's (not Ricardo's) "transformation problem": A radical reconceptualization. *History of Political Economy, 14*(4), 564–582.

Yagi, K. (1999). *Kindai Nihon no Syakai Keizaigaku* [In Japanese: Social economics in modern Japan]. Chikuma Shobo.

Yoshihara, N. (2017). A progress report on Marxian economic theory: On the controversies in exploitation theory since Okishio (1963). *Journal of Economic Surveys, 31*(5), 1421–1448.

CHAPTER 5

An Axiomatic Approach and the New Interpretation

5.1 Introduction

Recently, a meaningful development in the mathematical formulation of Marxian theory of exploitation has been provided by Roberto Veneziani and Naoki Yoshihara (Veneziani & Yoshihara, 2011a, 2011b, 2017; Yoshihara, 2008, 2010; Yoshihara & Veneziani, 2013), which was entitled an "Axiomatic Approach" (AA).

The AA uses the axiomatic method "in order to identify the desirable properties of a definition (and measure) of exploitation" (Veneziani & Yoshihara, 2017, p. 1610). First, by employing the setup of a general convex cone technology, the AA shows that the Fundamental Marxian Theorem does not hold generally outside the conventional setting of linear production economy or the von Neumann technology (Yoshihara, 2008). Furthermore, the AA has been extended to the labor theory of value in general starting with "some basic properties of labor values that are meant to capture some implications of the notion of labor values as measuring the labor embodied or contained in commodities" (Cogliano et al., 2018, p. 193). Notable from the perspective of this book is that the AA reaches a conclusion that "if the New Interpretation is adopted, then it is possible to establish a robust relation between exploitation and profits in general economic environments with heterogeneous labour" (Veneziani & Yoshihara, 2017, p. 1609). This was developed from the

D.-M. Rieu, *A Mathematical Approach to Marxian Value Theory*, Marx, Engels, and Marxisms,
https://doi.org/10.1007/978-3-031-07808-8_5

AA's position that "among the main approaches, only the 'New Interpretation' is shown to satisfy PECP [Profit-Exploitation correspondence Principle-Rieu] in general" (ibid., p. 1622).

This chapter deals with the AA focusing on its connection with a developed version of the New Interpretation (NI) given by Rieu (2008, 2009) and Duménil et al. (2009). In this context, the central issue is the application of the NI at the microeconomic level which necessarily leads to the issue of labor heterogeneity. It will be shown that behind the sophisticated mathematical analysis of the AA lies the NI's core insight of the Marxian value theory. Furthermore, the AA's analysis of heterogeneous labor requires a restricted assumption already discussed in Part I of this book.

The remainder of this chapter is structured as follows. Section 5.2 summarizes the basic economic model and the results on labor exploitation of the AA. Section 5.3 provides an intuitive explanation of the NI's labor exploitation condition. It will be shown that the refutation of the "General Commodity Exploitation Theorem" (Bowles & Gintis, 1981; Roemer, 1982) by the AA is nothing but another way of explaining the NI's intuition under more limited definitions. Section 5.4 analyzes the theoretical effect of introducing heterogeneous labor on the conclusion of the AA. It will be confirmed that the application of the NI at a microeconomic level requires the assumption of equal rates of surplus value. Section 5.5 concludes.

5.2 Basic Results of the Axiomatic Approach

The AA starts with the following basic setup of the economy.

An economy is specified as $E \equiv \langle H; (P, b); (\omega^{\upsilon})_{\upsilon \in N} \rangle$ with $H = W \cup N$. The production set $P \subseteq R_{-} \times R^{n}_{-} \times R^{n}_{+}$ is a closed convex cone with $0 \in P$.[1] H is the set of agents who trade n commodities. Every agent $\nu \in H$ has her initial endowments denoted as $\omega^{\upsilon} \in R^{n}_{+}$. H can be partitioned into two disjoint subsets, the working class W and the capitalist class N. Whereas the capitalists have some assets, the workers do not have any initial endowments. Namely, $N = \{\upsilon \in H | \omega^{\upsilon} > 0\}$ and $W = \{\upsilon \in H | \omega^{\upsilon} = 0\}$. Each worker is endowed with one unit of

[1] R is the set of real numbers, and R_{+}, R_{++}, and R_{-} are the set of non-negative, strictly positive, and non-negative real numbers. R^{n} is an n-dimensional vector space over R. The null vector is denoted as 0.

homogeneous labor. Standard assumptions such as the indispensability of labor as a factor of production and free disposal condition hold here (Yoshihara, 2010, p. 283).

For a given price vector p and wage rate $w > 0$, capitalists maximize profits subject to their wealth constraint. The following conventional definition of the equilibrium is adopted:

Definition 5.1. (Roemer, 1981, p. 41) A reproducible solution (RS) for the economy E is a pair $\left((p, w), (\alpha^v)_{v\in N}\right) \in R_+^{n+1} \times P$, where $p \in R_+^n \backslash \{0\}$ such that

(a) $\forall v \in N, \alpha^v \in P$ solves profit maximization problem;
(b) $\widehat{\alpha} \geq \alpha_0 b$, where $\alpha \equiv \sum_{v\in N}\alpha^v$ and $\widehat{\alpha} \equiv \overline{\alpha} - \underline{\alpha}$ (reproducibility);
(c) $pb = w$ (subsistence wage);
(d) $\underline{\alpha} \leq \omega$, where $\omega \equiv \sum_{v\in N}\omega^v$ (social feasibility).

Here $\alpha_0 \in R_+, \underline{\alpha} \in R_+^n, \overline{\alpha} \in R_+^n$, and $b \in R_+^n \backslash\{0\}$ denote the direct labor input, the inputs of produced goods, the output of the n commodities, and the consumption bundle for one unit of labor, respectively, and $\alpha \equiv (-\alpha_0, -\underline{\alpha}, \overline{\alpha}) \in P$.

The following two more definitions are worth examining in the context of this chapter.

Definition 5.2. (Yoshihara & Veneziani, 2013) Given an economy $E \equiv \langle H; (P, b); (\omega^v)_{v\in N}\rangle$, let $\left((p, w), (\alpha^v)_{v\in N}\right) \in R_+^{n+1} \times P$ be an RS for E. For each $c \in R_+^n$, with $pc \leq p\widehat{\alpha}$, let $\tau^c \in [0, 1]$ be such that $\tau^c\widehat{\alpha} \in B(p, c) \equiv \{x \in R_+^n | px = pc\}$. The labor embodied in c at the social reproduction point α is$\tau^c\alpha_0$.

Definition 5.3. (Yoshihara & Veneziani, 2013) Given an economy $E \equiv \langle H; (P, b); (\omega^v)_{v\in N}\rangle$, let $\left((p, w), (\alpha^v)_{v\in N}\right) \in R_+^{n+1} \times P$ be an RS for E. For any $\mu \in W$, who supplies one unit of labor and consumes b, let $\tau^b \in [0, 1]$ be defined as in Definition 5.2. Then, μ is exploited if and only if $\tau^b\alpha_0 < 1$.

A new definition of labor embodied is provided by Definition 5.2. As $p(\tau^c\widehat{\alpha}) = pc$ from the definition of *B(pc)*, "labor embodied" is changed as follows:

$$\tau^c\alpha_0 = \frac{pc}{p\widehat{\alpha}}\alpha_0 = \frac{pc}{m} \tag{5.1}$$

Here m denotes the NI's "monetary expression of labor time" (MELT) defined as the ratio of money value-added $(p\widehat{\alpha})$ to total direct labor input (α_0).

It must be noted that this notion of "labor embodied" represents a sort of redistributed value, neither Marxian labor value nor the NI's conceptualization.[2] More specifically, this definition implies that the weight of a certain commodity bundle in total prices of net product is equal to that in total quantity of labor embodied.

Suffice it to give a simple numerical example to show this point.

Example 5.1 Suppose a two-commodity economy with prices and physical conditions of production data: $p_1 = 10, p_2 = 5, w = 5, \alpha_0 = 200, \widehat{\alpha} = (100, 200), c = (50, 0)^T$.[3]

As $pc = 500$, $B(pc)$ represents the set of commodity bundles that cost exactly as much as 500. Then, τ^c is determined so as to satisfy the condition , $\tau^c\widehat{\alpha} = \tau^c(100, 200) \in B((10, 5), (50, 0)^T)$. Therefore, τ^c= 0.25.

By Definition 5.2, the "labor embodied" in c is $\tau^c\alpha_0 = 50$ (hours). Therefore, the relation, $\frac{pc}{p\widehat{\alpha}} = \frac{\tau^c\alpha_0}{\alpha_0}$ holds here.

On the other hand, Definition 5.3 gives the intuitive notion of labor exploitation which implies that an exploited agent contributes more labor than she retrieves from society. In so far as Definition 5.2 is adopted, it is consistent with the conventional Marxian concept of labor exploitation.

Based upon these two definitions, the following two theorems are derived.

Theorem 5.1 (Veneziani & Yoshihara, 2011a, 2011b) At the RS for E, every worker μ is exploited if and only if profits are positive.

Theorem 5.1 associated with Definition 5.3 extends the relation between labor exploitation and profit to the level of an individual worker. Although the NI's main subject area is the aggregate relationship between price and labor time, it also permits the microeconomic application of its concepts (Duménil et al., 2009). Therefore, Theorem 5.1 can also be examined in the context of the NI as will be shown later.

[2] As explained repeatedly in previous chapters, the NI relates the MELT to the definition of value of labor-power which is not applicable to other commodities. Especially, see discussion in Sect. 3.3 of Chapter 3 regarding a concept of "redistributed value.".

[3] For dimensional consistency, c should be 2×1 vector.

Theorem 5.2. (Yoshihara & Veneziani, 2013) There exist an economy E and an RS in which the equivalence between positive profits and the existence of commodity k-exploited agents does not hold. (Here the notion of commodity k-exploitation is defined in the same way as Definitions 5.2 and 5.3 with only a change of the numéraire from labor to commodity k.)

Theorem 5.2 is provided to refute the so-called "General Commodity Exploitation Theorem" which argues that any commodity other than labor-power, say peanut or iron, can be "exploited" in the traditional Okishio-Morishima approach (Morishima, 1973; Okishio, 1963). Also in Theorem 5.2, the meaning of commodity k-exploitation is ultimately based upon the novel definition of "labor embodied." Therefore, it should be noted that the trueness of Theorem 5.2 hinges on whether one accepts Definition 5.2.

5.3 The New Interpretation's Condition of Labor Exploitation

This section tries to offer an intuitive explanation of labor exploitation condition of the NI.

As value of labor-power (VLP) is defined as the ratio of money wage to the MELT in the NI,

$$VLP = \frac{w\alpha_0}{\frac{p\widehat{\alpha}}{\alpha_0}} = \frac{w\alpha_0}{p\widehat{\alpha}}\alpha_0 \leq \alpha_0 \tag{5.2}$$

The equality here holds when there is no profit, formally $w\alpha_0 = p\widehat{\alpha}$.[4] Now labor exploitation condition for an individual worker μ is as follows:

$$VLP^{\mu} = \frac{w\alpha_0}{p\widehat{\alpha}} < 1 \tag{5.3}$$

As *VLP* means wage share in the money value-added by definition in (5.2), labor exploitation condition is automatically satisfied. The equivalence between positive profits and the existence of labor exploitation, in other words, the Fundamental Marxian Theorem is simply presupposed from the start. This implies that the Fundamental Marxian Theorem (the

[4] It must be noted in passing that Eq. (5.2) does not need Definition 5.2.

form of Theorem 5.1 in the AA) is something that cannot be "proved" in the framework of the NI.[5]

The implication of the NI's labor exploitation condition can be stated more intuitively; as labor-power is not a commodity produced for profit, there is no distinction between gross and net product of labor-power. This is the theoretical foundation of the NI to define value of labor-power independently from consumption bundle. Mohun, one of the NI theorists, summarizes this point as follows:

> ...the unequal exchange forced by differing compositions of capital combined with the competitive equalisation of the rate of profit does not apply to the exchange of labour-power for a wage, because neither composition of capital nor rate of profit is involved in the 'production' of people. Hence in general the value of labour-power is the money wage divided by the monetary expression of labour-time. (Mohun, 2003, pp. 90–91)

As a thought experiment, suppose that there is a fictitious industry which "produces" labor-power commodity. Assume that no direct labor is needed to produce a unit of labor-power. Instead, wage bundle b is assumed to be the only input.

The MELT of this fictitious economy (m^f) will be:

$$m^f = \frac{p\widehat{\alpha} - w\alpha_0}{\alpha_0} < m \tag{5.4}$$

Therefore, value of labor-power in this economy (VLP^f) is:

$$VLP^f = \frac{w\alpha_0}{m^f} = \frac{w\alpha_0}{p\widehat{\alpha} - w\alpha_0}\alpha_0 \tag{5.5}$$

Labor exploitation condition for an individual worker μ is:

$$VLP^f = \frac{w}{m^f} = \frac{w\alpha_0}{p\widehat{\alpha} - w\alpha_0} < 1 \tag{5.6}$$

As easily can be seen, there is no guarantee that (5.6) is satisfied when there is positive profit. If wage share ($\frac{w\alpha_0}{p\widehat{\alpha}}$) is denoted as δ, (5.6) implies $\delta < 1/2$. Without doubt, this is not related to any meaning of labor exploitation. Furthermore, assuming that there is no profit, formally,

[5] This point has already been explained in Chapter 4. See Table 4.1.

$p\widehat{\alpha}= w\alpha_0$, m^f and VLP^f will be zero and infinity, respectively. This is a contradiction.

To show this intuition on the NI's labor exploitation condition excludes the "General Commodity Exploitation Theorem" in its own way, it will be useful here to check if commodity *k*-exploitation condition in the NI sense is satisfied. Instead of the MELT, one considers "monetary expression of commodity *k*" (m_k) as follows:

$$m_k = \frac{p\widehat{\alpha} - pb\alpha_0}{\underline{\alpha}_k} \tag{5.7}$$

This represents how many units of money correspond to a unit of commodity *k*. Therefore, the so-called commodity *k*-exploitation condition is as follows:

$$\frac{p_k}{m_k} = \frac{p_k\underline{\alpha}_k}{p\widehat{\alpha} - pb\alpha_0} < 1 \tag{5.8}$$

This condition does not necessarily hold even in case positive profit exists. As a matter of fact, it depends upon the input–output structure of the economy and is not related to the existence of positive profit in any meaningful way.

Example 5.2 Suppose the same economy as Example 5.1. Let commodity 1 be a numéraire. Now commodity 1-exploitation condition is

$$\frac{p_1}{m_1} = \frac{p_1\underline{\alpha}_1}{p\widehat{\alpha} - pb\alpha_0} = \frac{\underline{\alpha}_1}{100} < 1$$

$$\therefore \underline{\alpha}_1 < 100$$

Without doubt, this condition does not have any implication for "exploitation."

Conclusively, there is no room for the theory of general commodity exploitation in the NI framework. This implies that Theorem 5.2 is another way of describing the NI's central insight that there is fundamental asymmetry between labor-power and other commodities. However, as the NI does not require Definition 5.2, it is theoretically efficient than the AA in the sense that less assumptions and definitions are required to "prove" essentially the same results.

5.4 Labor Heterogeneity

In this section, the effect of introducing heterogeneous labor with different skills into the basic model of the AA is examined.[6]

Suppose that each worker is endowed with one unit of heterogeneous labor. There are k skilled workers whose labor produces the quantity of value σ_s per hour ($\sigma_s > 1$). The rest of the workers, $\alpha_0 - k$, are unskilled workers whose labor produces the quantity of value σ_u per hour ($\sigma_u < 1$). All the other conditions of Definition 5.1 such as total direct labor input, total wage fund, and total consumption bundle are kept unchanged, and therefore the economy E is still at the RS. As total value should be equal to total labor time, the following holds:

$$k\sigma_s + (\alpha_0 - k)\sigma_u = \alpha_0$$

$$\therefore (\sigma_s - \sigma_u)k = (1 - \sigma_u)\alpha_0 \tag{5.9}$$

If one assumes that skilled labor produces s (>1) times as much as unskilled labor does, (5.9) can be solved as

$$\sigma_s = \frac{s\alpha_0}{(s-1)k + \alpha_0}, \quad \sigma_u = \frac{\alpha_0}{(s-1)k + \alpha_0} \tag{5.10}$$

As total wage fund remains the same, the following must hold with the usual normalization condition, $pb = 1$:

$$kw_s + (\alpha_0 - k)w_u = \alpha_0 \tag{5.11}$$

Here w_s and w_u denote hourly wage of skilled and unskilled workers, respectively.

Assuming that skilled workers receive more wage than unskilled workers, formally $w_s = s^* w_u$ (s^*>1), (5.11) can be solved as

$$w_s = \frac{s^*\alpha_0}{(s^*-1)k + \alpha_0}, \quad w_u = \frac{\alpha_0}{(s^*-1)k + \alpha_0} \tag{5.12}$$

[6] This was originally hinted by Yoshihara (2008), albeit without formal analysis.

Adopting the NI's definition of value of labor-power, labor exploitation conditions for each group of workers are as follows:

$$\sigma_s > \frac{w_s}{m} \quad \therefore m\sigma_s = ms\sigma_u > w_s = s^* w_u \tag{5.13}$$

$$\sigma_u > \frac{w_u}{m} \quad \therefore m\sigma_u > w_u \tag{5.14}$$

Therefore, these two conditions are equal only if $s = s^*$; in other words, wage differential exactly reflects skill differences. If not, one group of workers may not be exploited, whereas the other group is exploited. Considering labor market segmentation such as the confrontation between regular and non-regular workers, the most plausible case in reality is $s < s^*$. In this case, if the following holds, skilled workers are not exploited, but "exploiters."

$$\frac{(s-1)k + \alpha_0}{(s^*-1)k + \alpha_0} < m < \frac{(s-1)k + \alpha_0}{(s^*-1)k + \alpha_0}\frac{s^*}{s} \tag{5.15}$$

A simple numerical example will be helpful to get the picture of the issue here.

Example 5.3 The MELT is assumed to be 20 dollars per hour. There are three groups of workers, high-skilled, average-skilled, and low-skilled, whose quantitative weights are 20, 30, and 50%, respectively. Hourly wages of each group are 20, 10, and 6 dollars, respectively. In this case, the weighted average of hourly wage is 10 dollars, which is equal to the hourly age of average-skilled workers. Therefore, the average value of labor-power in the sense of the NI is equal to 0.5, which makes the aggregate rate of exploitation 100%. If the NI's micro-level definition is applied, however, the value of labor-power of each group differs significantly. In the case of high-skilled workers, it will be 1, which means that those workers are not exploited. Only the workers with average and low skill are exploited.[7] Conclusively, every worker is not exploited.

Without a doubt, as exploitation is above all a collective phenomenon, it is doubtful if one can say that in this case skilled workers "exploit"

[7] While the rate of exploitation for the average-skilled workers is equal to the social average, low-skilled workers are super-exploited.

unskilled workers. However, it is obvious that Theorem 5.1 should be modified or generalized further in the case of heterogeneous labor.

This simple analysis shows that the equivalence between positive profits and labor exploitation of every worker, namely Theorem 5.1 does not hold in general. It also confirms that the conventional NI procedure is applicable on a sectoral level only with the assumption of equal rates of surplus value, or strictly speaking, the assumption that value expressions of labor time (how many hours of socially necessary abstract labor correspond to an hour of concrete individual labor) are proportional to wage rates.[8] According to the AA theorists, "although wages are necessary to convert different types of labour into a single unit, exploitation status can be determined prior to and independent of the prices of commodities, as in classical Marxian theory" (Veneziani & Yoshihara, 2017, p. 1616). As has already been discussed in Sect. 3.4.4 of Chapter 3, however, this is just "an abstract benchmark" (Foley, 2016, p. 382).

5.5 Conclusion

This chapter discussed the AA from the perspective of the NI, in particular its application at microeconomic level. It was shown that the AA extends the central insight of the NI. It is not certain whether the NI defines exploitation on a level of individual worker, which was originated from the methodological individualism adopted by Roemer (1982). However, the AA's definition of "labor embodied" is distant from the NI's concept of value. Furthermore, the AA's main results, at least discussed here, can be derived from the NI's intuition without sophisticated mathematical analysis. Lastly, it was shown that a contradiction occurs if labor heterogeneity is introduced into the framework of the AA. To avoid this problem, a more restricted assumption such as the equal rate of surplus value is required.

[8] For the derivation of this condition, see Sect. 3.4.3 in Chapter 3.

References

Bowles, S., & Gintis, H. (1981). Structure and practice in the labor theory of value. *Review of Radical Political Economics, 12*(4), 1–26.

Cogliano, J., Flaschel, P., Franke, R., Fröhlich, N., & Venezaini, R. (2018). *Value, competition and exploitation: Marx's legacy revisited*. Edward Elgar.

Duménil, G., Foley, D. K., & Lévy, D. (2009). A note on the formal treatment of exploitation in a model with heterogeneous labor. *Metroeconomica, 60*(3), 560–567.

Foley, D. (2016). What is the labour theory of value and what is it for?". In G. Freni, H. D. Kurz, A. M. Lavezzi, & R. Signorino (Eds.), *Economic theory and its history: Essays in honor of Neri Salvadori* (pp. 370–384). Routledge.

Mohun, S. (2003). The labour theory of value as foundation for empirical investigations. *Metroeconomica, 55*(1), 65–95.

Morishima, M. (1973). *Marx's economics*. Cambridge University Press.

Okishio, N. (1963). A mathematical note on Marxian theorem. *Weltwirtschaftliches Archiv, 91*, 287–299.

Rieu, D.-M. (2008). Estimating sectoral rates of surplus value: Methodological issues. *Metroeconomica, 59*(4), 557–573.

Rieu, D.-M. (2009). The "New Interpretation": Questions answered and unanswered. *Metroeconomica, 60*(3), 568–570.

Roemer, J. E. (1981). *Analytical foundations of Marxian economic theory*. Cambridge University Press.

Roemer, J. E. (1982). *A general theory of exploitation and class*. Harvard University Press.

Veneziani, R., & Yoshihara, N. (2011a). *Exploitation and profits: A general axiomatic approach in convex economies with heterogeneous agents* (IER Discussion Paper. Series, A. No. 556). The Institute of Economic Research, Hitotsubashi University.

Veneziani, R., & Yoshihara, N. (2011b). Strong subjectivism in the Marxian theory of exploitation: A critique. *Metroeconomica, 62*(1), 53–68.

Veneziani, R., & Yoshihara, N. (2017). One million miles to go: Taking the axiomatic road to defining exploitation. *Cambridge Journal of Economics, 41*(6), 1607–1626.

Yoshihara, N. (2008). *Roudou Sakusyu No Kousei Rriron Josetsu* (In Japanese, *An Introduction to the Welfare Theory of Labor Exploitation*). Tokyo: Iwanami Shoten.

Yoshihara, N. (2010). Class and exploitation in general convex cone economies. *Journal of Economic Behavior and Organization, 75*(2), 281–296.

Yoshihara, N., & Veneziani, R. (2013). Exploitation of labor and exploitation of commodities: A "New Interpretation." *Review of Radical Political Economics, 45*(4), 517–524.

PART III

Rate of Profit

CHAPTER 6

The Okishio Theorem

6.1 Introduction

The Okishio theorem (Okishio, 1961), alongside the Fundamental Marxian Theorem discussed in Chapter 4, is one of the representative achievements of mathematical Marxian economics. The Okishio theorem states that "if the real wage rate in terms of consumption goods is constant, and a new technique, which lowers unit costs in terms of the present price-wage (production price) configurations, is introduced into a basic sector, then the equal rates of profit must be higher when the new equilibrium is established" (Okishio, 2001, p. 493).[1]

Although the Okishio theorem has primarily been regarded as a denial of Marx's law of the tendency of the rate of profit to fall (TRPF), especially in Western literature, its implications are not as simple as they first appear. While technical changes and income distribution are indissolubly linked in reality, Marx's law of the TRPF tried to demonstrate that a falling rate of profit can result only from the specific character of technical changes, i.e., capital-using labor saving. The Okishio theorem,

[1] In the case of a non-basic sector, the rate of profit is unchanged, which in any case implies non-falling rate of profit. Okishio's distinction between basic and non-basic sectors is different from Sraffa's (1960) distinction between basic and non-basic goods. While wage goods are not basic goods in Sraffa's sense, they are produced in Okishio's basic sector.

D.-M. Rieu, *A Mathematical Approach to Marxian Value Theory*, Marx, Engels, and Marxisms,
https://doi.org/10.1007/978-3-031-07808-8_6

however, mathematically proved the impossibility of this situation. Therefore, merely focusing on the possibility of the falling rate of profit itself leads to a fruitless debate. Rather, it is useful to examine what implication the main thrust of the theorem has for the TRPF. In this sense, a recent critique of the theorem by the "Temporal Single-System Interpretation" (TSSI) is worthy of serious examination. Like its critique of the Fundamental Marxian Theorem discussed in Chapter 4, the TSSI also argues that "the Okishio theorem is simply false" (Kliman, 2007, p. 136) and furthermore, that the TRPF can be proved under general conditions. In addition to examining the TSSI's critique in order to pursue the original intention of the Okishio theorem, it will be necessary to return to Okishio's Japanese predecessor, Kei Shibata (1902–1986), who developed an original formulation of the Okishio theorem in the 1930s.

The remainder of this chapter is structured as follows. Section 6.2 examines the connection between Okishio and Shibata focusing on the creation of the so-called Shibata-Okishio theorem. From this connection, it will be possible to derive the theorem's counterfactual character. Section 6.3 examines the TSSI's critique of the theorem and shows that it is not an "internal refutation" in any sense. A more recent explanation of the falling rate of profit by the TSSI is also critically examined. Section 6.4 examines Okishio's work in his later years, in which he displayed a tendency toward a denial of his own theorem. What he truly meant is investigated in relation to the dynamics of competition.

6.2 The Shibata-Okishio Theorem

Let us start with the basic structure of the Okishio theorem (Bowles, 1981, pp. 183–184). Prices of production are determined by using the conventional notations as follows, where superscript 0 denotes the initial equilibrium before technical change.

$$p^0 = \left(1 + r^0\right)\left(p^0 A^0 + wl^0\right) \tag{6.1}$$

Adopting another conventional assumption that workers do not save and so, $w = pb$, where b denotes consumption bundles, Eq. (6.1) is changed into the following:

$$\frac{1}{1 + r^0} p^0 = p^0\left(A^0 + bl^0\right) \tag{6.2}$$

As p^0 is the left eigenvector of the matrix $A^0 + bl^0$, the rate of profit can be represented as

$$r^0 = \frac{1 - \lambda_{MAX}}{\lambda_{MAX}} \tag{6.3}$$

where λ_{MAX} is the maximal eigenvalue.

The Okishio theorem implies that the maximal eigenvalue of $A^0 + bl^0$ is greater than that of $A^1 + bl^1$ if the former is changed to the latter because of cost-reducing technical progress.[2] Here the most important point is that capitalists' technical choices are premised on current equilibrium prices, not on Marxian labor values. A rational capitalist only introduces technology that decreases the expected unit cost. This fact is the so-called issue of "micro-foundation."

With this background in mind, let us examine Shibata's discussion. In the 1930s, Shibata's research in the field of theoretical economics tended in basically two directions. First, the implications of value theory integrated his studies concerning Marxian value theory and Walrasian theory of general equilibrium. Second, the effect of technical change on the rate of profit is a prototype of the Okishio theorem. As Shibata (1934) is the representative article for the latter direction, let us follow the logic of this article by using general notations.

Shibata (1934) uses a Bortkiewicz-like model that is composed of three sectors. While sector 1 produces gold, which is both money and a luxury good, sector 2 and sector 3 produce production goods and consumption goods, respectively. However, as it is assumed that the organic compositions of capital are equal in sector 2 and sector 3, one of them is redundant regarding the formation of the general rate of profit.[3] On the other hand, the first low of the input coefficient matrix has all zero elements due to the assumption $a_{1j} = 0$. Suppose that $B = \left(b_{ij}\right) = A - \alpha I$ where α is a scalar. Since the first row of A contains entirely 0s, $b_{11} = -\alpha$ and $b_{1j} = 0 (j \neq 1)$. Using Laplace expansion, $|B| = -\alpha |B_{11}|$, where B_{11}

[2] Note that b is not changed after the introduction of a new technology, which is the basic assumption of the Okishio theorem. Without a doubt, it is possible for certain elements of $A^1 + bl^1$ to decrease with cost-reducing technical progress. Therefore, a simple application of the Perron–Frobenius theorem is not sufficient to prove the Okishio theorem (Hahnel, 2017, p. 129).

[3] It is not clear why Shibata constructed this unusual model. Most likely, he did so because he dealt with tedious numerical calculations without giving a general proof.

is the first leading principal minor of B, and therefore, eigenvalues of A are zero and the solutions of $|B_{11}| = 0$. According to the Perron–Frobenius theorem, $|B_{11}| = 0$ has nonzero real roots. Therefore, the maximal eigenvalue of A can be obtained merely by solving the equation, $|B_{11}| = 0$. Considering Eq. (6.3), sector 1 does not have any effect on the determination of the equilibrium rate of profit. Furthermore, the initial situation before the technical change in Shibata's model is characterized by the uniform organic composition of capital in all three sectors. Then, price becomes equal to value in every sector. In this sense, the objection may be raised that Shibata's model considered the issue of technical choice only in terms of the value aspect (Howard & King, 1992, p. 137). However, as Shibata assumed that technical change only occurs in sectors 2 and 3, the gold-producing sector (sector 1) has a different organic composition of capital from the other two sectors after the adoption of a new technology. Namely, Shibata's model introduces price-value deviation, and therefore, it is not a simple model that considers only the value aspect.

Shibata's examples can be easily represented using general notations as in Table 6.1. The first column shows that only a capital-using-labor saving technical progress, i.e., $\Delta a_{ij} > 0$, $\Delta l_j < 0$ is considered. Prices of commodities 2 and 3, strictly speaking, their relative prices in terms of gold (commodity 1) can change in any direction in the second column. However, $\Delta p_i \geq 0$ is impossible.

First, insofar as the criterion for technical choice is satisfied, $\Delta p_i > 0$ is impossible "except where the law of progressive increase of the cost of production rules" (Shibata, 1934, p. 66). Shibata argues here that a

Table 6.1 Shibata's "Instances" (1934)

Technical change	*Price*	*Rate of profit*	
$\Delta a_{ij} > 0, \Delta l_j < 0$	$\Delta p_i > 0$	$\Delta r < 0$	Impossible
	$\Delta p_i = 0$	$\Delta r = 0$	Impossible
	$\Delta p_i < 0$	$\Delta r > 0,\ \Delta b_j = 0$	Okishio theorem
		$\Delta r < 0,\ \Delta b_j < 0$	Shibata's falling rate of profit

rational capitalist will not introduce a new technology unless it decreases cost.[4]

Next, $\Delta p_i = 0$ is also an impossible case because "the elevation of the organic composition of capital to take place only where it brings surplus profit by lowering the cost of production—which, in the end, brings about a fall in price" (Shibata, 1934, p. 67).

In the end, only two cases are possible in reality. The case, $\Delta p_i < 0$ and $\Delta b_j = 0$ leading to $\Delta r > 0$ exactly corresponds to the situation described by the Oksihio theorem. Shibata formulated the essence of the theorem before Okishio by providing the logic for this case. This is why the theorem can be called the Shibata-Okishio theorem.

Now, the falling rate of profit is only possible "because the operation of the decline of the average rate of profit due to the increase of real wages (or the shortening of the working day) is superior in force to the operation of its rise on account of changes in the methods of production, there is a decline in the average rate of profit" (Shibata, 1939, pp. 71–72), which corresponds to the only remaining case in Table 6.1. This case can be interpreted as the contrapositive of the Okishio theorem implying "if the equilibrium rate of profit is known to have fallen ($\Delta r < 0$), the real wage must have increased ($\Delta b_j < 0$)."[5] This situation explains the counterfactual character of the Shibata-Okishio theorem. In another paper, Shibata explicitly noted this point:

> It simply shows that if the elevation of the organic composition of capital and the fall of the average rate of profit really happen at the same time, this phenomenon requires to be explained in a different way from the one which Marx adopted. (Shibata, 1939, p. 71)

This fact implies that Shibata was already aware of another important implication of the Okishio theorem, namely, the TRPF cannot be explained from the character of technical innovation independent of changes in income distribution or the value production process.

[4] Therefore, Groll and Orzech's (1989, p. 257) evaluation that the rise in productivity is essential feature in Shibata's model should be rejected. In another paper, to refute Tsuru Shigeto's criticism on his 1934 paper, Shibata illustrated the essentially same numerical example with $\Delta p_i > 0$ and $\Delta r < 0$ and wrote that "But evidently such is not what Mr. Tsuru or Marx has in mind" (Shibata, 1939, pp. 59–60).

[5] "If not-B, then not-A" is the contrapositive of "if A, then B." Here B means "the rate of profit does not fall", while "real wage rate remains constant" is described as A.

In Shibata, the theorem was connected to his alternative economic system beyond the contradiction of capitalism, which made people suspect that he was a fascist. Shibata (1943) argues that according to the "new economic logic" under "communal totality," it is possible to increase employment by setting wages higher than the marginal productivity of labor.[6] The central concept here was his "rate of income"[7] which can be written as $(V + S)/(C + V)$ according to Marx's notation, where C, V and S denote constant capital, variable capital, and surplus value. According to Shibata (1934, p. 34), technical progress is compatible with a decreasing rate of income, which means conflict between the economic welfare of the entire society and the objectives of capitalists. This fact can be simply shown from the definition of the rate of income as follows. Here q and e denote the organic composition of capital and the rate of surplus value, respectively.

$$\frac{V+S}{C+V} = \frac{1+S/V}{C/V+1} = \frac{1+e}{1+q} \tag{6.4}$$

An increase in q decreases the rate of income while the intensification of exploitation increases it. On the other hand, Marx's rate of profit, defined as $r = e/(1+q)$ can increase at the same time that the rate of income decreases when both q and e increase. Table 6.2 compares Shibata's trajectory of capital accumulation with a "trajectory à la Marx." The fact that these two cases coexist is the contradiction of capitalism, namely, that capitalists do not pursue the maximization of social welfare defined as the maximization of the rate of income.

[6] In counterpoint to the passage by Morishima in his memoir quoted in Sect. 4.3 of Chapter 4, Negishi (2009) evaluated Shibata's "new economic logic" positively from the perspective of theoretical economics. According to Negishi, Shibata's theory of communal totality is related to his critique of Böhm-Bawerk, rather than a populist theory for wartime. This reading may be all the more plausible because Shibata's postwar book (Shibata, 1959) tries to provide a general theory of communal totality.

[7] The "rate of income" ("Syotokuritsu" in Japanese) was one of the specific concepts that Okishio used to measure the degree of unequal exchange. He, unlike Shibata, defined it as income per unit of direct labor (Okishio, 1956, p. 54). Okishio's rate of income is conceptually identical to the monetary expression of labor time at the level of industry (Rieu & Park, 2020, p. 295).

Table 6.2 Shibata's and Marx's trajectories

	Organic composition of capital	*Rate of surplus value*	*Rate of profit*	*Rate of income*
Shibata's Case	↑	↑	↑	↓
Marx's Case	↑	↑	↑	N/A

Okishio reproduces Shibata's work with the exception that he provided a general proof of the theorem and a clear distinction between the "productivity criterion" and "cost criterion" for technical choice. In particular, the latter is important to understand his entire theoretical system.[8]

The productivity criterion and cost criterion can be written as (6.5) and (6.6), respectively.

$$\lambda^0 A^1 + l^1 \leq \lambda^0 A^0 + l^0 \tag{6.5}$$

$$p^0\left(A^1 + bl^1\right) \leq p^0\left(A^0 + bl^0\right) \tag{6.6}$$

While (6.6) indicates a "profitable" technical change, (6.5) can be regarded as a "progressive" technical change with a modification of λ^0 to λ^1 on the left-hand side (Cogliano et al., 2018, p. 226). For Shibata, the "productivity criterion" was related to the desirability of an economic system, which was not satisfied in capitalism due to the profit maximization behavior of capitalists.

Returning to Shibata's (1934) example, these two criteria can only be equal when $p_2/w_j = \lambda_2$. However, this situation is inconsistent with the condition that "there must be positive profit in every industry," namely, $p_j/w_j > \lambda_j$ (Okishio, 1961, p. 86).

Without a doubt, there is no reason to believe that every industry must have a positive profit in a real capitalist economy. Okishio, however, thought that this situation was necessary for the normal reproduction of a capitalist society and used it as one pillar of his Fundamental Marxian

[8] Furthermore, Okishio (1977a, p. 251) criticized Shibata for assuming the direction of price change at the start. However, if, one considers the fact that Shibata's exposition is based upon tedious numerical calculations and not upon a generalized model, this criticism does not seem decisive.

Theorem.[9] Okishio emphasized that the main objective of his Fundamental Marxian Theorem was to "prove the theory of surplus value without assuming equal exchange" (Okishio, 1995, p. 232), which originated from the difficulty of his first reading of Marx's *Capital* starting in light of the assumption of equal exchange, which was inconsistent with Japanese reality in the late 1940s.

It can be concluded that Okishio's theories are similar to Shibata's insight with regard to the falling rate of profit. Understanding the Shibata-Okishio theorem as a counterfactual situation was already nascent in Shibata's discussion. Furthermore, both scholars emphasized that the choice of technology is premised upon price terms, not upon value variables, which are invisible to capitalists. In Okishio's case, however, this issue of behavioral standards is a corollary to the Fundamental Marxian Theorem in that the latter shows how the existence of profit can be explained by the exploitation of labor in the invisible sphere.

6.3 A Refutation of the Temporal Single-System Interpretation's Critique of the Okishio Theorem

Beyond demonstrating that the Okishio theorem is internally refuted, the TSSI argues that the TRPF can be proved under general conditions. This argument implies that the falling rate of profit is not merely a possibility but a necessity, which leads to a sort of fundamentalist tendency. Regarding the static problem of the transformation of value into the price of production, there is no difference between the TSSI and the simultaneous single-system interpretation.[10] However, the TSSI argues that the intertemporal definition of value is needed to refute the so-called redundancy critique of Marxian value theory (Samuelson, 1971; Steedman, 1977). To show the necessity of the concept of labor value, it is necessary to explain something that cannot be seen only in the context of price variables, which is, according to the TSSI, to "prove" the TRPF. In other

[9] This fact indicates the level of abstraction at which Okishio's Fundamental Marxian Theorem works, which was often misunderstood. See Sect. 4.4 of Chapter 4.

[10] As shown in Chapter 3, this claim holds true in the case of the "New Interpretation" except that the price of constant capital deviates from the value of constant capital.

words, the refutation of the Okishio theorem is a core requirement to demonstrate the necessity of the value concept.[11]

Beneath the alleged proof of the TRPF lie the TSSI's alternative definitions of the "monetary expression of labor time" (MELT) and the rate of profit. The TSSI tries to show the inconsistency of the Okishio theorem by providing "counterexamples" (Kliman, 2007, p. 28).[12] In this vein, simple numerical examples have been provided to refute the theorem. In the following, after examining the TSSI's conception of time, these counterexamples are discussed in terms of three stages to demonstrate that the TSSI's refutation of the Okishio theorem is not "internal" in any sense. First, it will be shown that the one-sector model demonstrated is just a repetition of an already known fact, the law of the falling maximal rate of profit, rather than a counterexample to the Okishio theorem. Second, using a simulation analysis, it is shown that a two-sector example by Kliman and McGlone (1999) cannot refute the Okishio theorem. Finally, based on simulation results, a generalized relation among different definitions of the rate of profit is given.

6.3.1 *The Temporal Single-System Interpretation's Conception of Time*

A good place to start is to examine the TSSI's conception of time, which is different from the conventional approach. As already explained in Sect. 4.4 of Chapter 4, the TSSI's value and price of production are as follows:

$$\lambda_{t+1} = p_t A + l \tag{4.8}$$

$$p_{t+1} = p_t(A + bl)\left(1 + r_{[t,t+1]}\right) \tag{6.7}$$

Equation (6.7) differs from Eq. (4.9) in that the latter does not presuppose an equalized rate of profit. To consider TSSI's critique of the Okishio

[11] While Kliman (2011) interprets an economic crisis through the TRPF empirically, his work is ultimately based on the alleged refutation of the Okishio theorem.

[12] Kliman argues that "once the rate of profit is measured correctly, however, Marx's real rate of profit always falls…" (Kliman, 2007, p. 120). Without a doubt, a refutation of the Okishio theorem is not necessarily equal to a proof of the TRPF. Kliman's assertion is possible only with the change of the concept of the rate of profit, which will be discussed in the following sections.

theorem, however, Eq. (6.7) is appropriate because the theorem focuses on the general rate of profit. Note that $r_{[t,t+1]}$ is defined intertemporally, i.e., the profit in period $t+1$ is calculated on the invested capital in period t. It seems that historical cost rather than current cost is adopted here.

Interestingly, from the perspective of the conventional approach, Morishima already commented on these intertemporal formulations as if he had anticipated the TSSI:

> One might think that when the methods of production employed in period t are different from those which have been employed in period $t-1$, the λ's appearing on the left-hand side of the equations should be distinguished by subscript t from those on the right-hand side with $t-1$. However, in this case, those commodities which have been produced by the old methods of production and are used as factors of production in period t have to be re-evaluated at the new values, i.e., the amounts of labour that are required to produce these commodities by the new methods of production prevailing in period t, so that the same λ's appear on both sides of the value-determining equations. (Morishima, 1973, p. 14)

Theorists who maintain the TSSI, however, argue that their nonconventional definition of value and the general rate of profit does not violate any premise of the Okishio theorem because the theorem does not "explicitly invoke this constraint [simultaneous valuation-Rieu] as a premise" (Kliman & McGlone, 1999, p. 53). In this sense, this seemingly historical cost definition is one of the main pillars of the TSSI's alleged refutation of the Okishio theorem.

As the TSSI developed into a systematic interpretation beginning in the mid-1990s, however, historical cost developed into a more elaborate concept. The latest formulation of the TSSI's conception of time can be found in Kliman (2007). After providing a numerical example in Table 6.3, he explains the difference between historical cost and "pre-production reproduction cost."

> Let us first distinguish between *historical cost* and *pre-production reproduction cost*. In the example above, the input apple's pre-production reproduction cost is \$0.50, the cost (inclusive of profit) of producing an apple at the moment when this apple became an input into the production of applesauce. Imagine, however, that originally—when it was produced—this input apple cost \$0.60. Then \$0.60 is its historical cost. (Kliman, 2007, p. 96. Italics in original)

Table 6.3 Kliman's (2007) distinction between historical cost and pre-production reproduction cost

Time	*Yesterday, 2 p.m.*	*Today, 9 a.m.*	*Today, 1 p.m.*	*Today, 2 p.m.*
Event	The apple is produced	The apple is sold	The apple becomes an input into applesauce	The applesauce is produced
Cost of newly-produced apple	\$0.60	\$0.55	\$0.50	\$0.45
Cost concept	Historical cost		Pre-production Reproduction Cost	(Post-production) Replacement Cost

The concept of "pre-production reproduction cost" is notable since it means that the TSSI's formulation such as Eqs. (4.8) and (6.7) is not premised on the historical cost concept as usually understood. However, Kliman's (2007) example has unsolved problems.

As shown in Table 6.3, this example assumes that all the apples entered the production process at the given point of time, 2 p.m. yesterday, and that all the applesauce is produced at the given point of time, 2 p.m. today. However, this distinction is artificial because applesauce is constantly produced, and apples are used as input simultaneously. This situation is something like positing an artificial period, say $t+0.5$, between period t and period $t+1$. Furthermore, this example is a one-input one-output model. If there are inputs other than apples, the time should be divided further unless all the inputs entered the production process simultaneously. For example, another input, sugar may enter production at 1:30 p.m. If one considers fixed capital, this issue becomes more complicated. However minutely one divides time, several processes of production exist simultaneously, and therefore, we have many inputs with different vintages. In summary, the concept of "pre-production reproduction cost" is nothing other than a return to historical cost in a continuous time setting.[13] This situation is made clear by the fact that, even among

[13] See discussions concerning Freeman (1996, 1999) in Sect. 4.4.2 of Chapter 4.

the TSSI theorists, there is no consensus method for valuing commodities in the presence of stock of commodities, which leads to different calculations of the MELT (Potts, 2016).

It is necessary here to examine the TSSI's intertemporal definition of the MELT already introduced in Chapter 4, which distinguishes between the time of input and time of output.

$$m_{t+1} = \frac{p_{t+1}x_{t+1}}{\frac{p_t A_{t+1} x_{t+1}}{m_t} + l_{t+1}x_{t+1}} \tag{4.14}$$

Equation (4.14) is adopted by Akinci and Karahanogullari (2015, p. 771), who demonstrate a subtle difference from Kliman (2007, p. 191) since the latter, in our notations, uses $l_{[t,t+1]}$ instead of l_{t+1} in the denominator of the right-hand-side to faithfully reflect his concept of "pre-production reproduction cost." This difference is partly due to the TSSI's specific difficulty with integrating continuous reality into a discrete time framework. At any rate, this definition of the MELT plays an important role in the TSSI's alleged refutation of the Okishio theorem, especially regarding an alternative definition of the rate of profit.

6.3.2 *The Law of the Falling Maximal Rate of Profit: A One-Sector Model*

As a simple counterexample to the Okishio theorem, Kliman (2007, pp. 120–129) illustrated the so-called one-commodity corn model, as shown in Table 6.4. The last two columns are newly added here for further discussion. Kliman assumed that all net products are used as inputs

Table 6.4 Kliman's (2007) one sector example

Year	*Seed corn (SC)*	*Net product (NP)*	*Corn output (SC + NP)*	*rate of profit (r) (%)*	*Labor input (LL)*	*Technical composition of capital (SC/LL)*	*Organic composition of production (SC/NP)*
1	64	16	80	25.0	80	0.8	4.00
2	80	20	100	25.0	100	0.8	4.00
3	100	30	130	30.0	100	1.0	3.33
4	130	45	175	34.6	100	1.3	2.89

for the next year because wage and capitalist consumption are zero. As the new technology that raises the technical composition of capital is introduced in the 3rd year, the temporal rate of profit decreases while Okishio's material rate of profit increases.

First, it should be noted that a one-sector model is not appropriate to refute the Okishio theorem because it neglects price-value deviation,[14] which is one of the main motives of the theorem in providing a micro-foundation for the technical choices of capitalists. Furthermore, the example here assumes that workers work for free, i.e., that the wage rate is zero. In this special case, the law of the falling maximal rate of profit was already proven and emphasized by Okishio himself (Okishio, 1961, 1977b).[15] A crucial point is that no criterion for capitalists' behavior is considered in this law.

Another important issue in this example is that the organic composition of capital is not definable. In case $V = 0$, C/V does not have economic meaning, where C and V represent constant capital and variable capital, respectively. On the other hand, Okishio employed the "organic composition of production (OCP)" instead of the organic composition of capital, which "directly denotes the proportion between direct labor and indirectly necessary labor to produce production means" (Okishio, 1961, p. 87). If one intends to refute the Okishio theorem internally, therefore, a counterexample should be constructed to increasing OCP. However, as demonstrated in the last column of Table 6.4, the OCP is decreasing in this example.[16]

All these factors considered, Kliman's (2007) one-sector example cannot refute the Okishio theorem.

[14] As is well known, a strict price-value proportionality holds in a one-commodity world.

[15] If $w = 0$, prices of production are written as $p = (pA + wl)(1 + r) = pA(1 + r)$. As p is the left eigenvector of matrix A, $1 + r$ is the inverse of the maximum eigenvalue under conventional assumptions that A is indecomposable. Therefore, according to the Perron–Frobenius theorem, an increase in at least one element of A, which implies a capital-using technical change, increases the maximum eigenvalue. In other words, the maximal rate of profit decreases.

[16] As the OCP is $C/(V + S)$, it can be calculated in this zero-wage case. Okishio's intention to use the OCP was to make an indicator that is independent from the degree of exploitation. Therefore, even in the theoretically maximal exploitation case, the OCP is definable.

6.3.3 A Simulation Analysis for a Two-Sector Model

Kliman and McGlone (1999) provided a two-sector model to demonstrate that "cost-reducing, labor-saving technical change can cause a fall in the general rate of profit" (Kliman & McGlone, 1999, p. 51). The input–output structure of the model and the initial conditions are as follows.

$$A = \begin{pmatrix} 0.8 & 0 \\ 0.2 & 0 \end{pmatrix}, l = (0.2, 0.8), b = \left(0, \frac{11}{32}\right)^T, x = (55, 30)^T, p = (2.2, 0.8)$$

Good 1 is a production good while good 2 is a consumption good. Unlike Kliman's (2007) one-sector model, the nonzero real wage in each sector is equal to $11/32$ units of good 2. The gross output vector during the initial period consists of 55 units of good 1 and 30 units of good 2. It is additionally assumed that the physical input, i.e., good 1, and the output of each sector increase by 10% every period. To reflect labor-saving technical change, the labor input in each sector is assumed to increase by only 3.4% every period while the real wage remains constant. Under these assumptions, Kliman and McGlone (1999, p. 53) showed that the temporal rate of profit falls while the simultaneous rate of profit rises.

Above all, it should be noted that the OCP in Okishio's sense remains constant. From the data above, initial values of goods 1 and 2 are obtained from the equations, $44\lambda_1 + 11 = 55\lambda_1$ and $6\lambda_1 + 24 = 30\lambda_2$, and therefore, $\lambda_1 = 1$, $\lambda_2 = 1$. As the OCP is defined as the ratio of the value of physical input to the quantity of labor input, it is $44\lambda_1/11 = 4$ in sector 1 during the initial period and $6\lambda_1/24 = 0.25$ in sector 2. These magnitudes do not change over time under Kliman and McGlone's (1999) assumptions.[17] Therefore, the problem noted in Kliman's (2007) one-sector model reappears, which implies that one of the basic assumptions of the Okishio theorem is violated. As Okishio himself noted before the

[17] This is the case even if one applies the TSSI's value equation. To calculate the value magnitude from Eq. (4.8), the prices in the previous period should be given. Therefore, values at period 1 are obtained from $44 \times 1.1p_1 + 11 \times 1.034 = 55 \times 1.1\lambda_1$, $6 \times 1.1p_1 + 24 \times 1.034 = 30 \times 1.1\lambda_1$. In this way, we can get the time path of the OCPs, which eventually converge to the same level as in the conventional definition. Without a doubt, there are several initial periods during which the TSSI's OCP is greater than the conventional one. As demonstrated later, this movement, i.e., the gradual disappearance of the initial shock is typical regarding the TSSI values and rate of profit.

emergence of the TSSI, "there is no a priori reason to reject the possibility...of raising the productivity of labour without reducing L/C [the inverse of the OCP-Rieu] (Okishio, 1977b, p. 97)."

A related issue in this numerical example is that the capital-output ratio remains constant (Laibman, 1999, p. 29). Freeman and Kliman (2000, p. 264) argue that this issue is "a key 'stylized fact' in the economic growth literature'," which probably references Kaldor's "stylized facts." However, it is doubtful whether this situation remains the case in the context of recent capitalism. Furthermore, such a situation is inconsistent with the general understanding in Marxian theory of the TRPF as the interaction between the decrease in "capital productivity," the inverse of capital-output ratio, and the increase in profit share as a counteracting factor (Duménil & Lévy, 1993).

Before conducting a simulation, one more important issue regarding the MELT should be discussed. The TSSI theorists regard the increasing the MELT due to labor productivity increase as the main foundation of the refutation of the Okishio theorem.

> According to the Okishio Theorem, this change [labor-saving innovation – Rieu] raises the rate of profit measured in numeraire prices. However, this is only one consequence of the labour-saving innovation. It also increases the MELT, a result ignored by the Okishio Theorem. A rising MELT implies that symbol-money represents less labour-time, an effect I will call inflation of symbol-money. Inasmuch as this endogenous inflationary effect offsets the rise in the Okishian rate of profit, the innovation provokes a reduction in the profit rate measured in labour-time. Thus, the Okishian rate of profit can be interpreted as a nominal rate of profit, measured in terms of symbol-money. (Ramos-Martinez, 2004, p. 68)

Here it is notable that the TSSI theorists interpret the conventional rate of profit used by Okishio as the "nominal rate of profit" or "nominal price rate of profit" (Kliman, 2007, p. 129) while they pursue the movement of the rate of profit under an alternative definition reflecting the increase in the MELT.

Now we can conduct simulations according to two scenarios. The details of each scenario are summarized in Table 6.5. All the input–output structures and initial conditions are the same as those of Kliman and McGlone's (1999) two-sector model. Real wage rate is assumed to remain unchanged.

Table 6.5 Scenarios for simulations

	Inputs		*Output (B) (%)*	*MELT (B-A) (%)*
	Good 1 (%)	*Labor (A) (%)*		
Scenario 1 Growth rate	10	3.4	10	6.6
Scenario 2 Growth rate	10	3.4	9	5.6

The main focus of our simulations is to introduce the increasing MELT as the main foundation of the TSSI's critique of the Okishio theorem, and, in an additional step, to investigate what happens when the increasing OCP is introduced.

In Scenario 1, the MELT is assumed to be 1 at the initial period and increases by 6.6% every period, which is equal to the difference between the output increase and labor input increase. As the MELT is the product of price and labor productivity, its growth rate is roughly equal to the rate of inflation and the growth rate of labor productivity. The reason why the growth rate of the MELT is set to 6.6% here is to exclude "exogeneous inflation, unrelated to productivity growth" (Kliman, 2007, p. 130). This assumption is required not only to follow the TSSI but also to examine the TRPF that is independent of exogeneous factors other than technical change. Following Ramos-Martinez (2004), it is assumed that the simultaneous rate of profit and the temporal rate of profit are equal at the initial period.

In Scenario 2, unlike in Kliman and McGlone's (1999) example, Okishio's OCP is assumed to increase. As the growth rate of output is 9%, the MELT grows by 5.6% every period. Note that the capital-output ratio increases in accordance with the standard assumption.

Simulation results are illustrated in Figs. 6.1 and 6.2.[18] For comparison, the temporal rate of profit with constant MELT is also shown.

In Scenario 1, as illustrated in Fig. 6.1, Kliman and McGlone's (1999) result is maintained, in other words, the temporal rate of profit decreases

[18] Essentially identical simulations were conducted in Rieu (2009). However, in Scenario 2 here, the growth rate of output is assumed to be 9% which is smaller than the rate of 9.9% in Rieu (2009) to introduce a more conspicuous decrease in "capital productivity." Some minor calculation errors were also corrected here.

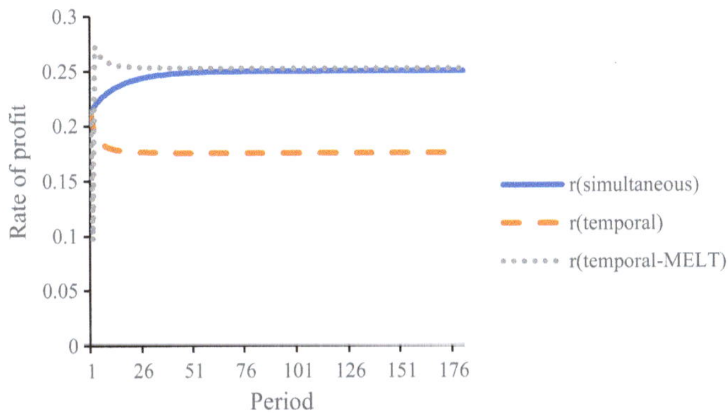

Fig. 6.1 Rates of profit: a constant OCP case

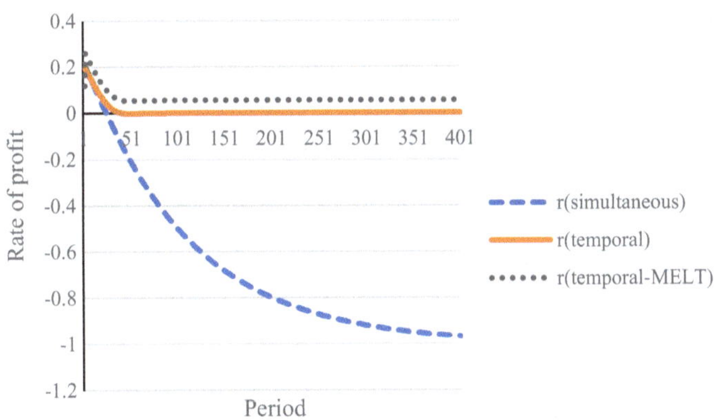

Fig. 6.2 Rates of profit: an increasing OCP case

while the conventional simultaneous rate of profit rises. However, introducing the MELT increase produces the interesting result that the temporal rate of profit initially soars but soon decreases and finally converges to a level that is higher than the simultaneous rate of profit. This result implies that the introduction of the endogenous MELT increase effect renders the TSSI's refutation of the Okishio theorem irrelevant.

In Scenario 2, we find a surprising result. While the temporal rate of profit approaches zero, the simultaneous rate of profit falls below zero at period 24. Considering the incentive of capitalists to introduce new technologies, capital accumulation would cease at this point. However, this result hints at the possibility that adding the increasing MELT assumption makes the simulation deviate from the framework of Okishio theorem. On the other hand, the main object of the simulation, i.e., the temporal rate of profit with the increasing MELT, shows convergence to a level that is exactly equal to the growth rate of labor productivity, 5.6% in this case. Therefore, in this case as well, the TSSI's refutation fails.

It is necessary to add that, as in Kliman's (2007) one-sector example, the TSSI's neglect of the micro-foundation of capitalists reappears in these simulations. Simply assuming autonomous growth for related variables may violate the cost criterion in the sense that capitalists are assumed to "invest according to a fixed rule, regardless of what happens to the price of output and to the profitability of investment" (Veneziani, 2004, p. 109).

6.3.4 *Generalization*

Based on simulations in the previous section, it is possible to proceed to a general analysis of the rates of profit as defined in different ways: simultaneous, temporal, and temporal with the MELT increase. The two latter cases present the TSSI's real rate of profit and nominal rate of profit, respectively.[19]

As the growth rate of the MELT (g_m) is approximately equal to the inflation rate (π) and the growth rate of labor productivity, i.e., the growth rate of the inverse of value (g_λ), the following relation holds.

$$(1 + g_m) = (1 + \pi)/(1 + g_\lambda) \tag{6.8}$$

Using Eq. (6.7), the nominal rate of profit (r^N) is defined as follows where x is the gross output vector.

$$r_{t+1}^N = \frac{p_{t+1}x - p_t(A + bl)x}{p_t(A + bl)x} \tag{6.9}$$

[19] Foley (2000) names these rates, respectively, the output (or material) rate of profit, the labor rate of profit, and the money rate of profit.

As the simultaneous rate of profit (r^S) presupposes a static equilibrium, i.e., $p_t = p_{t+1}$, it can be related to the nominal rate of profit as follows where π denotes the rate of inflation.

$$r_{t+1}^N = \frac{p_{t+1}x}{p_t(A+bl)x} - 1 = \frac{(1+\pi)p_t x}{p_t(A+bl)x} - 1 = (1+\pi)\left(1+r_{t+1}^S\right) - 1$$

$$\therefore 1 + r_{t+1}^N = (1+\pi)\left(1+r_{t+1}^S\right) \tag{6.10}$$

The real rate of profit (r^R) is defined as "the value or price rate of profit based on the prices that would exist if the MELT were to remain constant" (Kliman, 2007, p. 136). Therefore, it is defined as follows:

$$r_{t+1}^R = \frac{\frac{p_{t+1}}{m_{t+1}}x - \frac{p_t}{m_t}(A+bl)x}{\frac{p_t}{m_t}(A+bl)x} = \frac{m_t}{m_{t+1}}\frac{p_{t+1}x}{p_t(A+bl)x} - 1$$
$$= \frac{1}{1+g_m}\left(1+r_{t+1}^N\right) - 1$$

$$\therefore 1 + r_{t+1}^R = \frac{1+r_{t+1}^N}{1+g_m} \tag{6.11}$$

From (6.8), (6.10), and (6.11), the relation between the real rate of profit and the simultaneous rate of profit is as follows:

$$1 + r_{t+1}^R = \frac{1+r_{t+1}^N}{1+g_m} = \frac{1+\pi}{1+g_m}\left(1+r_{t+1}^S\right) = (1+g_\lambda)\left(1+r_{t+1}^S\right) \tag{6.12}$$

Using these relations among three different rates of profit, it is possible to formulate several propositions concerning the TSSI's critique of the Okishio theorem. These propositions are also represented by this chapter's notations.

(A) The Okishio theorem: Cost-reducing, not necessarily capital-using labor-saving, technical progress does not decrease the simultaneous rate of profit.

$$r_{t+1}^S \geq r_t^S \tag{6.13}$$

(B) "[T]he labour-saving innovation has two effects: it increases the nominal rate of profit but also raises the MELT, thereby reducing the capacity of symbol-money to represent labour-time. The Okishio Theorem takes only the first effect into account, neglecting the increase in the monetary expression of labour-time" (Ramos-Martinez, 2004, p. 76). "The law of the tendential fall in the rate of profit can be stated by saying that a labour-saving innovation provokes an increase in the MELT that is relatively greater than the increase in the nominal rate of profit" (Ramos-Martinez, 2004, p. 77). "A rising MELT does not cancel out the tendency of the rate of profit to fall" (Kliman, 2007, p. 129). Therefore, the real rate of profit decreases.

$$r_{t+1}^S \geq r_t^S, g_m > 0, \text{ and, } r_{t+1}^R < r_t^R \tag{6.14}$$

(C) "If the MELT grows at a constant rate, but values fall at an increasing rate as a result of a rising rate of productivity growth, the rate of inflation must decline, and the nominal rate of profit will tend to fall" (Kliman, 2007, p. 129).

$$g_m > 0, \frac{dg_m}{dt} = 0, g_\lambda < 0, \frac{dg_\lambda}{dt} < 0, \frac{d\pi}{dt} < 0, \text{ and } r_{t+1}^N < r_t^N \tag{6.15}$$

Now the TSSI's propositions (B) and (C) can be evaluated by using the generalized relations among three different rates of profit.

First, unlike (A), proposition (B) considers only labor-saving innovation which is not necessarily the same as cost-reducing innovation. In Kliman and McGlone's (1999) simulation, the unit cost of production decreases over time. However, this result excludes the existence of a new technology that is not capital-using labor-saving but merely cost-reducing. Almost all of the TSSI literature approaches the Okishio theorem in this way, which is related to the deficiency concerning a micro-foundation in the TSSI noted above.

Second, proposition (B) holds only if the simultaneous rate of profit and the temporal rate of profit are equal at the outset. Adopting Ramos-Martinez's (2004) assumption $\pi = 0$,[20] $r_t^R = r_t^S$ makes $1 + r_{t+1}^R = (1 + r_{t+1}^s)/(1 + g_m)$ from Eq. (6.12). Here $g_m > 0$ implies $r_{t+1}^R < r_{t+1}^S$, and therefore, r_{t+1}^R may be (but is not necessarily) smaller than r_t^R.

[20] It should be noted that Ramos-Martinez's (2004) "nominal rate of profit" means the simultaneous rate of profit. This claim is verified if the rate of inflation is zero, as is known from Eq. (6.10).

On the other hand, Eq. (6.10) can be rewritten as follows if the related variables are sufficiently small.[21]

$$r_{t+1}^N = \pi + r_{t+1}^S \tag{6.16}$$

The assumption of $\pi = 0$ makes $r_{t+1}^N = r_{t+1}^S$ here, which is equal to the assumption that the MELT increase is exactly canceled out by the value decrease. As explained above, this assumption is intended to exclude exogeneous inflation, only to consider "the endogenous inflationary effect" (Ramos-Martinez, 2004, p. 79).

Third, proposition (B) does not necessarily entail proposition (C).

Regarding (C), as seen in Eq. (6.8), $g_\lambda < 0$ and $dg_\lambda / dt < 0$ while the MELT is constant, implying that the rate of inflation is decreasing, i.e., $d\pi / dt < 0$. This situation implies that the TSSI's falling normal rate of profit is possible only in situations of "disinflation" (Kliman, 2007, p. 129). However, imposing an arbitrary time path of prices is not appropriate to explain the TRPF since Marx's original intention was to derive the tendency from the character of technology itself independent from any exogeneous shock. Furthermore, it is doubtful whether "values fall at an increasing result" indefinitely. As labor value approaches zero with the development of labor productivity, the growth rate of $1 + g_\lambda$ asymptotically approaches zero.[22] Therefore, unlike Kliman's (2007) assertion, the nominal rate of profit does not diverge from the simultaneous rate of profit indefinitely. Albeit in a different context, Moseley and Rieu (2009) also showed this point by conducting a simple simulation.

6.3.5 Summing Up

The TSSI's alleged refutation of the Okishio theorem requires both a change in the relevant concepts of the rate of profit and the imposition of an ad hoc assumption concerning the time path of prices. These requirements were confirmed by simulations of a two-sector model. Furthermore, in the case of the one-sector counterexample, an unusual

[21] If x is sufficiently small, $\ln(x + 1)$ is approximately equal to x. Therefore, taking the natural logarithm of both sides in (6.10) leads to (6.16).

[22] This situation is the case in Kliman and McGlone's (1999) simulation. In both sectors, the value of $1 + g_\lambda$ converges to 0.94.

assumption of zero wage renders such a counterexample redundant in that it simply shows the law of the falling maximal rate of profit.

More fundamentally, the TSSI does not consider the micro-foundation of technical change. The TSSI focuses on a corollary of the Okishio theorem, rather than the theorem itself. As already shown in Eqs. (6.5) and (6.6), "viable" technical change does not necessarily mean "progressive," and this fact has been emphasized repeatedly since Shibata's prototype of the theorem.

If the refutation of the Okishio theorem is to be "internal" in any sense, it must provide a counterexample to the theorem's given premises or demonstrate its logical inconsistency.[23] Alternatively, changing certain behavioral conditions to derive a different result could be a promising "external" critique (Foley, 1986; Park, 2005), one example of which is discussed in Sect. 6.4.2.

Since Okishio himself, in his later years, examined the validity of his assumptions, following his discussion will be helpful to understand the implications and limitations of the Okishi theorem. This will be done in the next section.

6.4 Whither the Okishio Theorem?

Once again, the Okishio theorem can be summarized as follows:

> The introduction of new technology, which yields a higher profit rate measured in terms of old equilibrium prices, raises the rate of profit under new equilibrium prices when the real wage basket is kept constant. (Nakatani & Hagiwara, 1997, p. 39)

In his last paper,[24] however, Okishio acknowledged the limitations of the theorem's two assumptions as follows:

[23] Commenting on Rieu's (2009) critique of the TSSI's understanding of the Okishio theorem, Kliman still argues that "any counter-example disproves a theorem if it satisfies *the theorem's* hypothesis—not Marx's hypotheses or Rieu's hypotheses—but not its conclusion" (Kliman, 2012, p. 288. Italics in original). This statement itself is literally true. However, as was shown above, the TSSI does not follow its own principle of the internal refutation.

[24] Okishio already published many papers in Japanese journals in a similar veins as Okishio (2001). See Okishio (1996, 1999).

> My critique of Marx's law of the tendency of the rate of profit to fall, the 'Okishio theorem', was based on the following questionable assumptions: (1) the constancy of the real wage rate and (2) the establishment of new production prices with positive profits. The present paper examined these assumptions. We obtained a negative answer. (Okishio, 2001, p. 501)

This section aims to shed light on the implications of the Okishio theorem, particularly with respect to these two assumptions. Despite the apparent denial of the theorem by its own creator, Okishio's study of the relation between technical progress and the rate of profit may be understood as a consistent research program comprising two successive stages.

6.4.1 *The Okishio Theorem as a Counterfactual Thesis*

The Okishio theorem has been misunderstood. Some researchers have thought that the theorem implies an actual increase in the rate of profit, while others have interpreted the TRPF as a necessary tendency.[25] The Okishio theorem negates Marx's TRPF, in the sense that it claims that a profit rate "fall is due to rising wages, not mechanization *per se*" (Kliman, 1996, p. 208). However, a frequently neglected implication of the Okishio theorem is that the falling rate of profit can, and actually does, result from a rise in the real wage rate. Okishio examines how introducing viable technology affects the equilibrium rate of profit by developing a counterfactual argument; he compares the normal state of the capitalist economy with a hypothetical state in which the real wage is constant. The rational core of the theorem, therefore, lies in its formulation of the contrapositive that "if the rate of profit falls in the long run, this must be because of a rise in the real wage rate" (Nakatani & Hagiwara, 1997, p. 41).

The following "minimal dynamic relationship" (Laibman, 1996, p. 47) suggests a positive correlation between the rates of change in the wage share (ω) and the ratio of labor demand (L_D) to labor supply (L_S). Here

[25] For example, Okishio was regarded as taking Marx's law to be an argument that the rate of profit must fall (Petith, 2005, p. 288). This inference seems to have been partly due to Okishio's explanation of Marx's TRPF as implying a decrease of the maximum rate of profit, as explained in Sect. 6.3.2. Although in a different context, Fleetwood (2012) correctly understands the meaning of the Okishio theorem as a "counterfactual event."

$\dot{x}$ represents the change rate over time of x.

$$sign\dot{\omega} = sign\left(\dot{L_D} - \dot{L_S}\right) \tag{6.17}$$

This relation may be a relevant starting point for formulating the capitalist dynamics that Okishio pursued. Biased technical change, accompanied by an increase in the composition of capital, necessarily causes $\dot{\omega}$ to be negative, as a result of the industrial reserve army effect. Therefore, in reality, no effective method exists for distinguishing the results of technical progress from changes in the labor market. Under the original setup of the Okishio theorem, all the advantages of technical progress are obtained by the capitalist, as the real wage is kept constant, and this fact highlights the theorem's counterfactual character. At this stage, however, it is unnecessary to criticize the theorem simply because it is static. Okishio separates the problem of comparative equilibria from the adjustment process to an equilibrium as follows:

> … 'the theorem' treats the problem of comparing the magnitudes of the equalized rates of profit between two equilibrium states. In that case, it is not necessary to discuss the disequilibrium process between the equilibrium states. It is not necessary for proving the result. (Okishio, 1994, p. 28)

6.4.2 *The Foley-Laibman Theorem*

As the Okishio theorem itself is one of several comparative static results that may be derived mathematically from certain assumptions, it cannot be refuted within the given framework. Although much has been written about the theorem, only the "benchmark" (Laibman, 1997) literature has clearly elaborated this point. Therefore, this literature can help us focus on the mutual relation between technical change and the labor market, rather than simply on the negation or vindication of the Okishio theorem.

By substituting the assumption of a constant wage share for that of a constant real wage, Roemer (1981), Foley (1986), and Laibman (1997) demonstrate the necessity of the falling rate of profit as a result of the introduction of viable technology.[26] Using Laibman's (1997) simple

[26] This claim may be called the "Foley-Laibman theorem" (Kang & Rieu, 2009). It must be noted that the Okishio theorem and the "Foley-Laibman theorem" are not incompatible. Kang and Rieu (2009) provided a synthesis of the two theorems.

Table 6.6 An example of one good economy

	K	W	P	$\Upsilon = W + P$	K/Υ	P/Υ	P/K
Initial state	800	300	100	400	2.00	0.25	0.1250
Okishio	920	300	148	448	2.05	0.33	0.1609
Roemer-Foley-Laibman	920	336	112	448	2.00	0.25	0.1217

example of one good macroeconomy, this result can be illustrated by means of the information provided in Table 6.6. Let K, W, P, and Y denote, respectively, the physical capital stock, the flow of wages, profits, and net output. In addition, note that K/Y is a proxy for Marx's organic composition of capital, which is equal to Okishio's "organic composition of production," as explained in Sect. 6.3.2. While the second row in the table reflects Okishio's assumption that the real wage remains constant at 300, the last row reflects an alternative assumption that the profit share (P/Y) is constant at 0.25. One may easily confirm that the profit rate, defined as P/K, decreases under this new assumption.[27]

In other words, there are two benchmarks in the existing literature, namely Okishio's constant real wage and Roemer-Foley-Laibman's constant wage share, each of which leads to different results. Therefore, "it is impossible to say a priori whether the process of technical change will raise or lower the profit rate" (Foley, 1986, p. 139). This new benchmark, however, requires a behavioral explanation. Foley (1986), in the context of the "New Interpretation" of Marxian value theory, argues that this shift implied a constant value of labor-power, which he defined as the product of the money wage and the "value of money."[28]

The assumption of a constant "value of money" is, however, too restrictive and arbitrary if technical change is the focus of analysis. Furthermore, Okishian generalization of the theorem through the modification of the constant real wage assumption into "a non-decreasing utility level of laborers" in the case of product innovation (Okishio, 1993; Nakatani & Hagiwara, 1997) puts this explanation into question. That is, introducing new products necessarily changes the "value of money," even

[27] If wages are assumed to be advanced, then the profit rate may be redefined without loss of generality.

[28] "Value of money" is the inverse of the "monetary expression of labor time." See footnote 4 in Chapter 3.

when the money wage is constant. If the "value of money" decreases as a result of product innovation, Foley's value of labor-power decreases with the constant money wage, which implies an increase in the rate of profit.

As a result, the procedure of holding "the value of labor power constant by holding the money wage and the value of money constant" (Foley, 1986, p. 138) is misleading. Ramos-Martinez (2004) first recognized this point. Ironically, however, he used his observation to refute the Okishio theorem by distinguishing "nominal" and "labor-time" rates of profit. His "labor-time rate of profit" was defined as the rate of profit when changes in the "monetary expression of labor-time" are taken into account. Since he, like other temporalists, changes the definition of the rate of profit itself, his inference is not a compelling challenge to the Okishio theorem as explained in Sect. 6.3.4. It is interesting to note that a special case of a "constant value of money" occurs when the internal composition of the wage basket is equal to that of the physical value-added, which is the case when Foley's definition of the value of labor-power is consistent with the conventional definition.

Theorem 6.1 If the internal composition of the wage basket is equal to that of the physical value added and workers' utility level does not decrease during the process of innovation, the New Interpretation's "value of money" remains constant.

Proof Suppose that all commodities, including the newly introduced $n+1$ th commodity, are both consumption goods and production goods. According to Okishio (1993) and Nakatani and Hagiwara (1997), to satisfy the assumption of non-decreasing utility level of workers, workers should be able to buy a new consumption bundle $(b_1, b_2, \ldots, b_n, b_{n+1})$ at the current prices (p_i) and wage (w). This situation is represented as follows:

$$w = \sum_{i=1}^{n+1} b_i p_i \tag{6.18}$$

At the new equilibrium prices (q_i), the following relation must hold.

$$w = \sum_{i=1}^{n+1} b_i q_i \tag{6.19}$$

Subtracting (6.19) from (6.18) produces the following:

$$0 = \sum_{i=1}^{n+1} b_i (p_i - q_i) \tag{6.20}$$

As Foley's (1986) "value of money" is the ratio of total working time to total monetary value-added, its constancy implies the following relation under the assumption of the constant total working time. Here y_i denotes the physical value-added of the ith sector.

$$\sum_{i=1}^{n+1} (p_i - q_i) y_i = 0 \tag{6.21}$$

Considering (6.20), it can be known that (6.21) holds only if the following is satisfied where k is a positive scalar.

$$(y_1, y_2, \ldots, y_{n+1}) = k(b_1, b_2, \ldots, b_{n+1}) \tag{6.22}$$

Equation (6.22) is the condition that the internal composition of the wage basket is equal to that of the physical value-added. (Q.E.D.)

On the other hand, Laibman (1997, p. 47) maintains that the new benchmark implies a "class struggle neutrality" condition. Although such an interpretation is appealing, it may be unreasonable if the utility level of workers is considered to be affected by wage share. This problem is related in part to the incompatibility of the assumption of a constant relative income share with a competitive labor market (Roemer, 1981, p. 136). The problem also relates to intersectoral competition, according to the following logic in Fig. 6.3, where r_i and ω_i represent the rate of profit and the wage share, respectively, in the ith sector:

In other words, suppose that the wage share in a particular sector declines relative to those in other sectors. Then, feeling that they are

$$\ldots \rightarrow \omega_i \neq \omega_j \rightarrow \text{movement of labor} \rightarrow r_i \neq r_j \rightarrow \text{movement of capital} \ldots$$

Fig. 6.3 The logic of inter-sectoral competition

being treated unfairly, workers would exert less effort or move to other sectors.[29] Either of these actions would result in a decline in the Marxian rate of exploitation. This decline, in turn, would lead to the counter-tendency of capital to pursue a higher rate of profit. Therefore, the benchmark concern may develop into a competitive process problem.

6.4.3 *Competitive Equilibrium and Prices of Production*

One of the most salient critiques of the Okishio theorem may be the following challenge:

> If the economy did not move towards the new equilibrium, or if the processes that produce technical change are themselves a function of being out of equilibrium, then how does the economy change? In either case the results of comparative statistics are worthless, since the equilibrium is never attained. (Fine, 1982, p. 115)

A similar critique is also put forward by the TSSI. As the following quotation shows, the TSSI regards the falling rate of profit as an observable tendency, while Fine (1982) does not.[30]

> [The Okishio theorem] relies crucially on the unproved assumption that the economy 'fully adjusts' to a new static equilibrium after mechanization. Under continuous mechanization, however, full adjustment will not occur and the Marxian profit rate can fall. (Kliman, 1996, p. 211)

In his later work, Okishio presents the problem of this line of thinking and actually tries to provide some relevant results (Okishio, 1996, 1999, 2001). In particular, Okishio (2001) shows that competition among capitals makes profit vanish under certain parameter values and other initial conditions. At the heart of Okishio's simulation model lies an emphasis on the interaction between capital mobility and the labor market, even in

[29] In the efficiency wage literature, whether a wage is "fair" can affect the effort level of workers. According to Akerlof and Yellen (1990), the wage-profit ratio is one of the most important determinants of a fair wage.

[30] See Sect. 7.2 of Chapter 7.

... → supply ≠ demand → changes of prices → changes of profit rates → movements of capital → new supply & new demand → ...

Fig. 6.4 Cross-dual dynamics

cases without technical change. Thus, the conventional stability condition, employed by Nikaido (1985) is no longer valid.[31]

Okishio's simulation results cast doubt on the reality of the Okishio theorem's second assumption. This fact seemingly leads to a negation of the theorem itself. However, Okishio's framework can be maintained if an interaction between technical change and the labor market is introduced in the competition process. This process has usually been conceptualized as following cross-dual dynamics between market prices and output changes, which operate through differential profit rates (Duménil & Lévy, 1993, p. 75) (Fig. 6.4).

Okishio's contribution is the addition of a new level of labor market dynamics to these conventional cross-dual dynamics. At this stage, the assumption of real wage constancy is called into question. In contrast to the first stage, an exhaustion of the labor supply (and, therefore, a rise in the real wage) is explicitly introduced.

6.4.4 *Concluding Remarks*

The Okishio theorem can be regarded as describing a counterfactual situation, namely the state of technical change in the context of a constant real wage. Under this interpretation, labor market dynamics concerning changes in the real wage may then be introduced during the discussions of the competitive process determining production prices. In other words,

[31] Nikaido's (1985) stability condition requires that the consumption goods sector's organic composition of capital be greater than that of the capital goods sector. Although this requirement contradicts the conventional wisdom of Marxian economics, the truth of Okisho's claim can be shown easily through the introduction of sectoral differences to the organic composition of capital into the simulation model of Okishio (2001). Even under the assumption that the consumption goods sector's organic composition of capital is greater than that of the capital goods sector, the sectoral rates of profit converge to zero due to the increase in real wage. The real wage was assumed to be constant in Nikaido's model, which implies that the equilibration process is considered to be independent of labor market characteristics.

Okishio tries to formulate a two-stage analysis beginning with a counterfactual argument. If one accepts this research strategy, then the Okishio theorem itself cannot be refuted, except for the argument of logical inconsistency. Although the implications of the Okishio theorem are limited on this interpretation, the theorem's original framework is nonetheless maintained, in the sense that the dynamic relation between technical change and the labor market is regarded as one of the most important elements in the competition process. The connection between the first and the second stages stems from the observation that the generalization of the hypothetical state necessarily turns the entire problem into an equilibration process.

In summary, although these two restrictive assumptions reduce the implications of the Okishio theorem to being a counterfactual, the theorem still has meaning, given that it introduces a new dimension into the formulation of competition dynamics. Furthermore, labor market dynamics are closely related to the institutional setting of the Fundamental Marxian Theorem discussed in Chapter 4.

References

Akerlof, G. A., & Yellen, J. L. (1990). The fair wage-effort hypotheses and unemployment. *Quarterly Journal of Economics, 105*(2), 255–283.

Akinci, U., & Karahanogullari, Y. (2015). Convergence of monetary equivalent of labour time (MELTs) in two Marxian interpretations. *Cambridge Journal of Economics, 39*(3), 769–781.

Bowles, S. (1981). Technical change and the profit rate: A simple proof of the Okishio theorem. *Cambridge Journal of Economics, 5*(2), 183–186.

Cogliano, J., Flaschel, P., Franke, R., Frölich, N., & Veneziani, R. (2018). *Value, competition and exploitation: Marx's Legacy revisited*. Edward Elgar.

Duménil, G., & Lévy, D. (1993). *The economics of the profit rate*. Edward Elgar.

Fine, B. (1982). *Theories of the Capitalist Economy*. Edward Arnold.

Fleetwood, S. (2012). Laws and tendencies in Marxist political economy. *Capital and Class, 36*(2), 235–262.

Foley, D. K. (1986). *Understanding capital: Marx's economic theory*. Harvard University Press.

Foley, D. K. (2000). Response to Freeman and Kliman. *Research in Political Economy, 18*, 279–283.

Freeman, A. (1996). Price, value and profit—A continuous, general, treatment. In A. Freeman & G. Carchedi (Eds.), *Marx and non-equilibrium economics*. Edward Elgar.

Freeman, A. (1999). *The limits of Ricardian value: Law, contingency and motion in economics*. Paper presented at the 6th mini-conference of International Working Group on Value Theory.

Freeman, A., & Kliman, A. (2000). Two concepts of value, two rates of profit, two laws of motion. *Research in Political Economy, 18*, 243–267.

Groll, S., & Orzech, Z. B. (1989). From Marx to the Okishio theorem: A genealogy. *History of Political Economy, 21*(2), 253–272.

Hahnel, R. (2017). A tale of three theorems. *Review of Radical Political Economics, 49*(1), 125–132.

Howard, M. C., & King, J. (1992). *A History of Marxian Economics* (Vol. 2). Princeton University Press.

Kang, N., & Rieu, D.-M. (2009). The case for reformulating Marx's theory of the falling rate of profit. *Political Economy Quarterly, 46*(3), 53–60.

Kliman, A. (1996). A value-theoretic critique of the Okishio theorem. In A Freeman & G. Carchedi (Eds.), *Marx and non-equilibrium economics*. Edward Elgar.

Kliman, A. (2007). *Reclaiming Marx's capital: A refutation of the myth of inconsistency*. Lexington Books.

Kliman, A. (2011). *The failure of capitalist production: Underlying causes of the Great Recession*. Pluto Press.

Kliman, A. (2012). Response to critiques of *The Failure of Capitalist Production*. *Marxism 21, 9*(4), 263–315.

Kliman, A., & McGlone, T. (1999). A temporal single-system interpretation of Marx's value theory. *Review of Political Economy, 11*(1), 33–59.

Laibman, D. (1996). Technical change, accumulation and the rate of profit revisited. *Review of Radical Political Economics, 28*(2), 33–53.

Laibman, D. (1997). *Capitalist Macrodynamics: A systematic introduction*. Macmillan.

Laibman, D. (1999). Okishio and his critics: Historical cost vs. replacement cost. *Research in Political Economy, 17*, 207–227.

Morishima, M. (1973). *Marx's economics*. Cambridge University Press.

Moseley, F., & Rieu, D.-M. (2009). A critique of Kliman and McGlone's two-commodity 'refutation' of the Okishio theorem. *Marxism 21, 6*(3), 318–328.

Nakatani, T., & Hagiwara, T. (1997). Product innovation and the rate of profit. *Kobe University Economic Review, 43*, 39–51.

Negishi, T. (2009). Shibata Kei Hakase to Shinkeizaironri [In Japanese: Dr. Kei Shibata and his economics of planning] *Nihon Gakusiin Kiyou* [Transactions of the Japan Academy], *63*(3), 197–213.

Nikaido, H. (1985). Dynamics of growth and capital mobility in Marx's scheme of reproduction. *Zeitschrift Für Nationalökonomie, 45*(3), 197–218.

Okishio, N. (1956). Kokuminsyotoku to Roudou [In Japanese: National income and labor]. *Kokumin Keizai Zassi* [Journal of National Economics], *94*(4), 48–64.
Okishio, N. (1961). Technical changes and the rate of profit. *Kobe University Economic Review, 7*, 85–99.
Okishio, N. (1977a). Marukusu Keizaikaku: Kachi to Kakaku no Riron [In Japanese, *Marxian economics: The theory of value and price*]. Chikuma Shobo.
Okishio, N. (1977b). Notes on technical progress and capitalist society. *Cambridge Journal of Economics, 1*(1), 93–100.
Okishio, N. (1993). Introduction of new products and the rate of profit [In Japanese]. *Journal of Osaka University of Economics, 44*(1), 1–11.
Okishio, N. (1994). Reply to critiques against the 'Okishio theorem' [In Japanese]. *Journal of Osaka University of Economics, 45*(3), 1–32.
Okishio, N. (1995). An interview with professor Okishio [In Korean]. *Iron* [Theory], *13*, 227–240.
Okishio, N. (1996). Production prices and competition [In Japanese]. *Journal of Osaka University of Economics, 47*(3), 1–14.
Okishio, N. (1999). On average rate of profit [In Japanese]. *Journal of Kwansei Gakuin University of Economics, 52*(3), 1–20.
Okishio, N. (2001). Competition and production prices. *Cambridge Journal of Economics, 25*(4), 493–501.
Park, C.-S. (2005). Testing Okishio's criterion of technical choice. *Research in Political Economy, 22*, 199–208.
Potts, N. (2016). Two temporal single system interpretation of Marx calculations of the MELT. *Marxism 21, 13*(2), 94–122.
Petith, H. (2005). Marx's analysis of the falling rate of profit in the first version of volume III of *Capital. Review of Political Economy, 17*(2), 269–290.
Ramos-Martinez, A. (2004). Labour, money, labour-saving innovation, and the falling rate of profit. In A. Freeman, A. Kliman, & J. Wells (Eds.), *The new value controversy and the foundations of economics*. Edward Elgar.
Rieu, D.-M. (2009). Has the Okishio theorem been refuted? *Metroeconomica, 60*(1), 162–178.
Rieu, D.-M., & Park, H. W. (2020). Unproductive activities and the rate of surplus value at the industry level in Korea, 1995–2015. *Journal of Contemporary Asia, 50*(2), 284–307.
Roemer, J. E. (1981). *Analytical foundations of Marxian economic theory*. Cambridge University Press.
Samuelson, P. (1971). Understanding the Marxian notion of exploitation: A summary of the so-called 'transformation problem' between Marxian values and competitive Prices. *Journal of Economic Literature, 9*(2), 399–431.
Shibata, K. (1934). *On the law of decline in the rate of profit* (pp. 61–75). Kyoto University Economic Review.

Shibata, K. (1939). *On the general profit rate* (pp. 40–66). Kyoto University Economic Review.
Shibata, K. (1943). A mathematical development of new economic logic [In Japanese]. *Keizai-ronsou* [Economic Review], *65*(1), 35–46.
Shibata, K. (1959). *Dynamic and dialectic theories of world capitalism.* Minerva Shobo.
Sraffa, P. (1960). *Production of commodities by means of commodities. Prelude to a critique of economic theory.* Cambridge University Press.
Steedman, I. (1977). *Marx after Sraffa.* New Left Books.
Veneziani, R. (2004). The temporal single-system interpretation of Marx's economics: A critical evaluation. *Metroeconomica, 55*(1), 96–114.

CHAPTER 7

Falling Rate of Profit: Falsifiable or not?

7.1 Introduction

This chapter aims to evaluate some aspects of Alfred Saad-Filho's interpretation of Marxian value theory (Saad-Filho, 2002, 2018), focusing on its implication on the law of the tendency of the rate of profit to fall (LTRPF). Saad-Filho's understanding of value theory essentially advanced the logic of Ben Fine, who intervened in the controversy between the "Fundamentalists" and the "Neo-Ricardians" on issues of Marxian economics in the 1970s (Fine & Harris, 1979). Saad-Filho and Fine's interpretation has centered on the concept of the organic composition of capital. Their joint textbook on Marxian economics (Fine & Saad-Filho, 2016), which has been coauthored since the fourth edition, succinctly summarizes "the organic composition of capital interpretation" (Moseley, 2016). We show that although their specific interpretation of the organic composition of capital sheds new light on related issues, it also has a serious limitation. Section 7.2 examines the essential elements of Saad-Filho's (and Fine's) understanding of Marxian value theory. Its logical difficulties regarding the organic composition of capital are stated in Sect. 7.3. Section 7.4 discusses the implications along limitations of the concept of an "abstract law" proposed by Fine, especially with regard to the TRPF. Section 7.5 concludes.

D.-M. Rieu, *A Mathematical Approach to Marxian Value Theory*, Marx, Engels, and Marxisms,
https://doi.org/10.1007/978-3-031-07808-8_7

7.2 Saad-Filho's Interpretation of Marxian Value Theory

Saad-Filho's interpretation of Marxian value theory was derived from Fine's methodological discussion in the 1970s. Simply put, the capitalist economy is regarded as an articulation of mutually connected but qualitatively separated spheres of production, exchange, and distribution. As the abstraction level of production is higher than those of exchange and distribution, Marx's economic categories proceed from the highest level of abstraction, production, to lower level with more concrete contents. Jeon's (2011) explanation is helpful to understand the gist of this methodology:

> This interpretation of Marx's method emphasizes the following three aspects. First, although concepts, laws, and tendencies in the sphere of production are determinate, they do not regulate realities unmediated and directly. Put differently, analysis of the production sphere, though it is important, should not be confused with the analysis of reality. Second, analyses of the spheres of exchange and distribution are premised upon that of the sphere of production. Concepts and tendencies specific to these spheres neither nullify nor supplant the analysis of the production sphere. Third, there is no fixed criterion for the qualitative distinction between the spheres of production and exchange. (Jeon, 2011, p. 315)

No Marxian economist has raised objections against the conventional proposition that production is more important sphere than exchange and distribution. Once Saad-Filho's (and Fine's) interpretation is positioned in controversial issues, its specific character emerges. From an analytic viewpoint, it is the discussion of the organic composition of capital in the interpretation that provides clarity on its contribution and limitations. Assigning some specific characteristics to Marx's concept of the organic composition of capital (OCC) and value composition of capital (VCC), the interpretation provides "non-standard" (Moseley, 2016, p. 333) solutions to the traditional issues of the transformation of values into prices and LTRPF.

In this interpretation, while the OCC is the concept "defined in production," the VCC is "a concept of exchange" (Saad-Filho, 2018, p. 96). Based on this distinction, the composition of capital in the Marxian procedure of transforming values into prices of production is argued to be OCC, not VCC. Therefore, the transformation problem is not a "problem" from the outset, but only a result of misinterpretation. Similarly, the LTRPF is regarded as not implying the actual fall in the rate of profit, because it is the OCC, not the VCC that capital-using, labor-saving technical progress does raise.

7.3 Organic Composition of Capital

What then lies at the heart of the distinction between the OCC and VCC?

First, it is self-evident that the technical composition of capital (TCC), defined as the physical ratio of means of production to labor, is unmeasurable owing to the so-called index problem (Fine & Saad-Filho, 2016, p. 90). As the means of production are composed of heterogeneous capital goods, it is impossible to represent the TCC as a single number without using any commensurable standard such as prices and values. The necessity of the VCC itself is derived from this commensurability problem. According to Saad-Filho's interpretation, the OCC is defined at the abstraction level of production where changes in values of constant and variable capital do not occur as a result of the development of labor productivity or are not reflected.[1]

A plausible definition consistent with this interpretation is to distinguish old values before change in labor productivity and new values after it. In other words, while the VCC is C_{t+1}/V_{t+1}, the OCC is equal to C_t/V_t, where C, V, and the subscripts denote the values of constant capital, variable capital, and periods, respectively. This definition seems consistent with the following paragraph by Fine and Saad-Filho:

> However, in general the values at the beginning of the circuit ('earlier values'), at which the inputs are purchased, are higher than those at which the output is sold ('later values'). Marx argues that the OCC reflects the TCC at the *initial* (higher) values of the component parts of capital, *before* the new technologies affect the value of the output, in which case the social OCC rises in tandem with the social TCC. In contrast, the VCC reflects the TCC at the *final* (lower) value of the elements of constant and variable capital, determined by the modified conditions of production and newly established in exchange. In other words, the OCC is measured at the time of production, while the VCC is determined in exchange and calculated

[1] "In a dynamic context, the OCC is the *ex ante* evaluation of the constant capital technically required per hour, while the VCC is the *ex post* ratio..." (Saad-Filho, 2002, p. 5).

> on the basis of the values newly established by the currently predominant technologies. It was in this context that Marx examined the law of the tendency of the rate of profit to fall. (Fine & Saad-Filho, 2008, p. 177. Italics original)[2]

According to Fine and Saad-Filho, therefore, while the OCC necessarily increases reflecting capital-using, labor-saving technical progress, the VCC may decrease, or at least will not increase proportionally with the OCC as a result of the decrease in the value of the means of production.

However, one important issue is neglected in this logic. Suppose that the circuit of capital starts at time 1 and ends at time 2. Fine and Saad-Filho argue that the OCC measured by the old value at time $t = 1$ is different from the VCC measured by the new value at time $t = 2$. If then, the typical situation is characterized by $OCC_1 > VCC_2$. Assuming a continuous circuit of capital, however, the starting point of time of the second circuit is the same as the ending point of time of the first circuit. Therefore, the VCC is equal to the OCC at the starting point of the new circuit of capital, because the elements of constant capital are sold and bought at the new value established through the exchange in the first circuit. In other words, $OCC_2 = VCC_2$ holds. Undoubtedly, this OCC is greater than the VCC at the ending point of the new circuit. Namely, $OCC_2 > VCC_3$ holds. However, as the value decrease in the elements of constant capital is already reflected, OCC_2 is smaller than OCC_1. As this is also the case in the next circuit of capital, the following relation holds.

$$OCC_1 > VCC_2 = OCC_2 > VCC_3 = OCC_3 > VCC_4 \ldots$$

$$\therefore OCC_1 > OCC_2 > OCC_3 > \ldots \tag{7.1}$$

It is clear from (7.1) that the OCC ultimately decreases insofar as the VCC decreases continuously. This implies that one of Fine and Saad-Filho's stylized facts—the decrease in the VCC combined with the increase in the OCC—cannot exist in the long run. Furthermore, in case the VCC also increases, there will be no significant analytical difference even if the OCC and VCC are not distinguished in Fine and Saad-Filho's

[2] This point is iterated in Saad-Filho (2002, p. 73. Italics original): "As the OCC is an immediate value-reflex of the TCC, it does *not* change if the TCC is kept constant, even if the value of the elements of capital changes."

sense. This point was implicitly noted by Kincaid in the controversy with Fine and Saad-Filho in the *Historical Materialism* journal:

> The VCC registers changes in the value and price of labour and means of production inputs and thus reflects alterations in the capital/labour ratio resulting from changes in productivity. However, VCC is still a measure which refers to a *production* process – and, once a new VCC is established, as competition forces other capitals to lower their prices, this new VCC will become established as the OCC of a new phase of production. This, in turn, is followed by a new VCC as further rounds of technical advance again alter productivity and costs of production. This point is obvious when we take a *re*-production perspective, and see, as Marx did, a sequence of repeated cycles: production → circulation → production → circulation, etc. Fine and Saad-Filho's analysis is too focused on a single phase of production at a given OCC, followed by productivity change, and a repricing process which is registered in VCC. Their procedure is misleading, and it is vital to focus on the production-reproduction sequence, not on production treated as an isolated moment. (Kincaid, 2007, p. 161. Italics original)

This calls for a distinction between the simultaneous and temporal rate of profit by the Temporal Single-System Interpretation (Kliman, 2007) because Fine and Saad-Filho's OCC and VCC correspond to the historical cost and the current cost, respectively.[3] As already shown, however, the trend of the OCC converges to that of the VCC in the long run.[4]

A plausible refutation of this critique from Saad-Filho is that the OCC and the VCC belong to mutually different levels of abstraction, and therefore are not commensurable. In this respect, the following statement is worth quoting:

[3] Using Marx's notations, historical cost is $C_{t-1} + V_{t-1}$ while current cost is $C_t + V_t$. For example, Ernst (1982), as a precursor of the Temporal Single-System Interpretation, argued that the historical rate of profit falls even when the current rate of profit rises. Note that the current rate of profit is the benchmark of capitalists for capital mobility between industries, considering that the historical cost, as sunk cost, is not included in the calculation of the expected rate of profit. If then, the VCC rather than the OCC in Saad-Filho's sense should be related to the Marxian transformation procedure. This may be another point of critique of Saad-Filho's interpretation on the transformation problem, which is beyond the scope of this chapter. For a summary and critique of Saad-Filho's interpretation, see Chapter 6 of Moseley (2016).

[4] Using a simple two-sector model, Moseley and Rieu (2009) also reached a similar result.

> The description of the difference between the VCC and the OCC in terms of new and old values is *conceptual rather than chronological*: at any moment in time some capitals will be entering the production process as others will be leaving it, while technical change is ubiquitous. What the distinction does is to draw upon, and build in a more complex context, the separation between the spheres of production and exchange .... In production, the two classes of capitalists and workers confront each other over the process of production and, as accumulation proceeds, *there is a tendency for the TCC to rise*. In exchange, capitalists confront each other as competitors in the process of buying and selling and, as accumulation proceeds, *there is a tendency for values to be reduced and for the VCC to decline*. (Fine & Saad-Filho, 2016, p. 93. Italic added)

Two points must be noted: First (Point A), the distinction between the OCC and VCC is not chronological. Second (Point B), the increase in the TCC and the decrease in the VCC are combined effects of the same technical change. It remains to be seen whether Points A and B are compatible. What was shown above is that Point B does not hold if one is premised upon the chronological conception of the OCC and VCC—in other words, if Point A is rejected. The other side of the coin is that accepting Point A makes it impossible to speak of Point B. This issue naturally leads to the examination of the concept of an "abstract law."

7.4 Tendency of the Rate of Profit to Fall as an "Abstract Law"

A good place to begin is Fine and Saad-Filho's interpretation of the LTRPF as an "abstract law":

> The OCC tends to rise over time because of the adoption of specifically capitalist methods of production, especially the use of machinery, in the context of competition within sectors and the systematic attempt to extract relative surplus value. This tendency of the OCC to increase is the source of the law as such, whilst the formation of the VCC is associated with the counteracting tendencies (CTs) to the LTRPF. The interaction between the law and the CTs is an essential aspect of the process of accumulation. This interaction forms more complex economic phenomena, but only for that stage of development of capitalism for which machine production is predominant. This implies that the LTRPF is not an empirical law in the narrowly predictive sense – it is, rather, an abstract law. It does not

give prospective (quantitative) indications about movements in the rate of profit, but it provides the basis on which more complex economic phenomena can be studied...(Fine & Saad-Filho, 2016, p. 96)

In their joint textbook, Fine and Saad-Filho more clearly argue that the OCC and the VCC cannot be compared on the same dimension, particularly with regard to the critique of the Okishio theorem, their main antagonist:

Now put the two processes together, introducing new technology and generalising it across other producers to form new prices. For Okishio, these processes are immediate empirical equilibrium phenomena. They do not interact with one another to give more complex and concrete outcomes; instead, they are *simply added together algebraically* to show a rise in profitability for the economy as a whole from one equilibrium to the next. Moreover, the two disequilibrium processes cancel each other out as processes of change and leave the system in harmonious equilibrium. Because of this, the Okishio approach cannot distinguish between the VCC and the OCC. Instead, it relies exclusively upon an equilibrium notion of the VCC which, nevertheless, is given the name organic composition. By contrast, for Marx, the law and the CTs are *abstract tendencies whose interaction is not some algebraic sum*, but a crisis-ridden path of accumulation which can be understood but not always anticipated. (Fine & Saad-Filho, 2016, pp. 107–108. Italics added)

Unlike Okshio, the process of introducing new technology and the price formation process are not regarded as "algebraically summated" in Fine and Saad-Filho's interpretation. As already noted in Chapter 6, the Okishio theorem provides a comparative static analysis of the effect of new technology introduced on the equilibrium rate of profit. However, Fine and Saad-Filho argue that it is meaningless to predict the direction of change in the rate of profit by comparing relative magnitudes of the elements, as they belong to different levels of abstraction. On the other hand, they argue that "the consideration of the LTRPF as an abstract law does not deny its empirical significance" (*Ibid.*, p. 101). It is not clear how one can find "the empirical significance" without a quantitative comparison of the OCC and VCC. Although the strict distinction of the levels of abstraction is important, any situation can be *ex-post* rationalized by arguing that the level of abstraction is different when it comes to empirical measurement. While this is a representation of the cautiousness involved in trying not to reach a hasty conclusion by simple algebraic comparison, it also means that nothing can be said of the empirical trend of the profit rate.[5] To explain everything, in most cases, is to explain nothing.

7.5 Concluding Remarks

Saad-Filho (2002, 2018) does not directly handle the issue of the LTRPF. However, his interpretation of value theory is not free from aforementioned problems. Saad-Filho's critique of the "New Interpretation" (NI) is a good example:

> This approach [NI-Rieu] has been developed in order to address the appearances directly, through a 'Marxian macroeconomics'. However, this important objective exacts a heavy toll. The NI has little analytical 'depth', emphasises exchange and distribution at the expense of production, and it eliminates the mediations and the complex relationship between value and price and surplus value and profit, treating them as if they were identical. As a result, the NI becomes unable to incorporate some of Marx's most important insights into the analysis, including technical change, accumulation, the credit system and crises, other than as exogenous accretions. (Saad-Filho, 2002, pp. 32–33)

The NI has played a vital role in applying the "monetary expression of labor time" to the estimation of Marxian ratios, such as the rate of surplus value. Therefore, it has gone too far to criticize that the NI as having "little analytical depth," but without specifying more concrete points.[6]

The most serious defect of Saad-Filho's interpretation is that it made Marxian value theory and related issues such as the LTRPF unfalsifiable claims. Undoubtedly, objection may be raised against the falsifiability criterion in the sense of Karl Popper. It is also true that Fine and Saad-Filho's interpretation brought about an openness to the LTRPF by

[5] Cullenberg (1994), albeit in the vein of the so-called "Postmodern Marxism," provided a conclusion similar to Fine and Saad-Filho's, at least, with regard to the empirical examination of the rate of profit.

[6] It must be noted that Saad-Filho's view on the New Interpretation was not necessarily negative in his 1996 paper (Saad-Filho, 1996). He admitted the NI's discussion on the so-called double-counting in the Marxian procedure of transforming values into prices of production. Later, however, in a joint paper with Fine (Fine et al., 2004, p. 16) which was republished in Saad-Filho (2018, p. 132), he argued that double counting is a "red herring" and "misplaced and misleading."

considering complicated elements affecting the rate of profit. However, one should run the risk of making Marxian value theory a degenerating research program in the Lakatosian sense by adhering to methodological discussions.

References

Cullenberg, S. (1994). *The falling rate of profit: Recasting the Marxian debate.* Pluto Press.

Ernst, J. (1982). Simultaneous valuation extirpated: A contribution to the critique of the neo-Ricardian concept of value. *Review of Radical Political Economics, 14*(2), 85–94.

Fine, B., & Harris, L. (1979). *Rereading capital.* Macmillan.

Fine, B., Lapavitsas, C., & Saad-Filho, A. (2004). Transforming the transformation problem: Why the "new interpretation" is a wrong turning. *Review of Radical Political Economics, 36*(1), 3–19.

Fine, B., & Saad-Filho, A. (2008). Production vs. realisation in Marx's theory of value: A reply to Kincaid. *Historical Materialism, 16*(4), 167–180.

Fine, B., & Saad-Filho, A. (2016). *Marx's capital* (6th ed.). Pluto Press.

Jeon, H. (2011). Translator's note. In A. Saad-Filho (Ed.), *The value of Marx* (Korean ed.). Chaekgalpi.

Kincaid, J. (2007). Production vs. realisation: A critique of Fine and Saad-Filho on value theory. *Historical Materialism, 15*(4), 137–165.

Kliman, A. (2007). *Reclaiming Marx's capital: A refutation of the myth of inconsistency.* Lexington Books.

Moseley, F. (2016). *Money and totality: A macro-monetary interpretation of Marx's logic in capital and the end of the 'transformation problem'.* Brill.

Moseley, F., & Rieu, D.-M. (2009). A critique of Kliman and McGlone's two-commodity 'refutation' of the Okishio theorem. *Marxism 21, 6*(3), 318–328.

Saad-Filho, A. (1996). The value of money, the value of labour power and the net product: An appraisal of the "new approach" to the transformation problem. In A. Freeman & G. Carchedi (Eds.), *Marx and non-equilibrium economics.* Edward Elgar.

Saad-Filho, A. (2002). *The value of Marx: Political economy for contemporary capitalism.* Routlege.

Saad-Filho, A. (2018). *Value and crisis: Essays on labour, money and contemporary capitalism.* Brill.

CHAPTER 8

Piketty After Marx

8.1 Introduction

This chapter reviews Thomas Piketty's *Capital in the Twenty-First Century* from the perspective of its relationship to Marxian economic theory, especially focusing on the tendency of the rate of profit to fall (TRPF) as an analytical tool. Regardless of the theoretical position, Piketty's analysis premised upon income-wealth data over several hundred years has an overwhelming aura. More importantly, however, it revived the long-run dynamics of capitalism which had been relatively neglected under the reign of the neoclassical mainstream economics. Piketty's analysis is in the same vein of the long-run dynamics pursued by Ricardo, Marx, and other classical economists in the sense that it provides a powerful implication based on simple relationships between several fundamental variables such as income distribution, rate of return on capital, and growth rate. Without a doubt, Piketty himself strongly negates the impact of Marx.[1] Furthermore, his interpretation on Marx is often stereotyped. For example, according to Piketty, "Marx's theory implicitly relies on a strict assumption of zero productivity growth over the long run" (Piketty,

[1] In his 2014 interview with *The New Republic*, Piketty said "I never managed really to read it [Marx's work-Rieu]...*The Communist Manifesto* of 1848 is a short and strong piece. *Das Kapital*, I think, is very difficult to read and for me it was not very influential" (Chotiner 2014).

D.-M. Rieu, *A Mathematical Approach to Marxian Value Theory*, Marx, Engels, and Marxisms,
https://doi.org/10.1007/978-3-031-07808-8_8

2014, p. 27), which is something like a version of the "breakdown" of the capitalist system. However, many aspects of Piketty's analysis can be related to Marx's insight. To use a metaphorical expression, the distance between Piketty and Marx is far much smaller than that between Piketty and the neoclassical economists.

In this chapter, both Piketty's understanding of Marx's economics and Marxists' critique of Piketty's book are examined. It is argued that Marx's theory and Piketty's theory are not necessarily incompatible. In particular, it is shown that the TRPF as an analytical tool can bridge the gap between Piketty's empirical result and its theoretical explanation.

8.2 Piketty and Marx

8.2.1 The Structure of Piketty's Model

Let us start with the summary of Piketty's basic model.

"The first fundamental law of capitalism" and "the second fundamental law of capitalism" are formulated as follows:

$$\alpha = r \times \beta \tag{8.1}$$

$$\beta = \frac{s}{g} \tag{8.2}$$

where α, β, r, s, and g denote, respectively, the share of income from capital in national income, the capital/income ratio, the rate of return on capital, the saving ratio, and the growth rate.

While Eq. (8.1) is an identity, Eq. (8.2) indicates that the capital/income ratio converges to a certain level in a steady state.[2]

Piketty's model is composed of Eqs. (8.1) and (8.2) combining a historical relation, $r > g$,[3] which resulted in the following conclusion:

> When the rate of return on capital significantly exceeds the growth rate of the economy (as it did through much of history until the nineteenth

[2] In other words, "this is an asymptotic law" meaning that "if a country saves a proportion of s of its income indefinitely, and if the rate of growth of its national income is g permanently, then its capital/income ratio will tend closer and closer to $\beta = s/g$ and stabilize at that level" (Piketty, 2014, p. 168).

[3] Historically this inequality holds with the only exception in the 20th century. See Figure 10.10 in Piketty (2014, p. 156).

century and as is likely to be the case again in the twenty first century), then it logically follows that inherited wealth grows faster than output and income. People with inherited wealth need to save only a portion of their income from capital to see that capital grow more quickly than the economy as a whole. Under such conditions, it is almost incompatible with the meritocratic values and principles of social justice fundamental to modern democratic societies. (Piketty, 2014, p. 26)

Namely, the following inequality resulting from Eqs. (8.1) and (8.2) shows that the greater α is the greater the difference between r and g.[4]

$$\alpha = s \times \frac{r}{g} \tag{8.3}$$

According to Piketty (2014, p. 165), the trend of β shows a U-shaped graph over the last 100 years, although some differences existed in Europe and the USA. However, as Eq. (8.2) only holds in a steady state and the values of α and β cannot be specified *ex-ante*, we do not know the exact future trajectory of β. Several scenarios can only be suggested according to the expected values of the increasing rate of population, productivity, etc.

Piketty's model is based on the relation between several variables which has conventionally been the object of Marxian economics.

First, Eq. (8.1) is essentially the same as Eq. (8.4) which was generalized by Duménil and Lévy (1993) and others. Here P, K, Y, and W denote, respectively, the total profit, the total capital stock, the monetary value-added, and the total wage.

$$r = \frac{P}{K} = \frac{Y}{K}\frac{P}{Y} = \frac{Y}{K}\left(1 - \frac{W}{Y}\right) \tag{8.4}$$

Therefore, the rate of profit is determined by "capital productivity" (Y/K)[5] and labor income share (W/Y). Using Piketty's notations,

[4] Milanovic (2014, p. 522) interprets that Piketty's model crucially depends on the inequality relationship $r > g$ because there exists a positive feedback loop between α and β. However, considering that it holds only in a steady state, Eq. (8.3) itself does not necessarily lead to greater α and β.

[5] Capital productivity with quotation marks implies that the terminology is used in a limited sense because Marxian economics does not regard capital as productive. See Park and Rieu (2020) for an interpretation of the meaning of productive and unproductive in Marxian economics.

Eq. (8.4) is $r = 1/\beta \times \alpha$. This is nothing other than "the first fundamental law of capitalism" except that the differences in the definition and measurement of capital will be explained later.

On the other hand, Eq. (8.4) is constructed by using proxy variables to check Marx's TRPF. Marx expressed the rate of profit in value terms as follows.

$$r = \frac{s}{c+v} = \frac{s/v}{c/v + 1} \tag{8.5}$$

In Eq. (8.5), capital-using labor-saving technical progress is described as the increase in the organic composition of capital (c/v), while the income distribution is described as the change in the rate of surplus value (s/v). In addition to the problem of transforming labor values into prices, "capital productivity" and "capital income share" (P/Y) can be regarded as proxies for c/v and s/v, respectively. The so-called "trajectories *à* la Marx" (Duménil & Lévy, 1993) describe the situation in which the rate of profit falls because the increase in the capital income share cannot offset the decrease in "capital productivity."

Marx distinguished the technical change and the interclass income distribution and tried to show the TRPF only by the former without resorting to the latter. As explained in Chapter 6, the Okishio theorem proved that it was theoretically impossible. Okishio's "organic composition of production" was intended to construct a concept that is independent of the change in the income distribution.[6]

Recently, Zarembka (2015) showed that the "materialized composition of capital" in the United States has been stable since 1956. Although this is a debatable calculation and should be examined further (Paitaridis & Tsoulfidis, 2012, 2015), it can be interpreted that a stylized fact, the falling rate of profit due to continuous mechanization, actually resulted from the intensification of exploitation (not from the mechanization itself), which is consistent with the moral of the Okishio theorem. On the other hand, the "organic composition of production" is equal to Piketty's β except for the issue of defining capital. While β showed an upward

[6] See the footnote 16 of Chapter 6. Shaikh (1987) developed the concept "materialized composition of capital" which was essentially the same as Okishio's organic composition of production. Moseley (1991), in his empirical studies on the rate of profit in the U.S., used the same concept for the composition of capital in the same vein of Okishio.

trend in the postwar U.S., the "organic composition of production" was almost constant. This is due to the differential definition of capital stock.

Next, there is no equivalent of Eq. (8.2) in Marx's theory. With regard to the TRPF, Piketty argued that "Marx totally neglected the possibility of the durable technological progress and steadily increasing productivity" (Piketty, 2014, p. 10) and, therefore, assumed a special case of zero or near-zero growth rate (ibid., p. 228). Considering that Marx consistently emphasized the development of productive forces in a capitalist society since *The Communist Manifesto* coauthored with Engels in 1848, it cannot be stated that $g \to 0$, and therefore $\beta \to \infty$ was his vision. This is the point where Piketty's interpretation of Marx became stereotyped.

8.2.2 Differences in Definitions

As the following quotes clearly show, the critical difference between Marx and Piketty lies in the definition of capital stock.

> In this book, capital is defined as the sum total of nonhuman assets that can be owned and exchanged on some market. Capital includes all forms of real property (including residential real estate) as well as financial and professional capital (plants, infrastructure, machinery, patents, and so on) used by forms and government agencies. (Piketty, 2014, p. 46)

As Piketty himself clarified (Piketty, 2014, p. 47), this definition indicates wealth. For example, slaves in the southern US before the Civil War are also included in capital.[7] Piketty's concept of capital as wealth has been the object of the most serious criticism, not only from Marxists such as Harvey (2014) and Fuchs (2014) but also from mainstream economists, such as Milanovic (2014). According to the conventional Marxian understanding that defines capital as a social relation, not a thing, Piketty's concept of capital is problematic. Milanovic (2014, p. 521) also criticizes Piketty for not distinguishing the wealth used in "unproductive" and "productive" activities.

[7] It must be noted in passing that Piketty's exclusion of the so-called "human capital" from capital is entirely consistent with Marx's distinction between labor and labor-power. He argues that "such an arrangement [a labor contract-Rieu] has to be limited in both time and scope" while "in slave societies, of course, this is obviously not true" (Piketty, 2014, p. 46).

However, a typical Marxist critique of Piketty's concept of capital should be reexamined from the following two aspects:

First, considering Marx's theory of the circuit of capital in the 2nd volume of *Capital*, Piketty's concept of capital can have a logical foundation. Marx emphasized the metamorphoses[8] of capital as money capital, productive capital, and commodity capital. Although Marx discussed a successive change of the forms from money to means of production, and further to commodity, he also emphasized that three different forms of capital coexisted at a given point in time. For example, it was emphasized that idle money capital was regularly released from the circuit of capital. The following reminiscence of former CEO of General Motors, Alfred Sloan, shows that this conception actually worked well in the consciousness of the capitalist.

> [W]e began calculating a month ahead what our cash would be each day of the month, taking into account the sales schedule, payrolls, payments for materials, and the like .... [T]his
>
> system ... enabled us to invest the excess cash, principally in short-term government securities. Thus we earned an income on money formerly kept as cash and so increased the efficiency with which we used our capital. (Sloan, 1963, p. 123, quoted from Saros, 2008, p. 208)

In this context, the Marxian concept of capital (the denominator of the rate of profit formula) should include the amount of idling money capital as well as the conventional capital stock. Therefore, the rate of profit in this sense would be somewhere between Piketty's rate of return on capital and the conventional Marxian rate of profit.[9] If one adopts this definition of capital, the Marxian rate of profit can fall while Piketty's rate

[8] Interestingly, Piketty (2014, Chapter 3) also used this terminology, which is seldom used in mainstream economics, although his emphasis is on the weight of housing or agricultural land in capital stock, which was somewhat different from Marx's context.

[9] In the case of the South Korea, the weight of land in the total national wealth is approximately 50%, much of which can be regarded as an investment to heighten the efficiency of capital in Sloan's sense. Then, it would be appropriate to include a large part of land in capital. In this sense, Harvey's (2014, p. 85) following comment should be cautiously applied, at least in the South Korean context: "Money, land, real estate, and plant and equipment that are not being used productively are not capital. If the rate of return on the capital that is being used is high, then this is because a part of capital is withdrawn from circulation and in effect goes on strike."

of return on capital remains constant. If W and K denote Piketty's capital (wealth) and the Marxian concept of capital, respectively, P/W may be stable, while P/K falls simultaneously. A sufficient condition for this is the decrease in the weight of the nonconventional part of capital, $W - K$. In this sense, it is impossible to refute Piketty's thesis from the perspective of Marx's TRPF like Maito (2014), who argued that Piketty's own data showed the TRPF in the Marxian sense.

Second, Piketty is not much different from Marx in that he considers the problem of inequality to be an issue between capital and labor. Without a doubt, Piketty does not abdicate the framework of the neoclassical production function. However, Piketty's definition of the rate of return on capital has the merit of showing that income inequality depends on wealth inequality; in other words, there is an increasing threat to the so-called meritocracy. Even in the case in which Marx's TRPF holds, in so far as Piketty's rate of return on capital stabilizes, inequality will be deepening. Although Marx did not think that any meritocratic value holds in a capitalist society,[10] adding some simplifying assumptions transforms Piketty's model into Marx's model. For example, adding Kaleckian assumptions that workers consume their entire incomes and capitalists invest all their profits makes $\alpha = s$ in Eq. (8.3), which leads to $g = r$, as in Morishima's (1973) "Marx-von Neuman model."

8.2.3 An Alternative Reading of Piketty

Now let us compute Piketty's capital-income ratio for the South Korean economy to provide an alternative reading of Piketty's analysis. As shown in Fig. 8.1, Piketty's β (that is, the capital-income ratio) declined in the aftermath of the 1997–1998 crisis and started to rise considerably in early 2000.[11] It decreased somewhat immediately after the 2008 global crisis but continued to exhibit an upward trend. It also stated to increase rapidly after 2017, which may have reflected the skyrocketing housing prices during this period, which have persisted until the moment of writing this

[10] To Marx, the production process of profit is the exploitation of the workers by the capitalists. Therefore, the intensification of the inequality by accumulated wealth has a secondary importance. This is why the chapter on "the so-called primitive accumulation" appeared at the end of the 1st volume of *Capital* as a historical addendum.

[11] The data used in Figs. 8.1 and 8.2 are obtained from National Accounts by the Bank of Korea, which is available at https://econs.bok.or.kr.

Fig. 8.1 Piketty's β in South Korea, 1995–2020

book.[12] The global phenomena of the expansion of income and wealth inequality pointed out by Piketty (2014) were also markedly observed in South Korea during 1995–2020.

Unlike Piketty's analysis, however, the income distribution can be examined from a different perspective in relation to the productivity and profitability of capital by relying on the decomposition formula of the rate of profit in Eq. (8.4). The trends of the related variables during the sample period are illustrated in Fig. 8.2, which confirms Rieu and Joo's (2014) result on the profit-rate dynamics of the Korean economy in 1995–2012. An increase in profit share constantly offset a decline in capital productivity, and therefore, prevented the falling tendency of the rate of profit from unfolding. In other words, the strengthening of capital's class power played a vital role in preventing the tendency of the profit rate to fall. This dynamic has changed since 2010 when capital productivity leveled off and both the rate of profit and the capital share in income started to

[12] This hints at the possibility of overestimating the rise of the capital-output ratio (Rowthorn, 2014). However, it must be added that, at least in South Korea, skyrocketing housing prices were the main cause of wealth inequality, in that the weight of residential assets is more than 70% in the asset portfolio of the average Korean household.

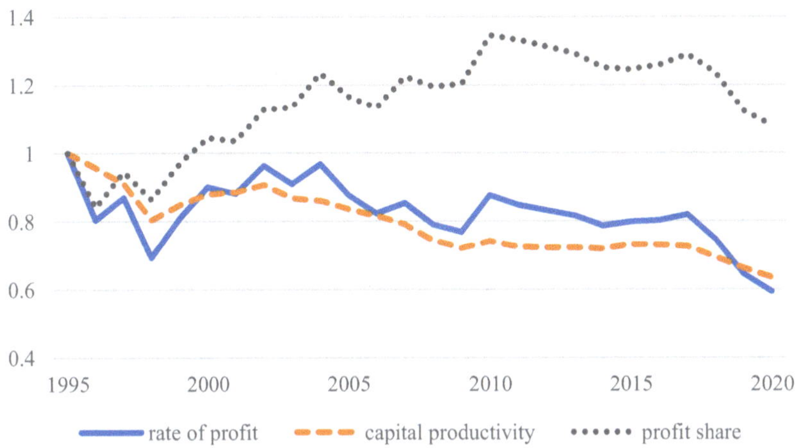

Fig. 8.2 The rate of profit, capital productivity, and profit share in South Korea: all industries, 1995–2020 (1995 = 1)

decrease. After 2017, however, partly due to the housing price inflation noted above, capital productivity also started to decrease. As the profit share started to decrease sharply, the rate of profit also decreased. Unlike in the earlier period, the decrease in Υ/K was not cancelled out by the increase in P/Υ, but was aggravated by the decrease in P/Υ, which led to the falling rate of profit.

In all, Figs. 8.1 and 8.2 indicate that the capital-income ratio, the profit share, and the rate of profit followed similar secular trends during the whole sample period. This result partly corresponds to Piketty's thesis on the co-movement of the wealth-income ratio and profit share until the early 2010s. Piketty (2014, p. 220) suggests that the positive correlation between the two is due to the elasticity of factor substitution being greater than one. However, data collected in the literature contradict Piketty's argument, making it empirically weak (see, for example, Rowthorn, 2014; Semieniuk, 2017). Rather, that the class struggle developed in favor of capital through neo-liberal structuration provides a better explanation at least for the South Korean economy during this period. Furthermore, after 2017, the trend changed somewhat drastically. This may be related to the appearance of the center-left government pursuing a sort of wage-led growth policy or the rapid rise in housing prices. Obviously, this alternative reading shows the possibility of interpreting the TRPF as an analytical tool to analyze capital accumulation based on the dynamic between class conflict and technical change.

8.3 Concluding Remarks

The simultaneous increase in α and β in Piketty's model requires that the elasticity of substitution be relatively high. From another perspective, this implies a nondiminishing marginal rate of return, which is proven by Piketty's historical data. This stability of the rate of return on capital is necessarily related to the critique of the marginal productivity theory of distribution. In *Capital in the Twenty-First Century*, Piketty hinted at this critique as follows:

> It is important to state clearly that the notion of marginal productivity of capital is defined independently of the institutions and rules—or absence of rules—that define the capital-labor split in a given society. For example, if an owner of land and tools exploits his own capital, he probably does not account separately for the return on the capital that he invests in himself. Yet this capital is nevertheless useful, and his marginal productivity is the same as if the return were paid to an outside investor. The same is true if the economic system chooses to collectivize all or part of the capital stock, and in extreme cases (the Soviet Union, for example) to eliminate all private return on capital. In that case, the private return is less than the "social" return on capital, but the latter is still defined as the marginal productivity of an additional unit of capital. Is it useful and just for the owners of capital to receive this marginal product as payment for their ownership of property (whether their own past savings or that of their ancestors) even if they contribute no new work? This is clearly a crucial question, but not the one I am asking here. (Piketty, 2014, p. 215)

The question is that the latter part of the quote is actually the same as that raised by Marx regarding the transformation of the productive power of social labor into the productive power of capital. However, Piketty stops here.[13] He excludes interclass politics from the elements determining the rate of profit by saying "in any case, the rate of return

[13] Although this issue necessarily leads us back to the Cambridge controversy on capital, Piketty stops again. See Galbraith (2014) for the critique of Piketty's neglect of the controversy. Considering that Piketty's objective is to explain the dynamic change in

on capital is determined by…first, technology…, and second, the abundance of capital stock" (ibid., p. 212). Following Marx's insight, however, class conflict around the production of surplus value, more broadly, the increasing power of capital brought by the increase in α should be pursued further.

Conclusively, Piketty's peculiar concept of capital and the neglect of the production process can be a practical strategy to empirically show the unequal distribution of wealth and explain its long-run dynamics. Although it is unclear whether he was conscious of it or not, the use of the neoclassical concept of the elasticity of substitution and the exclusion of "noneconomic" factors such as the class struggle, have a political effect in that his theory may be persuasive in mainstream economics. However, it is necessary to go beyond the narrow boundary of economics defined by the neoclassicals in order to explain the mutual dynamics between α and β. This is a research direction that may be called "Piketty after Marx," which was already anticipated as follows:

> But this expression [the equation (8.5) in this chapter-Rieu] by itself does not so much illuminate the determinants of the profit rate or its historical evolution as it serves as a framework for further investigation. It tells us where to look. Following such guide, a social grounding of the analysis of profits would go "behind" this formal expression for the profit rate to explain how and to what degree competition, class conflict, and other social forces determine the rate of exploitation and the organic composition of capital (along with an appropriate weighting scheme). (Bowles et al., 1986, p. 133)

References

Bowles, S., Gordon, D. M., & Weisskopf, E. (1986). Power and profits: The social structure of accumulation and the profitability of the postwar U.S. economy. *Review of Radical Political Economics, 18*(1–2), 132–167.

Chotiner, I. (2014, May 6). Thomas Piketty: I don't care for Marx—An interview with the left's rock star economist. *The New Republic*. https://newrepublic.com/article/117655/thomas-piketty-interview-economist-discusses-his-distaste-marx

wealth inequality, however, capital controversy can be set aside in the sense that the wealth inequality is measured by market prices in our daily lives.

Duménil, G., & Lévy, D. (1993). *The economics of the profit rate: Competition, crises, and historical tendencies in capitalism*. Edward Elgar.
Fuchs, C. (2014). Thomas Piketty's book 'Capital in the twenty-first century', Karl Marx and the political economy of the Internet. *triple C: Communication, Capitalism & Critique, 12*(1), 413–430.
Galbraith, J. K. (2014). *Kapital* for the twenty-first century? *Dissent*, Spring 2014. Available at: https://www.dissentmagazine.org/article/kapital-for-the-twenty-first-century. Accessed 1 Apr 2022.
Harvey, D. (2014). Afterthoughts on Piketty's *Capital in the twenty-first century*. *Challenge, 57*(5), 81–86.
Maito, E. E. (2014). *Piketty against Piketty: The tendency of the rate of profit to fall in United Kingdom and Germany since XIX century confirmed by Pikettys data* (MPRA Paper No. 55839).
Milanovic, B. (2014). The return of 'patrimonial capitalism': Review of Thomas Piketty's *Capital in the 21st century*. *Journal of Economic Literature, 52*(2), 519–534.
Morishima, M. (1973). *Marx's economics*. Cambridge University Press.
Moseley, F. (1991). *The falling rate of profit in the postwar United States economy*. St. Martin's Press.
Paitaridis, D., & Tsoulfidis, L. (2012). The growth of unproductive activities, the rate of profit, and the phase-change of the U.S. economy. *Review of Radical Political Economics, 44*(2), 213–233.
Paitaridis, D., & Tsoulfidis, L. (2015). Growth accounting of the value composition of capital and the rate of profit in the U.S. economy: A note stimulated by Zarembka's findings. *Review of Radical Political Economics, 49*(2), 303–312.
Park, H. W., & Rieu, D.-M. (2020). A mathematical formulation of the dual nature of unproductive labor. *Review of Radical Political Economics, 52*(4), 716–738.
Piketty, T. (2014). *Capital in the twenty-first century* (A. Goldhammer, Trans.). The Belknap Press of Harvard University Press.
Rieu, D.-M., & Joo, S. (2014). Marxian ratios after Piketty [In Korean]. *Review of Social and Economic Studies* [Journal of Korean Association for Political Economy], *45*, 161–183.
Rowthorn, R. (2014). A note on Piketty's *Capital in the twenty-first century*. *Cambridge Journal of Economics, 38*(5), 1275–1284.
Saros, D. E. (2008). The turnover continuum: A Marxist analysis of capitalist fluctuations. *Review of Radical Political Economics, 40*(2), 189–211.
Semieniuk, G. (2017). Piketty's elasticity of substitution: A critique. *Review of Political Economy, 29*(1), 64–79.
Shaikh, A. (1987). Organic composition of capital. In J. Eatwell, M. Milgate, & P. Newman (Eds.), *The new Palgrave: Marxian economics*. Palgrave Macmillan.
Sloan, A. P. (1963). *My years with general motors*. Doubleday.

Zarembka, P. (2015). Materialized composition of capital and its stability in the United States: Findings stimulated by Paitaridis and Tsoulfidis (2012). *Review of Radical Political Economics, 47*(1), 106–111.

PART IV

A New Research Direction

CHAPTER 9

Price-Value Relation with Stochastic Profit Rate and Labor Heterogeneity

9.1 Introduction

The main goal of this chapter is to provide a research guideline for generalizing the "New Interpretation" (NI) of the Marxian value theory (Duménil, 1980; Foley, 1982). Specifically, the chapter is a preliminary study to demonstrate the necessity of an integrated analysis of labor productivity which will be provided in Chapter 11.

As already discussed in Chapters 2 and 3, it is crucial to pursue how to estimate sectorally different rates of surplus value for the generalization of the NI. Duménil et al. (2009) presented a generalized NI model reflecting Rieu's (2008) suggestion which distinguishes the "value expression of labor time" (VELT) and the "monetary expression of value" (MEV). However, it remains to be seen whether one can successfully "derive" sectoral values from given observable data on market prices, sectoral rates of profit and technology (Rieu, 2009). This issue is necessarily related to the application of the NI at the microeconomic level. If measuring the rate of surplus value and the value-creating capacity of each labor category is simply a "pragmatic issue" (Foley, 2005, p. 41), it is necessary to go into "the hidden abode of production" (Marx, 1977, p. 123) to examine what actually happens in the creation of value and surplus value. Until we have an exact method for measuring labor intensity and complexity, however, there is no choice but to employ some

D.-M. Rieu, *A Mathematical Approach to Marxian Value Theory*, Marx, Engels, and Marxisms,
https://doi.org/10.1007/978-3-031-07808-8_9

simplifying assumptions. Most estimations of labor value assume that wage differentials are proportional to skill differentials, which leads to the uniform rate of surplus value. In Sect. 3.4.4, an alternative method of the inverse transformation starting from labor income share data was provided. That method, however, still has limitations in that it cannot directly estimate the VELT at the industry level.

Given the above situation, this chapter approaches the issue in a roundabout way using a simulation analysis. The greatest merit of a simulation analysis is to predict the basic structural relation when credible empirical data are not available. Adopting Greenblatt's (2014) methodology premised upon a "probabilistic political economy" (Farjoun & Machover, 1983), this chapter employs a simulation analysis of the linear economic model introducing labor heterogeneity, which also regards price, value, and the profit rate as random variables.

A standard of comparison in the simulation here will be the direct proportionality thesis between price and labor content. Shaikh (1984), Ochoa (1984), Tsoulfidis and Maniatis (2002), Cockshott and Cottrell (2005), and others have consistently reported that there is strong empirical regularity between price and labor quantity, which is directly and indirectly required to produce a certain commodity in different countries including East Asian countries (Han & Li, 2020; Tsoulfidis & Rieu, 2006). Despite the suspicion regarding "spurious correlation" (Kliman, 2002, 2004), this regularity was usually interpreted as implying that Marxian value is a good approximation for the even market price, not just an equilibrium price, such as the price of production. The proportionality result, however, is counterintuitive from the perspective of Marxian value theory because in this case the procedure of transforming values into prices of production becomes redundant.[1] Note further that the main purpose of Greenblatt (2014) whose basic model is adopted here, was to support this direct proportionality. The simulation analysis here, therefore, will examine whether price-labor content proportionality is maintained in the generalized NI.

To state the conclusion first, contrary to expectations, the direct proportionality between value and price does not disappear when only

[1] Shaikh, the main defender of this strand, however, has presented two interpretations of the transformation problem, one of which seems to be incompatible with the other arguing for price-value proportionality. See Moseley's (2021) discussion.

introducing sectorally different rates of surplus value, whereas it is dramatically weakened when introducing a differential value-creating capacity of labor. It is hoped that this small but surprising result will provide some hints for the generalization of the NI.

The remainder of the chapter is organized as follows. In Sect. 9.2, the basic model is introduced. In Sect. 9.3, the structure and results of the simulation are explained. Section 9.4 concludes the chapter.

9.2 Specification of the Model

The linear production model formulated in Sect. 2.5 of Chapter 2 will be used here. The whole chapter is devoted to a reduced form of the model (Duménil et al., 2009) in the sense that only one category of labor exists in each sector without loss of generality. Furthermore, each sector is assumed to produce one commodity. Therefore, the terms "*i*th commodity" and "*i*th sector" will be used interchangeably.

First, market prices are represented as:

$$p = (pA + lW)(I + R) = pA + v \tag{9.1}$$

Here $p, A, l, I,$ and v denote the market price vector $(1 \times n)$, the nonlabor input coefficient matrix $(n \times n)$, the labor input vector $(1 \times n)$, the identity matrix $(n \times n)$ and the money value-added vector $(1 \times n)$, respectively. Matrices of sectoral wages and profit rates are defined as $W = diag(w_1, w_2, \ldots, w_n)$ and $R = diag(r_1, r_2, \ldots, r_n)$. Note that (9.1) is not a set of price determining equations but an *ex-post* description of the market prices or using Roncaglia's (1978) metaphor of a "photograph" taken at a given moment in time.

Equation (9.1) can be changed in two ways:

$$p = lW(I + R)[I - A(I + R)]^{-1} = v(I - A)^{-1} \tag{9.2}$$

As is well known, the last equation in (9.2) implies that the commodity price is equal to the vertically integrated money value-added. Although (9.2) does not "determine" p but represents definitional relations, it provides the probability distribution of p_i's when the parameters on the right-hand side are randomly given.

On the other hand, value equations are represented as follows.

$$\lambda = \lambda A + l = \lambda A + \frac{1}{m} lW(I + E) \tag{9.3}$$

Here λ is a $1 \times n$ value vector and $E = diag(e_1, e_2, \ldots, e_n)$ where e_i denotes the rate of surplus value of the ith sector, and m is the MELT, which is defined as the ratio of total money value-added to the total labor time according to the NI.

Equation (9.3), like (9.1), describes a "photographed" relation between values and the sectoral rates of exploitation. Therefore, given parameters on the right-hand side produce the probability distribution of the λ_i's. The crux of our simulation is to compare these λ_i's with the p_i's calculated from (9.2).

Before delving into the equations to be used in the simulations, let us check the results of the usual simplifying assumption of the equalized rate of exploitation. As explained in Sect. 2.5 of Chapter 2, the uniform rate of surplus value, $e_i = \overline{e}$ makes the number of unknowns equal to that of equations. In other words, $I + E$ in Eq. (9.3) becomes $(1 + \overline{e})I$. Therefore, Eq. (9.3) is changed to:

$$\lambda = (\frac{1 + \overline{e}}{m})lW(I - A)^{-1} \tag{9.4}$$

Equation (9.2) can be rewritten with respect to total wages, lW:

$$lW = p[I - A(I + R)](I + R)^{-1} \tag{9.5}$$

Substituting (9.5) for (9.4) leads to:

$$\begin{aligned}\lambda &= \left(\frac{1 + \overline{e}}{m}\right)p[I - A(I + R)](I + R)^{-1}(I - A)^{-1} \\ &= \left(\frac{1 + \overline{e}}{m}\right)p[(I + R)^{-1} - A](I - A)^{-1} \end{aligned} \tag{9.6}$$

As $\overline{e}$ here is equal to the profit-wage ratio of the entire economy,[2] it is possible to solve for λ starting from observable data on the right-hand side, namely the MELT (m), the technological conditions of production (A), and the sectorally different rates of profit (R), all of which are *ex-post* parameters.

[2] Here, the distinction between productive and unproductive labor is assumed away for simplicity. When the distinction is introduced, the rate of surplus value will diverge from the profit-wage ratio. In the case of South Korea during the period 1995–2015, the gap between the rate of surplus value and the profit-wage ratio has grown while both experienced an upward trend (Rieu & Park, 2020, p. 292).

Now the issue is how to introduce labor heterogeneity into the basic equations above.

First, as heterogeneous labors may be exploited at different rates, assuming unequal sectoral rates of surplus value is a plausible way to introduce labor heterogeneity. In this case, unlike Eq. (9.6), the value equation becomes:

$$\lambda = \frac{1}{m} p[(I + R)^{-1} - A](I + E)(I - A)^{-1} \tag{9.7}$$

Equation (9.7) is a form of generalizing the NI in that sectorally different rates of exploitation are permitted, which will be called Generalization NI (1) in the next section.

Second, labor heterogeneity is introduced in the form of decomposing the MELT into the VELT and the MEV at the sectoral level as well as the aggregate level. As VELT is the ratio of transforming labor time into the quantity of abstract human labor, it represents the value-creating capacity of labor or "value productivity" explained in Chapter 2.[3] For analytical convenience, it can be assumed that $E(VELT_i) = 1$.[4] A simplifying assumption of homogeneous labor implies that $VELT_i = 1$ for all i's. However, accepting the differential value-creating capacity of heterogeneous labor means that $VELT_i$ will be greater (less) than 1 if labor in the ith sector is more complex (simpler) than the social average. As already shown by the following equation in Chapter 3, the equalized sectoral rate of surplus value is not identical to the equal $VELT_i$'s. Therefore, assuming different $VELT_i$'s is another way of introducing labor heterogeneity. Undeniably, in this case, relative $VELT_i$'s should not be equal to relative wages. In such a case, the rate of surplus value would be equalized,

[3] After acceping the distinction between the VELT and the MEV, Duménil et al. (2009, p. 564) called the product of the VELT and MEV the "monetary expression of concrete labor time" to differentiate it from the MELT in the existing NI literature. It remains to be seen whether this naming is consistent with Marx's own terminology about concrete and abstract labor. However, it is tentatively accepted in this book. On the other hand, the VELT should be a pure number because its dimension is "hour/hour" while the dimension of the MEV is "dollar/hour."

[4] Undeniably, it is possible to let $VELT_i = 1$ for the simplest labor type i. In that case, for all other types of labor, $VELT_j \geq 1\,(j \neq i)$. In any case, some way of measuring the level of complexity is necessary. This issue is not pursued further here because the aim of this chapter is to examine the theoretical effect of introducing differential value-creating capacity of labor. At this stage, it is sufficient to assume that $VELT_i$'s are randomly given.

and thereby labor heterogeneity would be nullified.

$$e_i = e_j \leftrightarrow \frac{VELT_i}{w_i} = \frac{VELT_j}{w_j} \tag{3.34}$$

Now according to the second method, the value equation becomes

$$\lambda = \lambda A + lM_I = lM_I(I - A)^{-1} \tag{9.8}$$

where M_I is a diagonal matrix whose main diagonal elements are $VELT_i$'s.

On the other hand, the relation between the monetary value-added and labor time is represented as

$$V = p(I - A) = lM \tag{9.9}$$

where V is a $1 \times n$ vector of value-added and M is a diagonal matrix whose main diagonal elements are $MELT_i$'s.

As the MELT is decomposed into the VELT and the MEV, the following relation holds where M_{II} is a diagonal matrix whose main diagonal elements are MEV_i's.

$$M = M_I M_{II} \tag{9.10}$$

MEV_i is the coefficient for transforming the value of the net product produced in the *i*th sector into the corresponding unit of money, i.e., money value-added, and therefore, the increasing (decreasing) MEV_i implies that the same amount of abstract labor is transformed into a higher (lower) price in the *i*th sector.[5]

Labor heterogeneity in this framework implies that the $VELT_i$'s and MEV_i's differ across sectors. Note that a uniform $MELT_i$ does not guarantee equalized $VELT_i$'s and MEV_i's as already explained in Chapter 3.

To illustrate this point, an extreme two-sector example will be helpful:

[5] As is well known, Marx, in his third volume of *Capital*, argued that the price of production is greater (smaller) than the monetary equivalent of value in the sectors with organic compositions of capital greater (smaller) than social average (Marx, 1981, p. 264). This means that the greater the organic composition of capital in the *i*th sector, the greater MEV_i is.

Suppose that the value-creating capacity of the labor in sector 1 is only half of the labor in sector 2, while the $MELT_i$'s are equal between the two sectors. In other words, sector 1 earns double the money that sector 2 earns with the same amount of value. A numerical example for this situation is $M = \begin{pmatrix} 1 & 0 \\ 0 & 1 \end{pmatrix}$, where $M_I = \begin{pmatrix} 0.5 & 0 \\ 0 & 2 \end{pmatrix}$ and $M_{II} = \begin{pmatrix} 2 & 0 \\ 0 & 0.5 \end{pmatrix}$. If one compares this composition of two matrices with the homogeneous labor case, namely, $M_I = M_{II} = I$, the implication of labor heterogeneity will be made clear.

Using Eqs. (9.8), (9.9), and (9.10), the value equation can be represented as a function of the physical conditions of production, market prices, and sectorally different $MELT_i$'s.[6]

$$\lambda = lM_I(I - A)^{-1} = lMM_{II}^{-1}(\mathrm{I} - \mathrm{A})^{-1} = p(I - A)M_{II}^{-1}(\mathrm{I} - \mathrm{A})^{-1} \tag{9.11}$$

Psotmultiplying bott sides of Eq. (9.11) by $(I - A)M_{II}$ yields

$$\lambda(I - A)M_{II} = p(I - A) \tag{9.12}$$

Equation (9.12) implies either that the sum of the monetary equivalent of values of the net product of the entire economy is equal to the total monetary value-added or that the MEV is defined with respect to the net product. This corresponds to axiom 1 of the NI in Chapter 3. This will be called Generalized NI (2) in the next section.

9.3 Simulation Analysis

9.3.1 Physical and Monetary Flows

To run a simulation, some structural relations regarding the physical and monetary flows of the economy should be established first. Price and value equations, (9.1) and (9.3) are not sufficient to proceed to a simulation because they do not provide information about quantities. Something such as an equilibrium condition for Marx's scheme of the reproduction will be needed.

[6] Note that M_I and M_{II} are nonsingular matrices because their main diagonals are all positive. Therefore, the inverse matrices of M_I and M_{II} exist.

This chapter adopts Greenblatt's (2014) stochastic model for simulations without any modification regarding physical and monetary flows. The reasons are twofold. First, the model has the merit of providing a solution to the problem of determining physical and monetary flows. Second, as Greenblatt (2014)'s main objective is to confirm price-labor content proportionality, it is useful as a starting point to examine the effect of labor heterogeneity. Furthermore, "the monetary equivalent of labor time"[7] is used as an important variable in the model. As the equilibrium conditions of physical and monetary flows are imposed to determine the total employment and sectoral labor inputs, it is not necessary to introduce any restrictive assumptions about production conditions such as constant returns to scale (Roberts, 2009, p. 592).

The basic structure of the model is as follows.

There are n industries or sectors, each of which produces only one commodity. Commodities 1, 2, ..., k are consumption goods, and commodities $k + 1$, $k + 2$,..., $k + n$ are production goods. There are two classes, capitalists and workers. Capitalists do not save. This is Marx's assumption of simple reproduction which does not cause any loss of generality.

Let us check physical flows first.

It will be useful here to refer to the equilibrium conditions for Marx's scheme of simple reproduction in the second volume of *Capital* which has the same structure as Grennblatt's (2014) model. They consist of two demand–supply equilibrium conditions for two departments: department I producing production goods and department II producing consumption goods.

Here the supply of production goods is represented as $\xi_i l_i$ $(i = k + 1, k + 2, \ldots, k + n)$ where ξ_i and l_i denote the physical productivity index and the employment quantity of the ith sector, respectively.[8] As the demand for the production good only comes from capitalists, and there is no demand for new investment due to the assumption of simple reproduction, it can be represented as the sum of $\xi_j l_j a_{ij}$'s $(j = 1, 2, \ldots, n)$

[7] As this concept is defined as the ratio of total money value-added to total labor time (Greenblatt, 2014, p. 526), it corresponds to NI's MELT.

[8] Greenblatt (2014)'s parameter ξ_i plays an important role here to introduce labor heterogeneity. This is similar to Ricci (2021, p. 110)'s distinction between the "labour expression of value" and the "monetary expression of value" in that the physical quantity of the commodity is used as a medium for connecting labor time and price.

where a_{ij} denotes the input coefficient defined in the conventional way. In a similar way, the supply of consumption goods is $\xi_i l_i$ ($i = 1, 2,\ldots, k$), while the demand for them is the sum of workers' demand, $l_i d_{ij}^W$ and capitalists' demand $l_i d_{ij}^K$ ($j = 1, 2,\ldots,n$), where d_{ij} denotes the demand for the ith commodity in the jth sector. The superscripts, W and K denote workers and capitalists, respectively.

Therefore, the demand–supply equilibrium condition is represented as follows.

$$l\Xi = l(D + A\Xi)^T \tag{9.13}$$

where $l = (l_1, l_2, \ldots, l_n)$ and $\Xi = diag(\xi_1, \xi_2, \ldots, \xi_n)$. D is the matrix representing the sum of the workers' demand for consumption goods, D_W and the capitalists' demand for consumption goods, D_K.

Equation (9.13) consists of n equations with n unknowns. The quantity of employment of each sector as well as of the entire economy is determined under the given input coefficients (A), demand conditions (D), and physical productivity data (Ξ). When postmultiplying both sides of (9.13) by Ξ^{-1}, l becomes the left eigenvector of $(D + A\Xi)^T\Xi^{-1}$ with the eigenvalue set to 1.

On the other hand, monetary flows run in the opposite direction to physical flows in the form of incomes and expenses. Equation (9.1) can be rewritten as:

$$p = (pA + lW)(I + R) = pA + \mu + \iota\Xi^{-1}W \tag{9.14}$$

where μ is the $1 \times n$ vector of sectoral markup per unit of commodity μ_i's and ι is an all-ones vector; and therefore, $\iota\Xi^{-1}W$ is a diagonal matrix whose main diagonal elements are $\frac{w_i}{\xi_i}$'s.[9]

Assuming that the budget constraints of capitalists and workers are satisfied with equality leads to $\mu_i\xi_i = \sum_{j=1}^n p_j d_{ji}^K$ and $w_i = \sum_{j=1}^n p_j d_{ji}^W$.[10] Combining these constraints with Eq. (9.14) produces the following relation. When the elements of P are given, z is solved as an

[9] As Ξ is a diagonal matrix, $\Xi^{-1} = diag(\xi_1^{-1}, \xi_2^{-1}, \ldots, \xi_n^{-1})$.

[10] As workers do not buy production goods, $\sum_{j=k+1}^n p_j d_{ji}^W = 0$, and therefore, $\sum_{j=1}^n p_j d_{ji}^W = \sum_{j=1}^k p_j d_{ji}^W$.

eigenvector of P with eigenvalue 1.

$$z = zP \tag{9.15}$$

where $z = (p_1, p_2, ...p_n, \mu_1, \mu_2, ..., \mu_n, w_1, w_2, ...w_n)$ and $P = \begin{pmatrix} A & \Xi^{-1}D_K^T & D_W^T \\ I & 0 & 0 \\ \Xi^{-1} & 0 & 0 \end{pmatrix}$.

As noted above, the MELT (m) can also be determined by

$$m = pDl^T / \sum_{i=1}^{n} l_i \tag{9.16}$$

The denominator is the sum of working hours, and the numerator is the sum of the total monetary value-added in the entire economy.

9.3.2 *Methods*

Monte Carlo simulation methods were used to verify the model. Although the essential structure is equivalent to that of Hahn and Rieu (2017), the simulation was performed 20,000 times to obtain a robust result here.

Greenblatt's (2014) basic simulation structure was reproduced in the simulation analysis as follows:

The number of firms is set to 64, half of which produce production goods, whereas the other half produce consumption goods. For each model, a simulation was run with random numbers generated from a uniform distribution. Nonzero elements of D_W, D_K and A are assumed to be within the interval [0.25, 0.75). For nonzero elements of Ξ, the interval [1, 3) is given. If D_W, D_K and A are given, then l and z can be solved for from (9.13) and (9.15).

The logical structure of simulations using this chapter's notation is illustrated in Fig. 9.1. In the first step, elements of nonlabor input coefficients, physical productivity data, and market demand conditions are randomly generated. From these parameter values, total employment and its sectoral composition, sectoral prices, wages, and profits are obtained to satisfy demand-supply equilibrium conditions. More important, the MELT, including its application at the sectoral level, is also obtained. In the next step, the crucial question is whether rates of surplus value

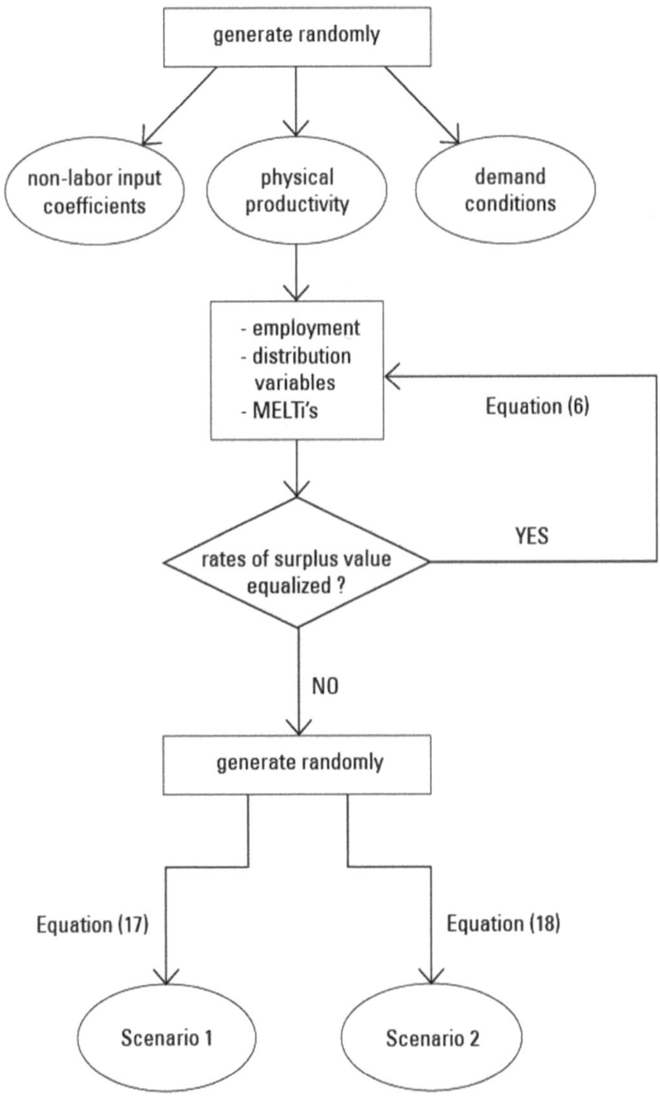

Fig. 9.1 Flow chart of simulations

are equalized. In the case of the uniform rate of surplus value, a simulation is not required. However, for the purpose of comparison, the price-value relation in this case will also be reported. The main focus here is to introduce labor heterogeneity by two methods, Generalized NI (1) and Generalized NI (2), which will be called Scenario 1 and Scenario 2, respectively.

Equations (9.7) and (9.12) are solved by simulations. Combining the demand–supply equilibrium conditions derived above with these two equations produces the following relations.

$$\lambda \Xi l^T = \frac{1}{m} p\left[(I+R)^{-1} - A\right](I+E)(I-A)^{-1}\Xi l^T \tag{9.17}$$

$$\lambda (I-A) M_{II} \Xi l^T = p(I-A)\Xi l^T \tag{9.18}$$

Equation (9.17) is for Scenario 1 while Eq. (9.18) is for Scenario 2.

To run a simulation, the sectoral rates of surplus value, e_i's are randomly given within a certain range. Although there are few credible data on the sectoral rates of surplus value, one can find estimates on the sectoral labor income shares as the first approximation. As explained in 3.4.4 of Chapter 3, the labor income share of sector i is a proxy, albeit a poor one, for $1/(1+e_i)$. According to Jeon and Joo (2015), the lowest labor income share in South Korea was estimated as 0.4288, whereas the highest was 0.6266 in 2013. This implies that the highest sectoral rate of surplus value was approximately 133.2 percent while the lowest rate was approximately 59.6 percent, and the ratio of the former to the latter was approximately 2.23. Considering these data, the range of e_i was set such that the highest was three times as large as the lowest in the simulation.

On the other hand, according to Eq. (9.18), the range of the $VELT_i$ is crucial. To yield the same degree of volatility as Scenario 1, $VELT_i$'s were given randomly and uniformly within the interval [0.5, 1.5) where $E(VELT_i) = 1$, and therefore the matrix M_I was determined.[11] As the

[11] Duménil et al. (2009, p. 563) provided the normalization condition, $\sum_{i=1}^{n} VELT_i l_i = \sum_{i=1}^{n} l_i$ in this chapter's notations. However, this condition is not needed for our purpose here. Even if $\sum_{i=1}^{n} VELT_i l_i = k \sum_{i=1}^{n} l_i$ (k $\neq$ 1), one can make new $VELT_i$'s by dividing old $VELT_i$'s by k. Then, the normalization condition would be satisfied. The matrix M_I in Eq. (9.8) would be $(\frac{1}{k})M_I$ in this case, and therefore, there will be no change in relative values.

matrix M was determined in the first step in Fig. 9.1, M_{II} will also be determined through Eq. (9.10). Finally, λ is determined in the Eq. (9.18).

A criterion for evaluating value-price deviation, Steedman and Tomkins's (1998) "physical quantity-free measure," will be adopted here not because of its exactness but because it has been widely used.[12] Steedmand and Tomkins's (1998) "distant measure" is

$$d = 2sin\frac{\alpha}{2} = \sqrt{2(1 - cos\alpha)},\ where\ tan\,\alpha = \frac{\sigma_{p*}}{\mu_{p*}} \tag{9.19}$$

where $p^* = \left(p_1^*, p_2^*, ..., p_n^*\right) = \left(\frac{p_1}{w_1\lambda_1}, \frac{p_2}{w_2\lambda_2}, ..., \frac{p_1}{w_n\lambda_n}\right)$. μ_{p*} and σ_{p*} denote the arithmetic average and the standard deviation of the p^* elements, respectively. The greater the d-value is, the greater the value-price deviation.

9.3.3 *Results*

Figure 9.2 illustrates the kernel density of profit rates. Kernel estimation methods were used to find the empirical distribution of the observed minimums, averages, medians, and maximums in 20,000 simulations. The average rate of profit was between 30 and 40 percent. The extreme values vary over an approximately threefold range, which was approximately one and half times greater than Greenblatt's (2014) results.

To check if the price-value proportionality was maintained, prices were regressed on values. The adjusted R^2 values of the regressions are shown in Fig. 9.3. For comparison purposes, the Standard NI in which the sectoral rates of surplus value are equalized is also illustrated. As the R^2's in this case are near 1, it is easily confirmed that the direct linear proportionality exists between value and price. In Scenario 1, similar to Greenblatt's (2014) simulation results, the adjusted R^2's still show a near normal distribution with its center equal to approximately 0.9. Only in Scenario 2 did this proportionality seem to disappear. This is the most important result of our simulation analysis in the sense that only the second method of introducing labor heterogeneity produces a qualitative change.

[12] The so-called "spurious correlation" literature mainly emphasizes that the proportionality or nondeviation thesis was a result of biases due to sectorally different physical quantities. Steedman and Tomkins (1998) attempted to remove this problem. However, it was also criticized by Díaz and Osuna (2009), who was refuted by Fröhlich (2012).

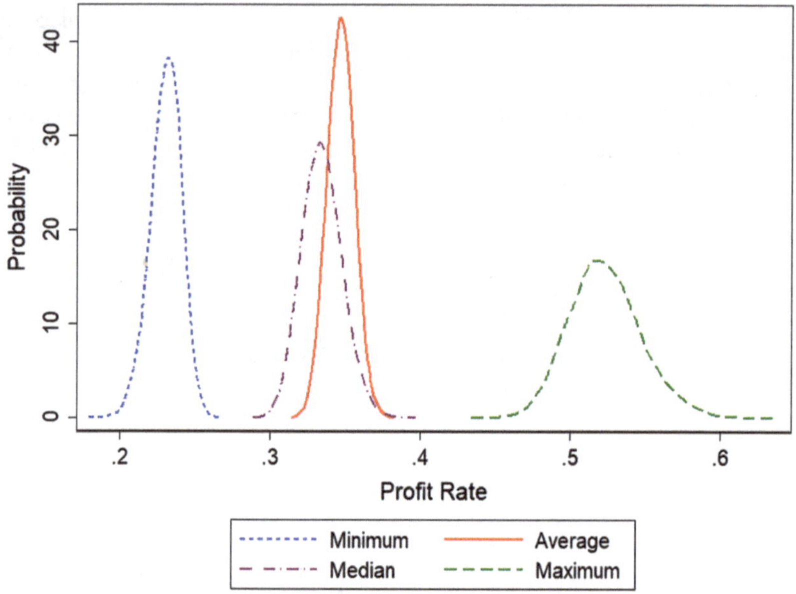

Fig. 9.2 Simulated density functions of profit rates

Finally, Table 9.1 illustrates Steedam and Tomkins's (1998) "distance measure" which was calculated as the average of all the simulations. Additionally, in the case of the d-value, only Scenario 2 showed a significantly greater magnitude, 0.1636 compared with the other two cases. This number is substantial. Unfortunately, however, it is not yet clear how a large d-value disproves price-value proportionality, although many empirical studies have been performed previously. The main thrust of the present chapter, however, is to show that not only does the d-value leap, but also the volatility of its distribution grows dramatically only in Scenario 2. Figure 9.4 illustrates the empirical distribution of the "distance measure" by the kernel density function.

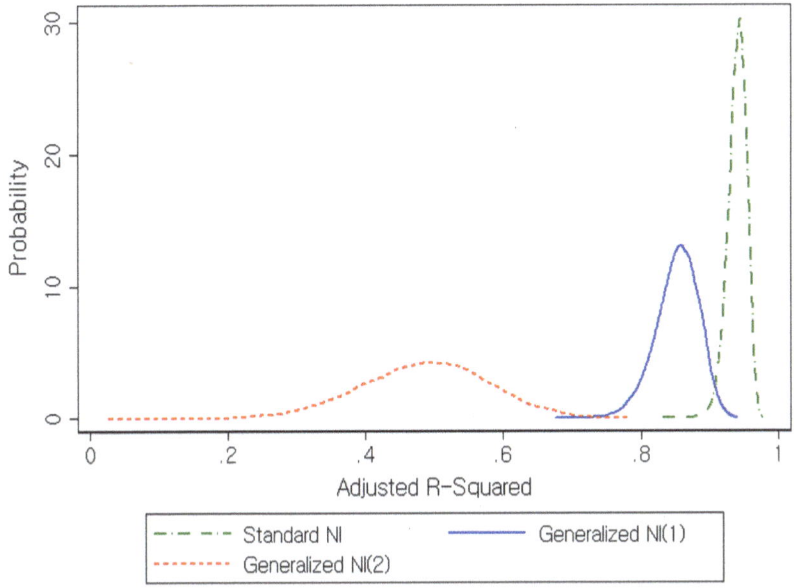

Fig. 9.3 Simulated density functions of adjusted R-Squared on price-value regression

Table 9.1 Price-value distance measure

	α^0	$\frac{\sigma_p^*}{\mu_p^*}$	$\alpha(radian)$	d
Standard NI	3.8119	0.0666	0.0665	0.0665
Generalized NI(1)	4.8626	0.0851	0.0849	0.0848
Generalized NI(2)	9.3815	0.1653	0.1637	0.1636

9.4 Conclusion

In this chapter, using a stochastic model developed by Greenblatt (2014), the effect of labor heterogeneity was examined by a simulation analysis.

As Marx himself explained in Volume 3 of *Capital*, a systematic divergence between value and price is one of the most important analytical results of Marxian value theory as a theory of price that differentiates

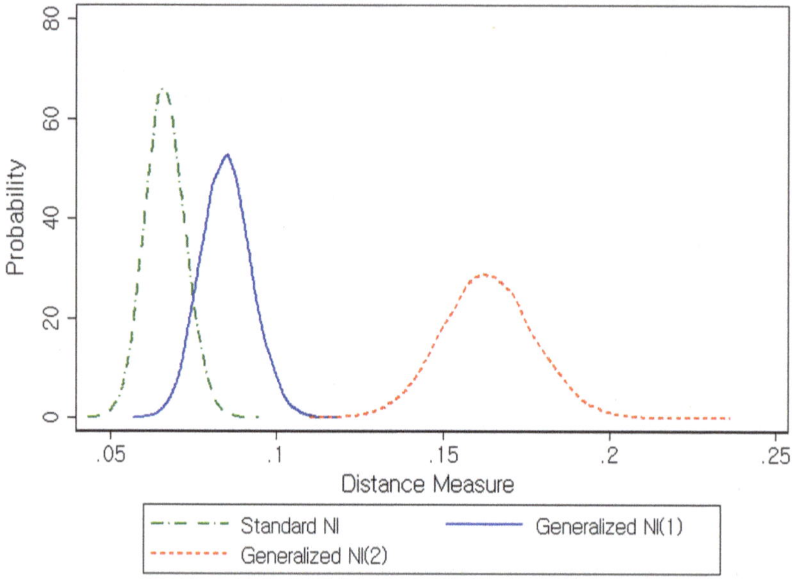

Fig. 9.4 Simulated density functions of distance measure on price-value deviation

it from Ricardian value theory. While the exact meaning of the price-value proportionality literature is still "obscure" (Foley, 2000, p. 19), it is obvious that the direct proportionality between price and value makes the value concept redundant, rather than proving the potential of the theory in explaining prices. Although the NI was purported to be a theory of aggregate macroeconomic variables at least in its early stage of development, the NI also implicitly provided a rule for value-price deviation at the microeconomic level as seen in Chapter 3.

The simulation results of this chapter are quite interesting in that merely introducing unequal sectoral rates of surplus value was not sufficient to produce value-price deviation. In Scenario 1, labor heterogeneity was introduced randomly with a threefold range in the sectoral rates of surplus value. In Scenario 2, to give the same degree of volatility, the sectoral value expression of labor was given randomly within the same interval. However, the effect on the relation between price and labor content was conspicuous in the latter case. To complement the results, observations using Steedman and Tomkins's (1998) "distance measure" were also provided. Contrary to Cogliano et al.'s (2022, p. 327) comments on a previous version of this chapter, merely introducing randomness does not necessarily lead to the weakened proportionality between value and price. Only in Scenario 2, in other words, in Generalized NI (2) where labor heterogeneity was introduced in the form of differential value-creating capacity of labor types, did value-price proportionality disappear.

The results of this chapter have an important implication for the generalization of the NI. Decomposing the MELT into the VELT and the MEV, in particular at the microeconomic level, is critical to refute price-value proportionality. In this sense, it supports this book's proposition that uneven sectoral development should be explained further by way of the decomposition of the MELT.

References

Cockshott, W. P., & Cottrell, A. (2005). Robust correlation between prices and labour values: A comment. *Cambridge Journal of Economics, 29*(2), 309–316.

Cogliano, J. F., Veneziani, R., & Yoshihara, N. (2022). Computational methods and classical-Marxian economics. *Journal of Economic Surveys, 36*(2), 310–349.

Díaz, E., & Osuna, R. (2009). From correlation to dispersion: Geometry of the price-value deviation. *Empirical Economics, 36*(2), 427–440.

Duménil, G. (1980). *De la valeur aux prix de production*. Economica.

Duménil, G., Foley, D. K., & Lévy, D. (2009). A note on the formal treatment of exploitation with heterogeneous labor. *Metroeconomica, 60*(3), 560–567.

Farjoun, E., & Machover, M. (1983). *Laws of chaos: A probabilistic approach to political economy*. Verso.

Foley, D. K. (1982). The value of money, the value of labor power and the Marxian transformation problem. *Review of Radical Political Economics, 14*(2), 37–47.

Foley, D. K. (2000). Recent developments in the labor theory of value. *Review of Radical Political Economics, 32*(1), 1–39.

Foley, D. K. (2005). Marx's theory of money in historical perspective. In F. Moseley (Eds.), *Marx's theory of money*. Palgrave Macmillan.

Fröhlich, N. (2012). Labour values, prices of production and the missing equalisation tendency of profit rates: Evidence from the German economy. *Cambridge Journal of Economics, 37*(5), 1107–1126.

Greenblatt, R. E. (2014). A dual theory of price and value in a meso-scale economic model with stochastic profit rate. *Physica A: Statistical Mechanics and Its Applications, 416*, 518–531.

Hahn, S. B., & Rieu, D.-M. (2017). Generalizing the new interpretation of the Marxian value theory: A simulation analysis with stochastic profit rate and labor. *Review of Political Economy, 29*(4), 597–612.

Han, C., & Li, M. (2020). Do labor values explain Chines prices? Evidence from China's input-output tables, 1990–2012. *Review of Radical Political Economics, 52*(1), 115–136.

Jeon, S. M., & S. Joo. (2015). Measuring labor income shares at the industry level for Korea (In Korean). *Journal of Korea Development Economics Association, 25*(4), 35–76.

Kliman, A. (2002). The law of value and laws of statistics: Sectoral values and prices in the US economy, 1977–97. *Cambridge Journal of Economics, 26*(3), 299–311.

Kliman, A. (2004). Spurious value-price correlations: Some additional evidence and arguments'. *Research in Political Economy, 21*, 223–238.

Marx, K. (1977). *Capital* (Vol. 1). Progress Publishers.

Marx, K. (1981). *Capital* (Vol. 3). Penguin.

Moseley, F. (2021). A critique of Shaikh's two interpretations of Marx's 'transformation problem.' *Cambridge Journal of Economics, 45*(3), 577–589.

Ochoa, E. (1984). *Labor-values and prices of production: An interindustry study of the U.S. economy, 1947–1972.* Ph.D. Dissertation, New School for Social Research, New York. UMI 8500220. Ann Arbor, Michigan.

Ricci, A. (2021). *Value and unequal exchange in international trade: The geography of global capitalist exploitation.* Routledge.

Rieu, D.-M. (2008). Estimating sectoral rates of surplus value: Methodological issues. *Metroeconomica, 59*(4), 557–573.

Rieu, D.-M. (2009). The "new interpretation": Questions answered and unanswered. *Metroeconomica, 60*(3), 568–570.

Rieu, D.-M., & Park, H. W. (2020). Unproductive activities and the rate of surplus value at the industry level in Korea, 1995–2015. *Journal of Contemporary Asia, 50*(2), 284–307.

Roberts, B. B. (2009). Ricardo: Standard commodity: :Marx: ? *Review of Political Economy, 21*(4), 589–619.

Roncaglia, A. (1978). *Sraffa and the theory of prices.* Wiley.

Shaikh, A. (1984). The transformation from Marx to Sraffa. In E. Mandel & A. Freeman (Eds.), *Ricardo, Marx, Sraffa: The Langston memorial volume.* Verso.

Steedman, I., & Tomkins, J. (1998). On measuring the deviation of prices from values. *Cambridge Journal of Economics, 22*(3), 379–385.

Tsoulfidis, L., & Maniatis, T. (2002). Values, prices of production and market prices: Some more evidence from the Greek economy. *Cambridge Journal of Economics, 26*(3), 359–369.

Tsoulfidis, L., & Rieu, D.-M. (2006). Labor values, prices of production, and wage-profit rate frontiers of the Korean economy. *Seoul Journal of Economics, 19*(3), 275–296.

CHAPTER 10

On Marx's Distinction Between Produktivkraft and Produktivität

10.1 Introduction

In Volume 1, Chapter 15[1] of *Das Kapital*, Marx identifies three factors—the length of the working day, labor intensity, and the productivity of labor—that determine the price of labor power and the relative magnitude of surplus value. Further, he performs a comparative static analysis on cases where one of them changes. For the first case, where the working day and labor intensity remain the same while the productivity of labor changes, Marx explains that the value is not altered, even if the amount of goods produced changes. In other words, "a working day of a given length always creates the same amount of value" (Marx, 1976, p. 656). Marx's explanation is easily understood when the productivity of labor shifts at the same rate in all sectors simultaneously. However, does this statement hold even if the productivity of labor changes only in a specific sector, or if the rates of change in the productivity of labor in several sectors are generally uneven? This question will be discussed in Chapter 11 and marks the starting point for the topic in the present chapter.

[1] Chapter 17 in the English edition. Hereinafter, the chapter classification of *Das Kapital* is based on the German edition.

D.-M. Rieu, *A Mathematical Approach to Marxian Value Theory*, Marx, Engels, and Marxisms,
https://doi.org/10.1007/978-3-031-07808-8_10

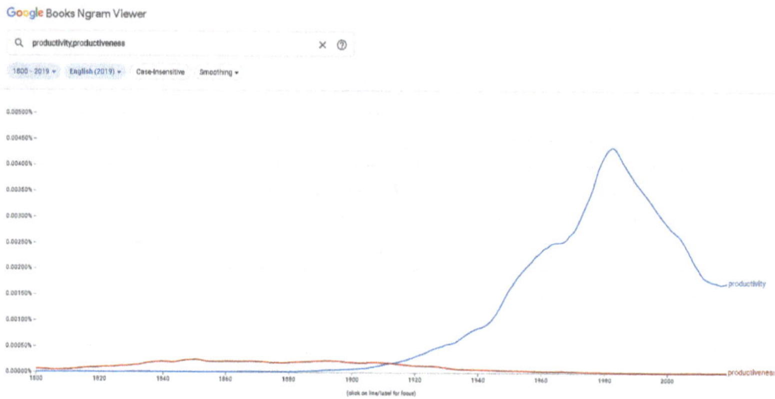

Fig. 10.1 Frequency of usage of the terms "productiveness" and "productivity"

The "productivity of labor" is the translation of the original German term "Produktivkraft der Arbeit," which literally translates as the "productive power of labor" or the "productive force of labor." Produkitvkraft was originally noted as "productivity" in the English translation released by Penguin Books, translated by Ben Fowkes. In another English translation by Progress Publishers in the former Soviet Union, the term was rendered as the somewhat unfamiliar term "productiveness."[2]

A review using Google Ngram Viewer in Fig. 10.1 indicated that "productivity" was not a commonly used term until the end of the nineteenth century, whereas "productiveness" was frequently used. Hence, we can deduce that the Progress Publishers' edition used the terminology from Marx's time, unlike the Penguin Books' edition. In fact, the Progress Publishers' edition claims that it is based on the first English version of *Das Kapital*, translated after Marx's death by Samuel Moore and Edward Aveling in 1887. However, this interpretation does not clearly answer the question. This is because, in *Das Kapital*, Marx also uses the term Produktivität.

[2] Reuten (2018, p. 134) noted this point as a mistranslation, arguing that Marx's "productive power of labour" and "productivity of labor" are not the same concept. Reuten's assertion is one of the central hypotheses tested in this chapter. Ruben (1988) had a similar view.

10.2 Produktivkraft Versus Produktivität

Was Marx using the terms Produktivkraft and Produktivität under strict conceptual distinction or were they used interchangeably as synonyms without any particular intention? Considering the nature of the German language, as well as Marx's inclination for being faithful to concepts, it is difficult to believe that either one was chosen and used depending on the instance.[3] Therefore, it is necessary to examine the use of the two words, with a focus on Volume 1 of *Das Kapital*, which was published and revised in Marx's lifetime.

Most notably, the intensification of labor is explained to increase Produktivität, which is classified as a factor separate from Produktivkraft. In other words, in "2. The Specialized Worker and His Tools" of Volume 1, Chapter 12 ("The Division of Labor and Manufacture"), there is a section that considers the increase in labor intensity to be the cause of rise in the productivity of labor.[4]

> [A] Die gesteigerte Produktivität ist hier entweder der zunehmenden Ausgabe von Arbeitskraft in einem gegebnen Zeitraum geschuldet, also wachsender Intensität der Arbeit, oder einer Abnahme des unproduktiven Verzehrs von Arbeitskraft. (Marx, 1867, p. 323)[5]

In quote [A], it is clearly stated that the intensification of labor is a factor that leads to an increase in the productivity of labor. The sentence is presented as follows in Ben Fowkes' translation; that is, like Produktivkraft, Produktivität is also translated as "productivity."

[3] Friedrich List distinguished the theory of productive forces (Produkitvkräfte) from the theory of value in *Das Nationale System der Politischenökonomie* (1841). In criticizing Adam Smith, List argued that "his investigations are limited to that human activity which creates material values..."; Further, by noting only physical labor as "productive forces" (Produkitvkräfte), he "laid the foundation for all the absurdities and contradictions" (List, 1909, p. 111). In short, for List, the stipulations that give positive meaning to Produkitvkräfte are already present. Thus, it is necessary to theoretically explore what kind of influence this attitude may have had on Marx.

[4] All the underlined areas have been added by the author to compare the original German term with the English or French translations.

[5] This quote was deemed especially important and was taken from the first edition of *Das Kapital*. It has been placed here to determine whether Marx used the term Produktivität from the start.

> [A-Ben Fowkes] The resulting increase of productivity is due either to an increased expenditure of labour-power in a given time—i.e., increased intensity of labour—or to a decrease in the amount of labor-power unproductively consumed. (Marx, 1976, p. 460)

Conversely, as seen in the following segment, the Progress Publishers' edition translated Produktivität as "productive power." It seems clear that it does not have the principle of choosing "productive power" only for "Produkitivkraft."

> [A-Progress] The resulting increased productive power is owing either to an increased expenditure of labor-power in a given time i.e., to increased intensity of labor or to a decrease in the amount of labor-power unproductively consumed. (Marx, 2015, p. 239)

Ultimately, quote [A] clearly states that the intensification of labor is a factor that leads to rise in the productivity of labor, and the interpretation that it leads to an increase in productive power is a deviation present only in the Progress Publishers' edition.

However, in Chapter 15, "Changes of Magnitude in the Price of Labor-Power and in Surplus-Value," Section IV-2 (B in the English edition) analyzes a case where labor is intensified, and the productive power of labor is deepened, while the length of the working day is simultaneously decreased ("Zunehmende Intensität und Produktivkraft der Arbeit mit gleichzeitiger Verkürzung des Arbeitstags"). The following compares the original German, Ben Fowkes' and Progress Publishers' editions, quoting a sentence from the text.

> [B] Gesteigerte Produktivkraft der Arbeit und ihre wachsende Intensität wirken nach einer Seite hin gleichförmig.. (Marx, 1975, p. 552)

> [B-Ben Fowkes] Increased productivity and greater intensity of labour both have a similar effect. (Marx, 1976, p. 666)

> [B-Progress] Increased productiveness and greater intensity of labour, both have a like effect. (Marx, 2015, p. 373)

In [B], the productive power of labor and labor intensity is treated as separate categories. In other words, the intensification of labor is not a factor that improves the productive power of labor.[6] Up until this point, it has been interpreted that the intensification of labor increases the productivity of labor (quote [A]), but does not increase the productive power of labor (quote [B]), based on which, productivity and productive power are different concepts; therefore, the translation of the Penguin Books' edition is rendered incorrect.

As such, when translating quote [A], did Progress Publishers—and even further back into the past, Moor and Aveling—simply mistranslate or deliberately translate the text as they did? To answer this question, the French translation of M.J. Roy (1875), which Marx himself supervised during his lifetime, was reviewed. The French version began to be published in 1872 as a series of fascicles, finishing in 1875. The subtitle of the French version contains the phrase "entirely revised by the author [entièrement revisée par l'auteur]." In the introduction to the French edition, Marx wrote, "Mr. J. Roy set himself the task of producing a version that would be as exact and literal as possible," and that "these alterations, introduced from day to day, as the book was published in parts, were not made with equal care and were bound to result in a lack of harmony in style..." As such, "whatever the literary defects of this French edition may be, it possesses a scientific value independent of the original and should be consulted even by readers familiar with German" (Marx, 1976, p. 105). Upon such a reference, the literary value of the French edition has been widely recognized (Anderson, 1983; Hayashi, 1975). The parts significantly revised in the French version compared to the first German edition were the chapters on the theory of value-form and capital accumulation. Nevertheless, as noted in the quote, Marx himself had complained regarding Roy's excessively literal translation. In a letter to F. Bolte on February 12, 1873, Marx grumbled, "this requires more effort than performing the entire translation myself" (Hayashi, 1975, p. 33).

Here, however, the two parts in question—Produktivität in [A] and Produktivkraft in [B]—are both translated as "productivité," whereas Produktivkraft in Chapter 1, as presented in [C] below, is translated as "force productive."

[6] Although he did not provide exegetical foundations, Ruben (1988, p. 10) also maintained that "Presenting labor intensity as a productive power certainly does not make any economic sense."

> [C] Der Wertgröße einer Ware bliebe daher konstant wäre die zu ihrer Produktion erheischte Arbeitzeit konstant. Letztere wechselt aber mit jedem Wechsel in der Produktivkraft der Arbeit. (Marx, 1975, p. 54)

> [C-Roy] La quantité de valeur d'une marchandise resterait évidement constante si le temps nécessaire à sa production restait anssi constant. Mais ce dernier varie avec chaque modification de la force productive du travail,... (Marx, 1875, p. 15)

Ultimately, in Volume 1 of the French edition that Marx himself supervised, Produktivkraft was only given a separate translation in explaining the value determination of commodities in earlier chapters, whereas in Chapter 15, the term was consistently translated as "productivity." Hence, there is, in fact, another edition unlike that of Progress Publishers (or the original edition translated by Moore and Aveling) and it is not a literal translation of the German version.

However, in Chapter 15 of the French translation by Jean-Pierre Lefebvre, which was published through textual verification by Étienne Balibar and others, Produktivkraft is translated as "force productive" instead of "productivité."

> [D-Lefebvre] Ceci étant supposé, il est apparu que les grandeurs relatives du prix de la force de travail et de la survaleur étaient déterminées par trois facteurs : 1. la longueur de la journée de travail ou grandeur extensive du travail ; 2. l'intensité normale, ou grandeur intensive, du travail qui fait qu'en un temps déterminé terminé tel quantum déterminé de travail est dépensé ; 3. enfin la force productive du travail, qui fait qu'en fonction du degré de développement des conditions de production, le même quantum de travail fournira dan le même temps un quantum plus ou moins important de produits. (Marx, 1993, pp. 581–582)

In sum, except for Roy's French edition, we can deduce that Marx used the term "productivity of labor" under a broader definition than the "productive power of labor." In other words, the scope covered by the productivity increase under capitalism is wider than that covered by the increase in productive power. In short, the intensification of labor cannot be regarded as a true increase in the productive power of labor. However, the question of interpreting Roy's choices for translation remains.

In a letter to Maurice Lachâtre, a publishing agent for the French edition, Marx expresses concern, writing, "the French public, always impatient to come to a conclusion, eager to know the connection between general principles and the immediate questions that have aroused their passions, may be disheartened" (Marx, 1976, p. 104), from which we can assume that he strove to explain the German conceptual terms. Fortunately, we found the part that confirmed this assumption, for which we may refer to a quote from "C. Intensification of labor" in Chapter 13, "Machinery and Large-Scale Industry."

> [E] Im allgemeinen besteht die Produktionsmethode des relativen Mehrwerts darin, durch gesteigerte Produktivkraft der Arbeit den Arbeiter zu befähigen, mit derselben Arbeitsausgabe in derselben Zeit mehr zu produzierien. Dieselbe Arbeitszeit setzt nach wie vor dem Gesamtprodukt denselben Wert zu, obgleich dieser unveränderte Tauschwert sich jetzt in mehr Gebrauchswerten darstellt und daher der Wert der einzelnen Ware sinkt. Anders jedoch, sobald die gewaltsame Verkürzung des Arbeitstags mit dem ungeheuren Anstoß, den sie der Entwicklung der Produktivkraft und der Ökonomisierung der Produktionsbedingungen gibt, zugleich vergrößerte Arbeitsausgabe in derselben Zeit, erhöhte Anspannung der Arbeitskraft, dichtere Ausfüllung der Poren der Arbeitszeit, d'h. Kondensation der Arbiet de Arbeiter zu einem Grad aufzwingt, der nur innerhalb des verkürzten Arbeitstags erreichbar ist. (Marx, 1975, p.432)

> [E-Roy] En genéral la plus-value relative est genée par une augmentatiton de la fertilité du travail qui permet à l'ouvrier de produire davantage dan le même temps avec la même dépense de force. Le même temps de travail continue alors à rendre la même valeur d'échange, bien que celle-ci se réalise en plus de produits don chaun, pris séparément, est par conséquent d'un prix moidre. Mais cela change avec la raccourcissement légal de la journée. L'énorme impulsion qu'il donne au développement du système mécanique et à l'économie des frais contraint l'ouvrier aussi à dépenser, au moyen d'une tension supérieure, plus d'activité dan le même temps, à resseirer les pores de sa journée, et à condenser ainsi le travail à un degré qu'il ne sauraít atteindre sans ce raccourcissement. (Marx, 1875, p. 177)

[E] is a section from a long paragraph that exceeds one page in the original German edition, which is divided into two paragraphs, and with the narrative significantly modified in the French edition. Based on this chapter's purpose, we can identify that the "productive power" of labor was modified for "fertilité" (fertility) in the first paragraph. In the second paragraph, "productive power" is replaced by the "development of the mechanical system [développement du système mécanique]."

While we are on this matter, let us look at some examples that include the use of Produktivität in Volume 1 of *Das Kapital*. A very interesting example is a section where Produktivkraft and Produktivität are used in the same sentence, as presented below.

> [F] Wenn es daher auf den ersten Blick klar ist, daß die große Industrie durch Einverleibung ungeheuerer Naturkräfte und der Naturwissenschaft in den Produktionsprozeß die Produktivität der Arbeit außerordentlich steigern muß, ist es keineswegs ebenso klar, daß diese gesteigerte Produktivkraft nicht durch vermehrte Arbeitsausgabe auf der anderen Seite erkauft wird. (Marx, 1975, p. 408)

> [F-Ben Fowkes] Therefore, although it is clear at the first glance that large scale industry raises the productivity of labour to an extraordinary degree by incorporating into the production process both the immense forces of nature and the results arrived at by natural science, it is by no means equally clear that this increase in productive force is not, on the other hand, purchased with an increase in the amount of labour expended. (Marx, 1976, p. 509)

Unlike in other parts, the Ben Fowkes' edition distinguishes between productivity and productive power probably because the two terms appear simultaneously. The Progress Publishers' edition also translates these terms into productiveness and productive force, respectively (Marx, 2015, p. 268), which is interesting in that it does not translate Produktivkraft as productiveness, unlike in other parts, but rather translates Produktivität as productiveness. Examining this part alone, there seems to be no consistent translation principle in the Progress Publishers' edition. [F] includes parts that are subtle and more difficult to interpret but can be read as not deviating from the findings mentioned in this chapter so far. In other words, if the productive power of labor is understood as a concept that is narrower than the productivity of labor, the expression stresses that the development of natural science causes an increase in the productive power of labor, not the productivity of labor accompanied by an increase in effort on the part of workers.

The following quote demonstrates that Produktivität bears a negative connotation.

[G] Die Differenz jedoch zwischen der Arbeit, die sie kostet, und der Arbeit, die sie erspart, oder der Grad ihrer Produktivität hängt offenbar nich ab von der Differenz zwischen ihrem eignen Wert und dem Wert des von ihr ersetzten Werkzeugs. Die Differenz dauert so lange, als die Arbeitskosten der Maschine und daher der von ihr dem Produkt zugesetzte Wertteil kleiner bleiben als der Wert, den der Arbeiter mit seinem Werkzeug dem Arbeitsgegenstand zusetzen würde. Die Produktivität der Maschine mißt sich daher an dem Grad, worin sie menschliche Arbeitskraft ersetzt. (Marx, 1975, p. 412)

[G-Ben Fowkes] However, the difference between the labour a machine costs and the labour it saves, in other words the degree of productivity the machine possesses, does not depend on the difference between its own value and the value of the tool it replaces. As long as the labour spent on a machine is such that the portion of its value added to the product remains smaller than the value added by the worker to the product with his tool, there is always a difference of labour saved in favour of the machine. The productivity of the machine is therefore measured by the human labour-power it replaces. (Marx, 1976, p. 513)

It should be noted that the expression "productivity of the machine [Die Produktivität der Machine]" is used in the second underlined term in [G]. As is well known, Marx's labor theory of value does not use the expression that machinery (i.e., capital) is productive. In that sense, Marx's use of Produktivität here seems to be a deliberate choice of vocabulary. The following expressions, appearing in the part noting the extension of the working day as the influence of mechanical production on workers, can be understood in the same context.

[H] Wenn die Maschinerie des gewaltigste Mittle ist, die Produktivität der Arbeit zu steigern, d.h. die zur Produktion einer Ware nötige Arbeitszeit zu verkürzen, ... (Marx, 1975, p. 425)

[H-Ben Fowkes] If machinery is the most powerful means of raising the productivity of labour, i.e. of shortening the working time needed to produce a commodity,......(Marx, 1976, p. 526)

Thus, we can assume that Marx was primarily trying to refer to the productive power of labor using the concept of productive power, and that he consciously chose the term "productivity" to refer to machinery.

Notwithstanding, the following phrases indicate that there are parts that leave room for doubt, in terms of reaching the same conclusion.

> [I] Hier wie überall muß man unterscheiden zwischen der größten Produktivität, die der Entwicklung des gesellschaftlichen Produktionsprozesses, und der größten Produktivität, die seiner kapitalistischen Ausbeutung geschuldet ist. (Marx, 1975, p. 445)

> [I-Ben Fowkes] Here, as everywhere else, we must distinguish between the increased productivity which is due to the development of the social process of production, and that which is due to the exploitation by the capitalists of that development. (Marx, 1976, p. 547)

For the interpretation presented in this chapter so far to be accurate, it appears that Produktivität in the first part should have been written as Produktivkraft. Without a doubt, even in this case, the interpretation in this chapter fits if the term is read in the sense of "so-called Produktivität" having a pejorative sense. This means that among the increases in productivity that are commonly referred to, it is necessary to distinguish between those arising from the development of social productive power and those from capitalistic exploitation. The production of absolute surplus value, including the intensification of labor, would belong to the latter.[7]

10.3 The Productivity of Labor and the Productive Power of Capital

According to the analysis in the previous section, we hypothesized that Produktivkraft mostly refers to the productive power of labor, and that Produktivität is used for factors of production other than labor power, such as machinery, or in a negative sense. A question that naturally arises at this point is whether there are cases to the contrary, where expressions of the productive power (Produktivkraft) of capital or productivity (Produktivität) of labor are used. Unfortunately, we found that such cases

[7] It is debatable whether labor intensification belongs to the production of absolute surplus value or not. Rhie (1999) argued that labor intensifiction is a form of the absolute surplus value in that it neither shortens the necessary labor time, nor increases labor productivity. Although Rhie's viewpoint seems to be conventional, it fails to distinguish between labor productivity and the productive power of labor.

are numerous. Below, we examine the corresponding phrases from the PDF file[8] of Volume 1 of *Das Kapital*.

10.3.1 The Productivity of Labor

The expression "productivity of labor (Produktivität der Arbeit)" or the "productivity of social labor [Produktivität der gesellscahftlichen Arbeit]" is used 32 times in the text. Among these instances, 20 cases remained after removing those related to production tools (361), machinery (425), and natural conditions (534, 535). These cases refer to historical products of pre-capitalistic eras (535); direct or indirect citations of economists such as Ricardo (534, 539, 546, 587, 854); and indirect narrative expressions in the subordinate clause daß of "the capitalist cries out [Es zetert]" (582).[9] These remaining 20 cases were classified into two types: Productivity of Labor A and Productivity of Labor B.

First, in the case of Productivity of Labor A, as in the previous section, there are no issues in interpretation if the productivity of labor is understood as the productive power of labor in a broad sense (two parts in 581, 583, 584, 632, 651, and 654). In addition, although the following phrase also uses the expression "social labor," it is not unreasonable to interpret it to mean that the improvement of productivity, as well as productive power in a narrow sense, leads to the accumulation of capital.

> [J] Die allgemeinen Grundlagen des kapitalistischen Systems einmal gegeben, tritt im Verlauf der Akkumulation jedesmal ein Punkt ein, wo die Entwicklung der Produktivität der gesellschaftlichen Arbeit der mächtigste Hebel der Akkumulation wird. (Marx, 2015, p. 650)

> [J-Ben Fowkes] Given the general basis of the capitalist system, a point is reached in the course of accumulation at which the development of the productivity of social labour becomes the most powerful lever of accumulation. (Marx, 1976, p. 772)

[8] The 1962 edition of Volume XXIII of Marx-Engels-Werke, released by the East German publisher Dietz Verlag, was used. Available at: https://marxwirklichstudieren.files.wordpress.com/2012/11/mew_band23.pdf (Accessesd April 5, 2022).

[9] In the following, numbers in parentheses denote page numbers in the German edition.

However, Chapter 15, the starting point of the research question in this chapter, contains the following phrases.

> [K] Der Arbeitstag von gegebner Größe stellt sich stets in demselben Wertprodukt dar, wie auch die Produktivität der Arbeit, mit ihr die Produktenmasse und daher der Preis der einzelnen Ware wechsle. (Marx, 2015, p. 543)

> [K-Ben Fowkes] Firstly, a working day of a given length always creates the same

> amount of value, no matter how the productivity of labour, and, with it, the mass of the product and the price of each single commodity produced may vary. (Marx, 1976, p. 656)

In fact, "Produktivkraft der Arbeit" is consistently employed in the titles of sections and paragraphs in Chapter 15, so it is difficult to understand why "Produktivität der Arbeit" is included in the text. Two more identical applications can be found in Chapter 15 (544, 547).

Productivity of Labor A was used in a total of 11 instances; most of them are understood to have been in a broader sense than productive power. Neverthless, the expression "productivity" was used in the text only in Chapter 15 when referring to comparative statics analysis.

Next, Productivity of Labor B was used in a total of 9 instances; Produktivkraft and Produktivität appear simultaneously in the same paragraph as "productivity of labor," similarly to the aforementioned quote [F]. Eight of them (two instances in 552 and 631, four in 650, and one in quote [F]) can be interpreted as using the productivity of labor in a broader sense than the productive power of labor, as with [F] in the previous section. Notwithstanding, the last instance, that is (i.e., the next section in Chapter 23, "The General Law of Capitalist Accumulation") is not easily interpreted.

> [L] Das Gesetz, wonach eine immer wachsende Masse von Produktionsmitteln, dank dem Fortschritt in der Produktivität der gesellschaftlichen Arbeit, mit einer progressiv abnehmenden Ausgabe von Menschenkraft in Bewegung gesetzt werden kann - dies Gesetz drückt sich auf kapitalistischer Grundlage, wo nicht der Arbeiter die Arbeitsmittel, sondern die Arbeitsmittel den Arbeiter anwenden, darin aus, daß, je höher die Produktivkraft der Arbeit, desto größer der Druck der Arbeiter auf ihre

> Beschäftigungsmittel, desto prekärer also ihre Existenzbedingung: Verkauf der eignen Kraft zur Vermehrung des fremden Reichtums oder zur Selbstverwertung des Kapitals. Rascheres Wachstum der Produktionsmittel und der Produktivität der Arbeit als der produktiven Bevölkerung drückt sich kapitalistisch also umgekehrt darin aus, daß die Arbeiterbevölkerung stets rascher wächst als das Verwertungsbedürfnis des Kapitals. (Marx, 2015, p. 674)
>
> [L-Ben Fowkes] On the basis of capitalism, a system in which the worker does not employ the means of production, but the means of production employ the worker, the law by which a constantly increasing quantity of means of production may be set in motion by a progressively diminishing expenditure of human power, thanks to the advance in the productivity of social labour, undergoes a complete inversion, and is expressed thus: the higher the productivity of labour, the greater is the pressure of the workers on the means of employment, the more precarious therefore becomes the condition for their existence, namely the sale of their own labour-power for the increase of alien wealth, or in other words the self-valorization of capital. The fact that the means of production and the productivity of labour increase more rapidly than the productive population expresses itself, therefore, under capitalism, in the inverse form that the working population always increases more rapidly than the valorization requirements of capital. (Marx, 1976, p. 798)

As Produktivkraft and Produktivität are perfectly interchangeable in this section, the assumption in this chapter cannot but falter yet again.

10.3.2 Productive Power of Capital

Now let us search for an example using the term "productive power of labor" for factors of production other than labor power. A total of 142 instances of Produktivkraft appeared when searching for Produktivkraft in the PDF file of Volume 1 of *Das Kapital* in the text alone, excluding the indexes and table of contents, among which 78 instances are usages of the "productive power of labor [Produkitivkraft der Arbeit]," which is directly modified by "der Arbeit." In addition, most cases refer to the productive power of specific labor, such as "seiner Arbeit," "ihrer Arbeit," or the "productive power of sewing or weaving [Produktivkraft der Weberei oder der Schneiderei],"or refer to the productive power of labor using a grammatical element as in "die Produktivkraft der sich in ihr verwirklichenden Arbeit [the productive power of labor realized in the product]".

In other words, the remainder (excluding cases that clearly refer to labor or the productive power of workers in meaning and those quoting others' writings) can be categorized into the following two types.[10]

> Productive Power of Capital A: cases where Productivkraft is used without a genitive case modifier, but refers to the productive power of labor in meaning because it is related to the issue of value production.
>
> Productive Power of Capital B: cases related to the proposition of converting the productive power of social labor into that of capital.

In short, unlike the "productivity of labor" in the preceding paragraph, "productive power" could be interpreted according to the originally established hypothesis, without significant difficulty. However, Type B, appearing in eight instances according to the search in this chapter, should be noted with interest. Among them, the three phrases that directly use the expression "productive power of capital [Produktivkraft des Kapitals]" are quoted as follows:

> [M1] Die Produktivkraft, die der Arbeiter als gesellschaftlicher Arbeiter entwickelt, ist daher <u>Produktivkraft des Kapitals</u>. (Marx, 1975, p. 353)
>
> [M2] Wie die durch die Kooperation entwickelte gesellschaftliche Produktivkraft der Arbeit als <u>Produktivkraft des Kapitals</u> erscheint,...(Marx, 1975, p. 354)
>
> [M3] Die aus der Kombination der Arbeiten entspringende Produktivkraft erscheint daher als <u>Produktivkraft des Kapitals</u>.,...(Marx, 1975, p. 354)
>
> [M1-Ben Fowkes] Hence the productive power developed by the worker socially is the <u>productive power of capital</u>. (Marx, 1976, p. 451)

[10] Marx uses the expressions "the productive power of the spinning machine [Die Produktivkraft seiner Spinnmaschine]" and "the productive power of the machine [die Produktivkraft der Maschine]" when quoting A. Ure, his main target of criticism (Marx, 1975, p. 581). In Ure's book, the terms are originally translated as "the productive power of his spinning machine" (Ure, 1835, p. 317) and "the productive power of the machine" (ibid., p. 320), respectively, but we can safely assume that Marx understood them in a negative manner.

> [M2-Ben Fowkes] Just as the social productive power of labour that is developed by co-operation appears to be the productive power of capital,...(Marx, 1976, p. 453)

> [M3-Ben Fowkes] Hence the productive power which results from the combination of various kinds of labour appears as the productive power of capital.(Marx, 1976, p. 481)

In other words, the term "productive power of capital" is used in Type B; however, this does not mean that capital bears productive power, but rather that the productive power of labor under capitalism is transformed into that of capital. "Transforming" in this sense also indicates that it is not a substantive change but occurring as such in the consciousness of the capitalist society. The following phrase (which explains the same content in detail) demonstrates Marx's idea better, even though the expression "productive power of capital" is not used directly.

> [N] Weil die gesellschaftliche Produktivkraft der Arbeit dem Kapital nichts kostet, weil sie andrerseits nicht von dem Arbeiter entwickelt wird, bevor seine Arbeit selbst dem Kapital gehört, erscheint sie als Produktivkraft, die das Kapital von Natur besitzt, als seine immanente Produktivkraft. (Marx, 1975, p. 353)

> [N-Ben Fowkes] The socially productive power of labour develops as a free gift to capital whenever the workers are placed under certain conditions, and it is capital which places them under these conditions. Because this power costs capital nothing, while on the other hand it is not developed by the worker until his labour itself belongs to capital, it appears as a power which capital possesses by its nature—a productive power inherent in capital. (Marx, 1976, p. 451)

10.4 Conclusion

Thus far, we have hypothesized that Marx strove to distinguish between Produktivkraft and Produktivität strictly, at least in Volume 1 of *Das Kapital*.

First, Marx's constant emphasis on the transformation of the social productive power of labor performed for free, into the productive power of capital under capitalist conditions can be interpreted to mean that capitalist exploitation is a more severe issue than just the increase in the expenditure of labor, such as labor intensification.

Next, Marx deliberately avoids using the word Produktivkraft for factors of production (i.e., machinery) other than labor power. As we presume in this chapter that Produktivität would have been used in a negative sense, Produktivität was used instead of Produktivkraft for machines, other than in the sections quoted. As is well known, in the labor theory of value, factors of production other than labor power are considered "unproductive" in the sense that they do not produce value. Thus, Produktivkraft was not used for "unproductive" factors of production.

It remains to be seen whether the three instances in the text of Chapter 15 and one in Chapter 23 (which were addressed in Sect. 10.3.1) can be interpreted consistently. However, the analysis in this chapter offers some insight into the discussion of the next chapter, which is the concluding part of the book.

References

Anderson, K. (1983). The "unknown" Marx's capital, Volume I: The French edition of 1872–75, 100 years later. *Review of Radical Political Economics, 15*(4), 71–80.

Hayashi, N. (1975). *A study on the French edition of Das Kapital*. Otsuki Shoten. [In Japanese].

List, F. (1909). *The national system of political economy* (Sampson S. Lloyd, Trans.). Longmans, Green and Co.

Marx, K. (1867). *Das Kapital* (Vol. 1). Verlag von Otto Meissner.

Marx, K. (1875). *Le Capital* (M. J. Roy, Trans.). Entièrement révisée par l'auteur.

Marx, K. (1906). *Capital* (Vol. 1, Engels & E. Untermann, Ed., S. Moore & E. Aveling, Trans.). Charles H. Kerr and Co.

Marx, K. (1975). *Das Kapital* (Vol. 1). In Marx-Engels-Werke (Bd. 23). Dietz Verlag.

Marx, K. (1976). *Capital* (Vol. 1). Penguin Books.

Marx, K. (1993). *Le Capital*. Quadrige/PUF.

Marx, K. (2015). *Capital* (Vol. 1). Progress Publishers. https://www.marxists.org/archive/marx/works/download/pdf/Capital-Volume-I.pdf. Accessed 5 Apr 2022.

Reuten, G. (2018). Marx's conceptualization of value in Capital. In M. Vidal et al. (Eds.), *The Oxford handbook of Karl Marx*. Oxford University Press.

Rhie, J. (1999). Labour intensity and surplus value in Karl Marx: A note. *History of Economic Ideas, 23*(3), 181–191.

Ruben, P. (1988). Produktivkraft und Produktivität in ökonomischen Maβrten. *Deutsche Zeitschrift für Philosophie, 36*(3). Online version is available at: http://www.peter-ruben.de/schriften/economy/Ruben%20-%20Produktivkraft%20in%20oekonomischen%20Massarten.pdf. Accessed 1 Apr 2022.

Ure, A. (1835). *The philosophy of manufactures*. Charles Knight, Ludgate-Street.

CHAPTER 11

Toward an Integrated Analysis of Labor Productivity

11.1 Introduction

In Marxian economics, it can be said that "the value magnitude of a unit of a certain commodity gives the social and standard measure for the labor productivity in the production of the commodity" (Okishio, 1965, p. 29). This idea was faithfully reflected in Izumi's (2014) concept of "Total labor productivity" (TLP).[1] TLP is defined as the inverse of the quantity of direct and indirect embodied labor in each sector calculated by using the input–output data. Flaschel et al. (2013, p. 381) also argue that "the classical–Marxian indices" are an appropriate concept for measuring labor productivity, which is the same as the TLP. Their work has been developed into an ambitious project providing "a general approach to price and value theory which identifies a research program in the classical-Marxian tradition" (Cogliano et al., 2018, p. 381). Uni (1998, p. 26) is also notable in that he defines the increasing rate of "labor productivity" by the decreasing rate of Pasinetti's (1988) "vertically integrated labor coefficient." Although he does not use the term "labor value," Uni

[1] Although they do not explicitly use the terminology, Nakajima and Izumi (1995) provides an empirical study based upon the "total labor productivity." See also Matsuda (1980) for connecting the labor value concept with labor productivity in the same vein of Okishio (1965).

D.-M. Rieu, *A Mathematical Approach to Marxian Value Theory*, Marx, Engels, and Marxisms,
https://doi.org/10.1007/978-3-031-07808-8_11

(1998) actually adopts the same concept as Izumi (2014) and Cogliano et al. (2018).

However, the value estimation by use of the input–output data has a weakness in adjusting the qualitative difference of concrete labor.[2] In the conventional literature, it was assumed that the qualitative adjustment did not make any large difference or labor with higher wages was regarded as more skilled labor in proportion to the wage difference (Flaschel et al., 2013; Ochoa, 1984). To date, at least, there is no consensus about how to measure the quality of labor let alone how to gather concrete data. Theoretically, however, the quantity of direct and indirect embodied labor without qualitative adjustment cannot be regarded as labor value in the Marxian sense.

On the other hand, Flaschel et al. (2013) showed that "the classical-Marxian indices" and monetary value-added productivity have different trends using German data. This is also confirmed in the case of Korea-China-Japan by Izumi's (2014) TLP. The main objective of this chapter is to develop these studies into a further study on uneven development and unequal exchange between sectors. In particular, as a continuation of the discussions in Part I, the conventional input–output data analysis will be integrated into the New Interpretation's concept of "monetary expression of labor time" (MELT) which was decomposed into "value expression of labor time" (VELT) and "monetary expression of value" (MEV).

The rest of the chapter is structured as follows. Section 11.2, as a continuation of Chapter 10, focuses on the interpretation of Marx's *Das Kapital* to understand the exact meaning of "Produktivkraft der Arbeit" (productive power of labor). It will be shown that a careful reading of Marx's text can have significant implications for an empirical estimation of labor value considering labor intensity, labor complexity, etc. As this issue is also related to the concept of "value productivity" tentatively suggested in Part I, Sect. 11.3 discusses it more specifically. Based on this discussion, the determining factors of the sectoral VELTs and MEVs are explained. In Sect. 11.4, the dynamics between the VELT and MEV are examined. Section 11.5 summarizes the main thrust of this chapter, which combines the MELT at the industry level and value estimation by use of the input–output table. A simple estimation will be illustrated using the

[2] This is also the case in estimating value-added productivity, not only Marxian labor value. See OECD (2001), pp. 46–49.

South Korean data. Section 11.6 concludes by suggesting a new research direction that synthesizes the two strands of Marxian value theory.

11.2 How to Read the Volume i of *Das Kapital*

The value magnitude of a certain commodity is determined by labor time, labor intensity, and labor complexity. Nevertheless, in the earlier part of *Capital*, Volume 1, Marx wrote "for simplicity's sake we shall henceforth account every kind of labour to be unskilled, simple labour; by this we do no more than save ourselves the trouble of making the reduction" (Marx, 1977, p. 32). Therefore, in Chapter 17 of the Volume 1 of *Das Kapital*, "changes of magnitude in the price of labour-power and in surplus-value," and the complexity of labor are not examined, but only length of the working day, intensity of labor, and productiveness[3] of labor are treated.

First, as follows, the intensification of labor increases the quantity of value produced.

> Hence the length of the working day being constant, a day's labour of increased intensity will be incorporated in an increased value, and, the value of money remaining unchanged, in more money. (Marx, 1977, p. 370)

Marx argues that "value remains unchanged, for each article costs the same labour as before" (*Ibid.*, p. 370). To reach this conclusion, Marx's "labor" should be interpreted as "effective labor." Effective labor can be represented as εl, where ε and l denote, the coefficients of labor intensity and labor time, respectively. If labor is intensified $k(> 1)$ times and therefore, the quantity of commodities produced increases by k times, the quantity of effective labor per unit of commodity remains unchanged because ε is equal to k.

In the case of labor intensification, however, if it happens "simultaneously and equally in every branch of industry, then the new and higher degree of intensity would become the normal degree for the society, and would therefore cease to be taken account of" (*Ibid.*, p. 370). In other words, the intensification of labor results in an increase in the quantity of value produced only when it happens in some industries or generally

[3] As already noted in Chapter 10, "productiveness" is English translation of "Productivkraft" in the edition of *Capital* by Moscow-based Progress Publishers. It was translated into "productivity" in the 1976 Ben Fowkes translation published by Penguin.

Table 11.1 The intensification of labor

	Working day	*Value–Price*	*Produced quantity*
Before	12 hours	6 shillings	6 units
After	12 hours	8 shillings	8 units

when it happens unevenly across industries. In this sense, Marx's own numerical example (*Ibid*., p. 370) should be interpreted as the situation in which labor is intensified only in one industry.

Table 11.1 summarizes this situation. Suppose that the working day is 12 hours and the quantity of value produced is 6 shillings in a certain industry.[4] Now assume that the labor in this industry is intensified to increase the produced value quantity to 8 shillings. Marx did not mention how much commodities are produced. Assuming the unit value is 1 shilling, then the quantity of labor with a higher degree of labor intensity would be changed to 1.5 hours from 2 hours per unit of commodity with a lower degree of labor intensity.

From the discussion above, it is known that the direct and indirect quantities of labor required to produce a certain commodity calculated from the input–output table would decrease if labor intensification happened in the concerned industry. Using usual notations, the quantity of embodied labor per unit of the jth commodity[5] is the jth element of the row vector $l(I - A)^{-1}$. If only the labor in the jth industry is intensified, then l_j would produce more than one unit of the jth commodity; otherwise, it can be safely assumed that l_j, as the quantity of direct labor required to produce one unit of the jth commodity, would decrease. However, "the value created varies with the extent to which the intensity of labour deviates from its normal intensity in the society" (*Ibid*., p. 370). Therefore, if labor is intensified in a certain industry, the direct and indirect embodied labor in the industry would decrease faster than the social average.

Labor complexity, although Marx himself did not give a detailed analysis, can also be analyzed using a similar line of reasoning. If labor

[4] As is well known, prices are assumed to be proportional to value in Volume 1 of *Das Kapital*.

[5] For analytical simplicity, it is assumed that each industry produces only one commodity.

complexity increases to the same degree simultaneously in all industries, the quantity of value produced would remain unchanged. With the increase in labor complexity only in a certain industry, *ceteris paribus*, the quantity of direct and indirect embodied labor in the industry would decrease. If labor complexity develops unevenly across industries, the quantity of value produced will change in proportion to the degree to which the labor complexity of the concerned industry deviates from the social average. In other words, the labor complexity in a certain industry increases faster than the social average, and its quantity of direct and indirect embodied labor will decrease faster than the social average.

Last, let us examine the issue of the productive power of labor. First, it should be noted that Marx's concept of "Produktivkraft der Arbeit" is different from labor productivity which is usually regarded as monetary value-added productivity in modern economics. As Flaschel et al. (2013) or Izumi (2014) showed, the trend of the conventional measure of labor productivity at a sectoral level is markedly different from that of the TLP or the classical-Marxian measure. This is because value-added productivity can change even when there is no change either in technology or the volume of production (Izumi, 2014, p. 188).[6] Izumi (2014, pp. 20–21) argued that an increase in labor productivity should imply a decrease in the direct and indirect quantities of embodied labor from the perspective of the allocation of social total labor because one cannot recognize the labor productivity increase if the decrease in direct labor replaced by a certain machine is smaller than the indirect labor required to produce that machine.[7]

In Chapter 1 of the Volume 1 of *Das Kapital*, Marx argues that the increase in the productive power of labor does not result in a change in the quantity of value created.

[6] This point was also noted by Flaschel et al. (2013) in the form that value-added based labor productivity is also affected by relative prices and the structure of final demand.

[7] See also Cogliano et al. (2018, pp. 217–218) for a mathematical formulation of "axioms" on labor productivity which is essentially in the same vein of Izumi's (2014) idea.

Table 11.2 The increase in the productive power of labor

Year	*Working day*	*Value–Price*	*Produced quantity*
2015	12 hours	6 shillings	6 units
2020	12 hours	6 shillings	12 units

> Since productive power[8] is an attribute of the concrete useful forms of labour, of course it can no longer have any bearing on that labour, so soon as we make abstraction from those concrete useful forms. However then productive power may vary, the same labour, exercised during equal periods of time, always yields equal amounts of value. But it will yield, during equal periods of time, different quantities of values in use; more, if the productive power rises, fewer, if it falls. The same change in productive power, which increases the fruitfulness of labour, and, in consequence, the quantity of use values produced by that labour, will diminish the total value of this increased quantity of use values, provided such change shorten the total labour time necessary for their production; and *vice versa*. (Marx, 1977, p. 33)

Just as in the case of labor intensity, what if the productive power of labor power develops unevenly across industries? Suppose that the productive power of labor increases only in an industry,[9] other things being equal, to produce 12 units of the commodity in 2020 from 6 units in 2015. It is also assumed, as Marx explained, that the sum of prices remained 6 shillings because the unit price was cut in half. As the input–output table is made using price data, not physical input–output flow data, one can estimate the quantity of direct and indirect labor per a certain amount of money, say ten thousand dollars. However, as shown in Table 11.2, the direct and indirect embodied labor quantity per price in the base period (2015) decreases to 1 hour from 2 hours in 2020. This implies that the direct and indirect labor quantity calculated by the input–output table is cut in half in the industry. In other words, the increase in the productive power of labor in a certain industry will be followed by a decrease in

[8] In the Penguin edition, this was translated into "productivity" (with a quotation mark) (Marx, 1976, p. 137). As noted above, this can be misleading in the sense that "productivity" has a specific meaning in modern economics.

[9] This is not an unusual assumption because Marx "posits no mechanism for inter-sectoral generalisations of the development of the productive powers" (Reuten, 2017, p. 15).

the quantity of direct and indirect labor embodied faster than the social average.

It is shown by the above analysis that if the direct and indirect quantities of embodied labor in a certain industry calculated from ordinary input–output data decrease, then one of the following three situations happens in that industry: labor intensification, an increase in the complexity of labor, or an increase in the productive power of labor. In reality, some combinations of these three situations may cause a decrease in the direct and indirect quantity of embodied labor; for example, the simultaneous decrease in labor intensity and the increase in labor complexity (if the latter effect surpasses the former effect).

If one assumes an unusual situation in which labor intensity, labor complexity, and the productive power of labor change proportionately in all industries, the direct and indirect labor quantities in all industries would change in the same proportion. However, this cannot be conceptualized only by the concept of labor productivity. In this sense, a more neutral expression such as "decreasing labor content" (Farjoun & Machover, 1983) will be desirable. Flaschel et al. (2013, p. 387) explained that "labour productivity with regard to good *i* increases if and only if the amount of labour directly and indirectly embodied in good *i* decreases." However, unless the labor complexity and labor intensity are included in the definition of labor productivity, a decrease in the direct and indirect labor quantity is a necessary condition, not a sufficient condition for an increase in labor productivity.[10]

It should be noted that the same issue also appears in monetary value–added based productivity concept. Although the intensification of labor or the increase in labor complexity does not cause a decrease in labor time measured by the clock hour, it will increase money value-added, and therefore, value-added-based productivity will increase. Without a doubt,

[10] Labor complexity may be included in labor productivity in a wider sense. However, labor intensity is not. Mavroudeas and Ioannides (2011, p. 431) argues that "a change in the technical conditions of production…usually involve a reduction of the "pores" of labour, i.e., the "dead," non-utilized segments of time during the work-hour" and in this sense the labor intensification should be included in the relative surplus-value production. If this is the case, labor intensity can also be included in the productive power of labor in a wider sense. However, this is inconsistent with not only the conventional Marxian literature but also our common-sense on the concept of the productive power of labor. See Chapter 10.

Table 11.3 Equalization of the rates of profit

Industry	*Constant capital*	*Variable capital*	*Surplus value*	*Value*	*Profit*	*Price of production*
I	800	200	200	1200	300	1300
II	700	300	300	1300	300	1300
III	600	400	400	1400	300	1300

unlike value-added-based productivity, the direct and indirect labor quantity reflects changes in the process of value production, and therefore, it is not related to the transformation of values into prices caused by interindustry mobility of capital or any other accidental changes in market conditions.

This point can be illustrated in Table 11.3 using Marx's model of prices of production.[11] For example, in the case of industry I, monetary value-added as the sum of variable capital and surplus value is equal to 400, and it becomes 500 as the sum of variable capital and profit after profit-rate-equalization. This implies that money value-added-based productivity also changes due to interindustry capital mobility.

11.3 Value Productivity

To start, it is helpful to elaborate on the concepts of value productivity and the VELT that were discussed in Chapters 2 and 3. Notably, Basu (2021, p. 67) explicitly employed the concept of "value productivity," defined as "the reciprocal of the total amount of labour needed to produce a commodity." If one understands this "value productivity" as the ratio of a certain commodity to the direct–indirect labor required to produce it, it can be determined by all the social and technical conditions of production that affect the "tensor of exploitation" (Lipietz, 1982), such as skill and labor intensity. As Basu admitted, this concept is

[11] Table 11.3 adopts Izumi (2014)'s explanation. Although Izumi (2014, pp. 187–190) gave a more elaborate model by distinguishing fixed part and circulating part of constant capital, etc., the model is simplified here only to show the basic concept. Additionally, the so-called transformation problem is assumed away here.

Table 11.4 The decomposition of the MELT: two cases

Sector	*Labor time*	*Case A*		*Case B*	
		VELT	*MEV*	*VELT*	*MEV*
I	20 hours	1	1	1.25	0.8
II	60 hours	1	1	1	1
III	100 hours	1	1	0.8	1.25
Total	180 hours	1	1	0.9167	1.1167

tantamount to Flaschel et al.'s (2013) definition of labor productivity.[12] Though Basu (2021, p. 66) distinguishes between the "use-value productivity of concrete labour" and "the value productivity of abstract labour," the latter seems to be a sort of tautology in the sense that abstract labor as a substance of value by definition always produces one unit of value per unit of time. When represented mathematically, it is always equal to one. However, one can have another concept of value productivity that indicates how much value is produced during a unit of time. The work of Duménil et al. (2009, pp. 1–2) is another rare example of the use of the term "value productivity." They define it as the relative capability of different types of concrete labor to create value. As the VELT measures the quantity of value produced per clock hour, we may use the VELT and value productivity interchangeably.

As emphasized repeatedly throughout this book, it is crucial to introduce the decomposition of the MELT into the MEV and the VELT at a sectoral level. the simple numerical example in Table 11.4 based on Chapter 3 is helpful: there are three departments, or sectors, each consisting of whole labor time amounting to 20, 60, 100 hours, respectively.

Case A is a Gouverneur (1990)-Itoh (2021)-like economy in that all the labor in each sector is homogeneous from the perspective of value production and market exchange. In this case, the decomposition of the MELT into the MEV and the VELT does not add new implications. In Case B, although the MELTs of all three sectors are equal to 1, the internal compositions of these MELTs are different. For example, the

[12] In the Japanese literature on Marxian value theory, this concept, although it was called "labor productivity" rather than "value productivity", has a long tradition beginning with Okishio (1965).

quantity of value produced by sector I is 1.25 times that produced in sector II; moreover, this sector takes less money on the market, namely, 0.8 times that taken by sector II. The reverse is truc in sector III. However, the MELT of the entire economy remains at 1 in Case B. Therefore, when focusing only on the aggregate MELT, one cannot capture the differences between the two cases. This clearly shows that the decomposition of the MELT is important only at the sectoral level with heterogeneous labor and market power.

With these issues in mind, let us examine the determining factors of the MEV and the VELT on a sectoral level.

First, sectoral MEVs are closely connected with the transformation of values into prices of production by which, for example, a sector with a high organic composition of capital would obtain a greater portion of the money equivalent to its value than the amount of value it produced. Therefore, sectoral differences in the organic composition of capital are the main determinant of sectoral MEVs. However, Marx's transformation procedure in *Capital*, volume 3, is premised on the assumption of the free mobility of capital across sectors. If this "perfect competition"[13] assumption is loosened, many other factors could cause differences among the sectoral MEVs. For example, sector III in Case B has an above average MEV due to some sort of market power strong enough to offset the profit-rate-equalizing forces. If the "degree of protection" (Gouverneur, 1983) rises in a certain sector, the MEV of that sector will increase. Credit availability is another element that determines the magnitude of the sectoral MEVs. Large firms with high profitability and much fixed capital, which may be used as collateral, have an increased debt capacity, and it is relatively easy for them to finance new investments with loans (Rajan & Zingales, 1995). Big businesses have enough bargaining power to impose below-market-prices on the subcontractors, as is often the case in South Korea. In small open economies, the exchange rate is another important determining factor.[14] Depreciation increases the MEVs of exporting sectors by improving their terms of trade. However, for analytical convenience, it is regarded as a financial element here. All these elements are

[13] This is only for terminological simplicity. It must be noted that, unlike Cogliano's (2021, p. 4) criticism, the neoclassical notion of "perfect competition" is not reintroduced into Marxian economics here.

[14] The author thanks to Hiroshi Ohnishi for noting this point.

summarized as follows.

$$MEV_i = f(OCC_i, DP_i, F_i) f_1 > 0,\ f_2 > 0,\ f_3 > 0 \qquad (11.1)$$

here MEV_i, OCC_i, DP_i, and F_i represent the MEV, the organic composition of capital, the degree of protection, and the financial capability including credit availability of the *i*th sector, respectively.

Second, the sectoral VELT is related to the determination of the value magnitude of a commodity, which is discussed in Marx's *Capital*, Volume 1. Although Marx discussed labor intensity and labor productivity in this volume, labor complexity or skill levels should also be considered. As skilled or complex labor produces more value than unskilled or simple labor within a unit of time, the former has a greater VELT than the latter. In other words, the coefficient used to reduce a clock hour of skilled labor to abstract labor time is greater than that that used to reduce unskilled labor, which implies that value productivity is greater in the former case. Labor intensity and labor productivity are also important factors in the context of determining VELT. These two factors are considered here with regard to the value aspect, not only the use value aspect. In contrast to Marx's argument that a given amount of labor time always produces the same amount of value irrespective of labor intensity and labor productivity, the quantity of value produced may increase if a change happens only in a certain sector or, more generally, happens unevenly across sectors. An increase in the labor intensity of a certain sector without changes in all the other sectors implies that the focal sector produces more use value and, in most cases, earns more revenue within a given period of time. Therefore, the VELT of the sector increases.[15] In the same way, if a certain sector becomes more (use-value) productive than all the other sectors, it is implied that the VELT of the sector increases.[16]

[15] Again, Basu (2021, pp. 73–75) is a rare exception who notes the impact of labor intensity on the value of commodities. His distinction between the "value-creating and use-value handling capacity of intensified labour" gives much insight into the issue, although his conclusion is quite different from this chapter's explanation.

[16] In the literature on Chinese Marxian economics, there is a long-standing debate on the proposition that labor productivity is directly proportional to the quantity of value created per unit of time (Meng, 2011).

In summary, $VELT_i$ can be represented as follows:

$$VELT_i = g(LS_i, LI_i, LP_i) g_1 > 0, g_2 > 0, g_3 > 0 \quad (11.2)$$

where in the ith sector, LS_i, LI_i, and LP_i denote the skill index of labor, labor intensity, and labor productivity, respectively.

11.4 The Dynamics Between the Monetary Expression of Value and the Value Expression of Labor Time

Now based on (11.1) and (11.2), the different types of sectors can be classified as shown in Table 11.5. Here m_{AVE} and v_{AVE} denote the social average of MEV_i and $VELT_i$, respectively.

As there are two standards, namely, MEV_i and $VELT_i$, we have 2×2 types of sectors.

Both the MEV_i and the $VELT_i$ of Type I sectors are below the overall social averages. This implies that not only the combined effect of the organic composition of capital and the degree of protection etc. shown in (11.1) but also the combined effect of labor skill, labor intensity, and labor productivity shown in (11.2) drives these sectors below the average social level. On the other hand, Type IV sectors have above average MEV_i and $VELT_i$ values. Type II and Type III are interesting cases in that the relative MEV_i and $VELT_i$ are in opposite positions. Therefore, the contradictory tendencies within these sectors prohibit their MELTs from rising above the social average. An example of a Type II sector is a rapidly developing industry with strong competition pressures, while sunset industries with high entry barriers are Type III sectors.

By classifying sectors or industries into the four groups shown in Table 11.5, the process of uneven development can be examined. For example, the effects of monetary policy, such as quantitative easing, work differently within different sectors. As Saros (2007) and Moseley (2011) showed, under an inconvertible money system, the MELT is determined

Table 11.5 Four types of sectors

	$MEV_i < m_{AVE}$	$MEV_i > m_{AVE}$
$VELT_i < v_{AVE}$	Type I	Type III
$VELT_i > v_{AVE}$	Type II	Type IV

by the quantity of money forced into circulation. In this case, an increase in the quantity of money increases the MELT, which is inconsistent with the conventional Marxian view, namely, that the values of produced commodities determine the quantity of money, not the other way round. This theoretical difficulty can be eliminated only if the effect of changes in the quantity of money is analyzed at the industry level rather than the aggregate level. In this sense, the decomposition of the MELT into the MEV and the VELT is crucial to allow Marxian monetary theory to escape from the trap of the quantity theory of money (Rieu et al., 2014).

11.5 Example: The South Korean Case

The MELT of the *i*th industry, $MELT_i$ represents how much money corresponds to a clock hour in the *i*th industry. Nakatani (1994, pp. 74–75), following Okishio, called this concept "the rate of income"[17] at the industry level and regarded it as an index for unequal exchange between industries. In other words, if a certain industry has a higher income rate than the social average, the direct labor of that industry obtains the benefit through the market exchange. In this section, we try to develop this idea more concretely.

First, by comparing the change rate of the $MELT_i$ over time ($\dot{m}_i$) with the social average ($\dot{m}$),[18] it is possible to pursue the change in the relative power of money acquisition in the *i*th industry. Namely, the difference between $\dot{m}_i$ and $\dot{m}$ is a criterion for classifying industries. Furthermore, denoting the inverse of the direct and indirect labor quantity as π_i, the difference between its rate of change ($\dot{\pi}_i$)[19] and the change rate of its social average ($\dot{\pi}$) can be added as additional criterion. Table 11.6 shows the classification of industries according to the two criteria.[20]

[17] For details on this concept in the literature of Japanese Marxian economics, see footnote 7 of Chapter 6.

[18] As the denominator of the $MELT_l$ is direct labor time, its social average should be defined as the weighted average with the weight being direct labor time of each industry.

[19] Note that this is generally greater than zero if one adopts "the decreasing labor content" (Farjoun and Machover, 1983; Flaschel et al., 2013) as a necessary tendency of capitalist society.

[20] This table is constructed in the similar vein of Table 11.5. However, this is tangible in the sense that all the variables here can be directly calculated from the ordinary input–output data and SNA.

Table 11.6 Four types of industries based on the change rate

	$\dot{m}_i < \dot{m}$	$\dot{m}_i > \dot{m}$
$\dot{\pi}_i < \dot{\pi}$	Type I	Type III
$\dot{\pi}_i > \dot{\pi}$	Type II	Type IV

Table 11.7 Types of industries: South Korea, 1990–1995–2000

	1990–1995	*1995–2000*
Agriculture, forestry, and fisheries	I	I
Mining and quarrying	II	IV
Textile products and leather products	IV	IV
Nonmetallic mineral products	IV	IV
General machinery and equipment	IV	II
Electronic and other electric equipment	IV	IV
Precision instruments	IV	II
Transportation equipment	II	II
Construction	IV	II

In the industries belonging to Type I, both the decreasing rate of the direct and indirect labor quantity and the increasing rate of the ability of money acquisition is smaller than the social average. On the other hand, Type IV industry shows a faster decreasing rate of labor content and an increasing rate of money acquisition, which is characterized by fast technological progress and the intensification of market power.

Interesting cases are type II and type III industries in the sense that there is a divergence between the two criteria. In the case of type II, the direct and indirect labor quantity decreases faster than the social average while market power is decreasing compared to the social average. In other words, the intensification of labor, the increase of labor complexity, and the development of the productive power of labor are faster than the social average, however, the ability of money acquisition on the market is growing slower-than-average or even decreasing. Type III is exactly the inverse case.

This classification in the South Korean example is shown in Table 11.7 whose data are summarized in Tables 11.8 and 11.9.[21]

Table 11.8 The increasing rates of total labor productivity: South Korea, 1990–1995–2000 (annual rate, %)

	1990–1995	*1995–2000*
Agriculture, forestry, and fisheries	5.91	1.56
Mining and quarrying	16.30	8.34
Textile products and leather products	12.90	9.10
Nonmetallic mineral products	13.34	8.63
General machinery and equipment	12.64	7.03
Electronic and other electric equipment	17.72	13.76
Precision instruments	9.72	7.93
Transportation equipment	13.44	7.58
Construction	12.68	5.68
Average[a]	8.74	5.03

[a]The weights are based on the quantity of direct labor

Table 11.9 Monetary expression of labor time at the industry level: South Korea, 1990–1995–2000

	1990(A)	*1995(B)*	*2000(C)*	*B/A*	*C/B*
Agriculture, forestry, and fisheries	3198.78	6150.94	8555.24	1.9283	1.3909
Mining and quarrying	8560.37	7021.32	34,167.01	0.8202	4.8662
Textile products and leather products	2159.85	5218.54	10,622.90	2.4162	2.0356
Nonmetallic mineral products	5607.28	11,531.15	19,519.39	2.0565	1.6928
General machinery and equipment	5272.84	10,972.72	16,740.73	2.0810	1.5257
Electronic and other electric equipment	4739.81	13,473.92	27,500.58	2.8427	2.0410
Precision instruments	3416.97	8333.56	11,777.32	2.4389	1.4132
Transportation equipment	7597.60	14,381.69	21,697.76	1.8929	1.5087
Construction	6752.66	16,753.54	14,726.16	2.4810	0.8790
Average[a]	4748.39	9347.00	15,803.42	1.9685	1.6907

Data sources 1990–1995–2000 Link Input–Output Tables, Bank of Korea an Survey Report on Wage Structure, Korean Ministry of Labor
[a]The weights are based on the quantity of direct labor

All industries except agriculture, forestry, and fisheries are characterized by faster-than-average decreasing rate in the labor content, i.e., $\dot{\pi}_i > \dot{\pi}$ while the change rate of the ability of money acquisition differs across industries. It is predictable that agriculture, forestry, and fisheries belong to type I. Textile products and leather products, nonmetallic mineral products, electronic and other electric equipment, and transportation equipment industries consistently showed the same type characteristics. However, in the cases of general machinery and equipment, precision instruments, and construction, the types were changed to type II in 1995–2000 from type IV in 1995–2000. Conversely, in the case of mining and quarrying, the direction of change was reversed, from type II to type IV in the same periods. The concrete causes for these changes should be studied further. However, probably the financial crisis of 1997–1998, in particular, caused some structural change within the manufacturing industry. For example, the breakdown of real asset prices through the period of crisis must have affected the ability of money acquisition in the construction industry.

In summary, the classification of industries according to the two criteria in Table 11.6 hints at the possibility of further research on the uneven development of industries by combining traditional input–output data and the NI's MELT analysis. This analysis can lead us to go beyond the confirmation of the fact that the TLP or the classical-Marxian productivity measure is totally different from the monetary value–added-based measure of labor productivity.

11.6 Conclusion

The main theoretical points of this chapter may be summarized as follows.

First, sectoral MELT is determined according to the dynamics between the sectoral MEV and the VELT over time. Furthermore, a key element of explaining this dynamic is found in the decomposition of the MELT into the MEV and the VELT. In summary, uneven development across industries is determined through interactions between the spheres of value production and market exchange. This recognition leads us to examine

[21] As data sources have a difference in the industry classification due to changes in the South Korean statistics in 1991 and 2000, Table 11.7 summarizes the only industries whose classifications are same in the two datasets.

the distinction between the MEV and the VELT further in pursuing the main research goal of this book.

Second, we tried to show that labor value is not a metaphysical and abstract but a pragmatic concept for the analysis of the real economy. When it is possible to identify some aspects that are different from the usual mainstream analysis, the analytical implication of the labor theory of value will be clarified. Once again it should be emphasized that the analysis in this chapter is the first step for specifying the distinction between "monetary expression of value" and "value expression of labor" which were provided either at a pure theoretical level in Part I or a simulation analysis in Chapter 9.

Last but not least, a new research direction was provided to integrate the two strands of Marxian value theory, the so-called dual system approach and the so-called single system approach which were usually regarded as incompatible. Izumi (2014) represents the former strand and the analytical tool of the "monetary expression of labor time" is one of the representative achievements in the latter strand.

References

Basu, D. (2021). *The logic of capital: An introduction to marxist economic theory*. Cambridge: Cambridge University Press.

Cogliano, J., Flaschel, P., Franke, R., Frölich, N., & R. Veneziani. (2018). *Value, competition and exploitation: Marx's legacy revisited*. Cheltenham. Edward Elgar.

Cogliano, J. F. (2021). Marx's equalized rate of exploitation. Department of Economics, University of Massachusetts Boston, Working paper 2021–01.

Duménil, G., Foley, D. K., & Lévy, D. (2009). A note on the formal treatment of exploitation in a model with heterogeneous labor. *Metroeconomica, 60*(3), 560–567.

Farjoun, E., & Machover, M. (1983). *Laws of chaos: A probabilistic approach to political economy*. Verso.

Flaschel, P., Franke, R., & Veneziani, R. (2013). Labour productivity and the law of decreasing labor content. *Cambridge Journal of Economics, 37*(2), 379–402.

Foley, D. (2005). Marx's theory of money in historical perspective. In *Marx's theory of money* (Eds.). Palgrave Macmillan.

Gouverneur, J. (1983). *Contemporary capitalism and Marxist economics*. Rowman & Littlefield Publishers.

Gouverneur, J. (1990). Productive labour, price/value ratio and rate of surplus value: theoretical viewpoints and empirical evidence. *Cambridge Journal of Economics, 14*(1), 1–27.

Itoh, M. (2021). *Value and crisis: Essays on Marxian economics in Japan* (2nd ed.). Monthly Review Press.

Izumi, H. (2014). *Calculation of the quantity of embodied labor and basic economic indices* (In Japanese). Otsuki Shoten.

Kliman, A. (2011). *The failure of capitalist production: Underlying causes of the great recession*. Pluto Press.

Lipietz, A. (1982). The so-called transformation problem revisited. *Journal of Economic Theory, 26*(1), 59–88.

Marx, K. (1976). *Capital*, volume 1. Penguin Books.

Marx, K. (1977). *Capital*, volume 1. Progress Publishers.

Matsuda, K. (1980). *The theory of labor productivity* (In Japanese). Chikuma Shobo.

Mavroudeas, S., & Ioannides, A. (2011). Duration, intensity and productivity of labour and the distinction between absolute and relative surplus-value. *Review of Political Economy, 23*(3), 421–437.

Meng-Jie. (2011). The plus-sum relations between capital and labor in the creation of value: a new Marxian explanation based on the proportional theory of value creation (In Chinese). *Economic Research Journal*, *46*(4).

Meng, J. (2015). Two kinds of MELT and their determinations: Critical notes on Moseley and the New Interpretation. *Review of Radical Political Economics, 47*(2), 309–316.

Mohun, S. (2004). The labour theory of value as foundation for empirical investigations. *Metroeconomica, 55*(1), 65–95.

Moseley, F. (2011). The determination of the "monetary expression of labor time" ("MELT") in the case of non-commodity money. *Review of Radical Political Economics, 43*(1), 95–105.

Nakajima, A., & H. Izumi. (1995). Economic development and unequal exchange among nations: Analysis of the U.S., Japan, and South Korea. *Review of Radical Political Economics*, *27*(3), 86–94.

Nakatani, T. (1994). *Economics of Value, Price and Profit*. Keio Shobo/ (In Japanese).

Ochoa, E. (1984). Labor values and prices of production: an interindustry study of the U.S. economy, 1947–1972. Ph.D. Dissertation. New School for Social Research.

OECD. (2001). *Measuring productivity—OECD manual: Measurement of aggregate and industry-level productivity growth.*

Okishio, N. (1965). *The basic theory of capitalist economy* (In Japanese). Otsuki Shoten.

Pasinetti, L. L. (1988). Growing subsystems, vertically hyperintegrated sectors and the labour theory of value. *Cambridge Journal of Economics, 12*(1), 125–134.

Rajan, R. G., & Zingales, L. (1995). What do we know about capital structure? Some evidence from inter-national data. *Journal of Finance, 50*(5), 1421–1460.

Reuten, G. (2017). The productive powers of labour and the redundant transformation to prices of production: a Marx-immanent critique and reconstruction. *Historical Materialism, 25*(3), 3–35.

Rieu, D.-M. (2008). Estimating sectoral rates of surplus value: Methodological issues. *Metroeconomica, 59*(4), 557–573.

Rieu, D.-M., Lee, K., & Ahn, H.-H. (2014). The determination of the monetary expression of concrete labor time under the inconvertible credit money system. *Review of Radical Political Economics., 46*(2), 190–198.

Saros, D. (2007). The price-form as a fractional reflection of the aggregate value of commodities. *Review of Radical Political Economics*, *39*(3), 407–415.

Uni, H. (1998). *Structural change and capital accumulation.* Yuhikaku Publishing. (In Japanese).

Index

D.-M. Rieu, *A Mathematical Approach to Marxian Value Theory*, Marx, Engels, and Marxisms,
https://doi.org/10.1007/978-3-031-07808-8

T

V

Kolibri 360 GmbH
Ferdinand-Jühlke-Straße 7
99095 Erfurt, Deutschland
produktsicherheit@kolibri360.de